Constructing Crime

Law and Society Series
W. Wesley Pue, General Editor

The Law and Society Series explores law as a socially embedded phenomenon. It is premised on the understanding that the conventional division of law from society creates false dichotomies in thinking, scholarship, educational practice, and social life. Books in the series treat law and society as mutually constitutive and seek to bridge scholarship emerging from interdisciplinary engagement of law with disciplines such as politics, social theory, history, political economy, and gender studies.

A list of the titles in this series appears at the end of this book.

Edited by Janet Mosher and Joan Brockman

Constructing Crime
Contemporary Processes of Criminalization

UBCPress · Vancouver · Toronto

20 19 18 17 16 15 14 13 12 11 10   5 4 3 2 1

Printed in Canada on FSC-certified ancient-forest-free paper (100% post-consumer recycled) that is processed chlorine- and acid-free.

Library and Archives Canada Cataloguing in Publication

Constructing crime : contemporary processes of criminalization / edited by Janet Mosher and Joan Brockman.

(Law and society series 1496-4953)
Includes bibliographical references and index.
ISBN 978-0-7748-1819-3

1. Criminology – Canada. 2. Crime – Sociological aspects – Canada. 3. Criminal behavior – Canada. I. Mosher, Janet E. (Janet Eaton) II. Brockman, Joan III. Series: Law and society series (Vancouver, B.C.)

HV6807.C65 2010	364.971	C2010-901062-0

Canadä

UBC Press gratefully acknowledges the financial support for our publishing program of the Government of Canada (through the Canada Book Fund), the Canada Council for the Arts, and the British Columbia Arts Council.

This book has been published with the help of a grant from the Canadian Federation for the Humanities and Social Sciences, through the Aid to Scholarly Publications Programme, using funds provided by the Social Sciences and Humanities Research Council of Canada.

This book has been published with the assistance of the Ontario Problem Gambling Research Centre.

UBC Press
The University of British Columbia
2029 West Mall
Vancouver, BC V6T 1Z2
www.ubcpress.ca

Contents

Acknowledgments

We are grateful to the former Law Commission of Canada not only for its funding of the case studies on "what is a crime?" that comprise this collection but also for its legacy of critical engagement with law. Each of the contributors benefited from the opportunity to work with the commission on this project, and we are particularly indebted to Steven Bittle for his support, leadership, and collegiality. This volume benefited from the thoughtful, encouraging, and critical commentaries of three anonymous reviewers and from the assistance provided by students Diana Morokhovets and Sarah Mohamed. Finally, we are indebted to Randy Schmidt and Megan Brand of UBC Press, whose guidance, encouragement, and good humour were critical to the completion of the project.

Constructing Crime

Introduction

Janet Mosher and Joan Brockman

This volume of essays marks the last work of the Law Commission of Canada (LCC) before its funding was removed in 2006, forcing its doors to close in December 2007 (Le Bouthillier 2007, 113). The first president of the commission, Roderick A. Macdonald (2007, 118), observed that the LCC, which was created in 1996, had survived only half as long as its predecessor, the Law Reform Commission of Canada (LRCC) (1971-93). Macdonald, along with the second president of the LCC, Nathalie Des Rosiers (2007), and the third and last president, Yves Le Bouthillier (2007), have all written insightful comments about the origins and demise of the LCC. According to Macdonald (2007, 123), the LCC had a radical mandate:

(a) to work towards the development of new concepts of law and new approaches to law; (b) to develop measures to make the legal system more efficient, economical and accessible; (c) to stimulate critical debate in, and the forging of productive networks among, academic and other communities in order to ensure cooperation and coordination in law reform initiatives; and (d) to work toward the elimination of obsolescence and anomalies in the current law.

Although the LRCC had a similar mandate, it slipped into a bureaucratic form "focussed on legislative change and [became] increasingly duplicative of the work of the policy development branch of the Department of Justice" (*ibid.*). Macdonald and others tried to avoid this pitfall by using the LCC's mandate to examine a much broader concept of law than what is commonly referred to as "law in the books."[1] Rather, law in action, which is often interpreted as the discretion of agents of enforcement, also includes "the normative commitments that shape the way most people live their lives" (*ibid.*, 134). The study of law should include how people engage or disengage with the law and with each other. The LCC (2003b, 7) provided examples of how we influence each other's behaviour without invoking the law – for example, "a man encourages a friend to stop smoking cigarettes. Newspaper articles caution against the rise of childhood obesity."

This volume marks the posthumous and final publication of the LCC's work on its "what is a crime?" project that was launched in 2001. True to its commitment to focus on law in action, the consultation phase began with an online debate, which the Canadian public, as well as experts from several countries, were invited to join, and it continued with roundtable discussions organized across the country and studies requisitioned by the commission. As part of its Legal Dimensions Initiative on "what is a crime?" the LCC commissioned six multidisciplinary research projects that were subsequently published by UBC Press in a volume of essays entitled *What Is a Crime? Defining Criminal Conduct in Contemporary Society* (Law Commission of Canada 2004).[2] The research projects explained and illustrated "the political nature of crime, from the enactment of legislation (immigration crisis and middle-class copyright infringement) to the variable enforcement of its provisions (insurance fraud, bad-humour jokes, and criminal negligence in administering water standards)" (Des Rosiers and Bittle 2004, xvii). Although very diverse in their subject matters, many focused on how unequal enforcement of the law affects the more vulnerable people in our society (*ibid.*, xvii) and concluded that the "culture of criminalization" is "indeed a dangerous strategy" (*ibid.*, xxii).

Drawing on these research papers and other consultations, the LCC (2003b, 4-5) drafted a discussion paper in 2003 that called upon Canadians to reflect on questions such as what does "unwanted behaviour" mean in Canada; do we tend to resort too readily to penal law to control behaviours; what are the consequences of excessive reliance on penal strategies; and what strategies would be more consistent with our democratic values for the treatment of unwanted behaviours? The commission hypothesized that "the current ways in which we define and respond to unwanted behaviour may not be appropriate. In general a *reflex* to criminal law has come to dominate," and it is "a dangerous strategy" (*ibid.*, 5). The commission was interested in the process of defining someone as criminal rather than the law itself and made a direct appeal to Canadians, both experts and social groups, to consider the impact of prohibiting unwanted behaviours through the *Criminal Code*.[3]

In 2003, the LCC (2003a, 1) commissioned another series of multidisciplinary case studies to examine "factors that contribute to the definition of 'unwanted' or 'criminal' behaviour, and the mechanisms and techniques that are / have been employed in response to certain behaviour." Realistically, the LCC stated that the project was not expected to "produce *the* definitive answer in terms of what constitutes a 'crime' or 'unwanted behaviour' [or] a roadmap for dealing with or responding to what often represents complex social issues" (*ibid.*, 1). Rather, the LCC hoped that these projects would assist it in developing "an analytical framework for reflecting on the processes that underlie and inform responses to unwanted behaviour, and the impacts of choosing various response and control mechanisms" (*ibid.*, 2). Unfortunately, funds were pulled from the LCC before it had an opportunity to prepare its report to Parliament. The five case studies in this collection are the result of the LCC's final consultation before its unfortunate demise.

These case studies draw upon original empirical research to elucidate the questions posed by the commission as part of its "what is a crime?" project. The case studies interrogate these questions from a range of disciplinary vantage points – sociology, law, criminology, Aboriginal studies – and through varied research methodologies. Each of the case studies provides a detailed interrogation of "crime" and of "criminalization" in radically different sites: social assistance or welfare receipt; billing practices of health care professionals; traditional harvesting by Aboriginal persons; interactions among social housing residents; and gambling activities. These varied sites help to illuminate both the contradictions and commonalties in "crime" and its deployment, including in the rationalities (ways of thinking) and technologies (ways of acting) employed to both construct and control "crime" within these varied and particular sites (Garland 1997).

At the broadest level, each of the case studies invites and engages a range of questions about criminalization processes. The terminology of "criminalization" has become increasingly commonplace, particularly in analyses of neo-liberal governance, yet its meaning is often less than precise. The case studies reveal three central ways in which criminalization may be understood and its parameters sketched. While these three approaches are by no means mutually exclusive, delineating each of them with some precision assists in sharpening an analysis of criminalization processes and in unpacking the concept of "crime." The first of these approaches focuses upon criminalization as the formal categorization of behaviour as "crime," the second looks beyond categorization to law in action, emphasizing the experiential over the definitional, and the third examines the act of governing through the idea of crime and how the very concept of crime is deployed to govern vulnerable populations.

Criminalization as Categorization
As employed by some, criminalization simply captures a categorization or classification choice – the choice to legislatively define (usually, through the exercise of the federal criminal law power) particular unwanted or undesirable conduct as a "crime." As Louk H.C. Hulsman (1986) notes, integral to the choice to define behaviour as "crime" is the logic of individual responsibility and the preference for a particular style of social control (punishment), a particular professional context, and a specialized organizational setting (criminal justice).

As with the earlier collection of case studies (Law Commission of Canada 2004), the studies in this collection reveal that the characterization of behaviour as "crime" is neither natural nor eternal. There is, as Hulsman (1986) points out, no ontological reality of crime. Rather, the characterization of particular conduct or behaviour as a "crime" is but one of many ways to construct and order social reality. Thus, "crime" is not the object of criminal justice policy but, rather, is produced by it (*ibid*.). The socially constructed and contingent nature of the categorization of behaviour as "crime" is well illustrated in the case studies of gambling, incivilities in social housing, and Aboriginal harvesting.

Originally criminalized as a vice and placed in the same class as soliciting for the purposes of prostitution, gambling today is condoned by the government and has become a legal and legitimate leisure activity, as shown by Colin Campbell, Timothy Hartnagel, and Garry Smith in Chapter 5, "The Legalization of Gambling in Canada." Yet gambling outside the parameters set by government continues to be a vice. The co-existence of legal and illegal gambling provides a poignant illustration that "criminal" status is the result of choice rather than being intrinsic to the quality of the activity itself. The political nature of this choice was very much revealed by the acrimonious battle between federal and provincial levels of government in the mid-1980s over the regulation of lotteries and lottery schemes – a battle that was settled through the granting of exclusive power to the provinces to license various gambling activities, with the provinces, in turn, agreeing to provide a calculated share of their profits to the federal government.

Similarly, the case study of incivilities reveals the choice entailed in the categorization of behaviour as "crime." Rather than being a question of decriminalization, as in the case study of gambling, the central problem posed by Frédéric Lemieux and Nadège Sauvêtre in Chapter 4, "Incivilities: The Representation and Reactions of French Public Housing Residents in Montreal City," is whether the "incivilities" encountered in daily life among public housing residents in Montreal – noise, graffiti, minor damage to property – should be characterized as "crime" and whether the social relations among tenants are best managed through the criminal justice system or some other means. Challenging the reflex to criminalization that is evident in the emerging development of new police "call codes" that detail a lengthy list of incivilities, Lemieux and Sauvêtre seek a deeper understanding of the representations of, and reactions to, incivilities by residents of social housing and, in particular, whether these representations and reactions are mediated by the management modes of different housing providers.

To interrogate the effects of these different modes of housing, the authors conducted a study of some 364 French-speaking inhabitants in the city of Montreal, living in five different areas of the city and in two forms of social housing with different management modes: low-income housing, which is publicly managed, and housing co-operatives, which are managed primarily through participatory, collective tenant structures. The interviewers presented tenants with a list of unwanted behaviours classified as "incivilities." The list included certain legally punishable infractions such as theft and vandalism, along with behaviours that are more associated with a lack of civility, such as graffiti, noisy neighbours, and spitting in lobbies. The respondents were asked a range of questions, including how frequently they had experienced each of these incivilities, how seriously they regarded them, and what they would do, or had done, when confronted with such behaviours. The authors found that the management mode was the most convincing element in accounting for differences in the frequency of uncivil behaviour, in the perceived seriousness of this behaviour, and in the preferred intervention when such behaviour occurs. Those individuals in co-operative housing were more inclined to do nothing and, if they did react, were less likely to pursue a formal intervention strategy than those in the publicly managed low-income housing group. Those in co-operative housing reported being exposed (as either witnesses or victims) less frequently to "incivilities" than did the low-income housing group, and greater exposure was correlated with an increased likelihood of opting for formal strategies. The authors also found that those in low-income housing reported lower levels of social cohesion and lower levels of informal social control than those in co-operative housing.

These various findings led the authors to the conclusion that the form of management within social housing plays an important role in relation to the degree of social cohesion and informal social control, which, in turn, mediates the levels of incivility and response patterns. In light of this finding, Lemieux and Sauvêtre suggest that public actors should "focus on interventions that stimulate the vitality of pro-social mechanisms in difficult neighbourhoods rather than implementing strategies that run a strong risk of further *codifying* and *judicializing* social relationships." They resist the turn to categorizing incivilities as "crime" by both questioning the efficacy of criminal justice regulation and illuminating the possibilities of alternative forms of regulation. The argument is made that selecting the right management form within social housing offers a more promising route to increasing the informal mechanisms of social control and, consequently, to reducing incivilities.

In Chapter 3, "Pimatsowin Weyasowewina: Our Lives, Others' Laws," Lisa Chartrand and Cora Weber-Pillwax reveal how various forms of legal regulation have criminalized Aboriginal peoples. The narratives of those who participated in the research project – approximately 100 First Nations, Métis, and non-status Aboriginal persons in four geographical regions in northern Alberta – movingly depict the Aboriginal harvesting practices that are integral to both cultural survival and physical sustenance. Traditional practices including hunting, trapping, fishing, and gathering, as well as the sharing of the fruits of these practices with family and other community members, are foundational expressions of Aboriginal peoples' social and cultural existence and are deeply intertwined with Aboriginal spirituality. Moreover, in a social context of often-profound poverty, they are practices that are essential to physical survival.

A variety of legal regimes, ranging from quasi-criminal hunting and fishing regulations to contractual arrangements between the state and resource developers, severely curtail, unduly structure, or prohibit these practices. Tellingly, the study by Chartrand and Weber-Pillwax challenges a view of criminalization that limits the understanding of "crime" to only those behaviours defined and proscribed by the formal criminal law (in Canada, the federal *Criminal Code*). In contrast, their research invites us to consider the common attributes between the formal criminal law and other forms of regulation (both legislation and contractual legal obligations). They explore the relationship between these legal instruments not as constitutional scholars seeking to analyze whether, for example, a province has exceeded its jurisdiction by attempting to exercise the federal criminal law power but, rather, as ethnographers seeking to understand the lived experiences of Aboriginal harvesters. Understood in this way, behaviour becomes a "crime" not only when it is defined through the exercise of the formal criminal law power by federal legislators but also when regulation – whatever its source – is characterized by particular features, including the prohibition or curtailment of harvesting practices, significant levels of surveillance, punitive sanctions, and discourses of criminality.

Chartrand and Weber-Pillwax reveal the contingent nature of "crime" by challenging the reader to imagine different possibilities. They turn on its head the categorization of "criminals" and "crime" by rhetorically asking, "if the right of a people to live is taken away from them for financial benefits to another, does this not constitute a crime against humanity in some definition, in some generation, in some location, and in some future?" The authors map out an array of alternative modes of regulatory options for effectively managing the resources that are so integral to traditional Aboriginal harvesting practices, demonstrating that there exists a range of tools and revealing plainly that the criminal law (or other forms of law sharing its features) is neither indispensable nor always desirable. In laying bare the constructed and contingent nature of "crime," these case studies call out for an explanation of why it is that particular behaviours are selectively categorized as "crime." Although the gravity of social harm is frequently offered by political actors as the underlying rationale, the various case studies in this collection, and perhaps most powerfully the Afterword by Marie-Andrée Bertrand, challenge the plausibility of this explanation. The case studies suggest that a variety of other interests and motivations often underpin the selective categorization of particular behaviours as "crime" and particular actors as "criminal." Campbell, Hartnagel, and Smith observe that in common law countries such as Canada, Australia, the United Kingdom, and New Zealand, and in several American states, the construct of gambling as a "crime" or an "inherently bad thing" crumbled when the governments of these countries discovered the financial benefits to be reaped from legalization. The "de-criminalization" of gambling was very much in the financial interests of the state since the state stood to profit from gambling's legalization.[4] Significantly, as these authors note, the changes to the *Criminal Code* did not remove all forms of gambling entirely from its ambit but, rather, simply vested in the provincial and territorial governments the power to grant exemptions to the general criminal prohibitions. This new regulatory regime has created a multi-billion-dollar legal gambling industry from which all levels of government have profited, leading the authors of the study to conclude that the role of the criminal law has been "principally to consolidate provincial authority over gambling as a revenue-raising instrument and to expand its availability rather than restrict it in any meaningful sense."

The social harms that are inherent in many gambling activities have received relatively little attention. To the contrary, the authors conclude that "perhaps the most crucial policy issue concerns the potential conflicts of interest that arise for provincial governments when they both regulate and promote gambling," a conflict that pits revenue maximization priorities against social responsibilities and in which economic exigency almost invariably wins. Pressured by citizen groups and victims' families, governments have had to step up and assume (some) responsibility for the undesirable effects of gambling, and attention has been most decidedly upon the "problem gambler," and a new cadre of professionals has emerged to fashion his or her treatment. These new professionals, whose status and survival are dependent upon the victims of gambling, have a vested interest in the lax consumer protection measures that presently characterize Canada's gambling policy. Significantly, the state has located the "problem" not in the activity of gambling but, rather, in the flawed players who are seemingly incapable of adequate self-responsibilization. Problem gamblers are depicted as the antithesis of *homo prudens*, the responsible, self-sufficient, entrepreneurial consumer capable of rationally exercising choice to maximize his or her own interests (Garland 1997, 185; Snider 2000, 177; Coleman 2003, 22). Rather, the problem gambler is a person out of control who requires treatment and correction.

While, historically, the criminalization of gambling may well have been aligned with the interests of organized religion and the newly industrialized state in a disciplined workforce, contemporary forms of de-criminalization and regulation protect the fiscal interests of the state. In other words, the choice to categorize forms of gambling as non-criminal protects the financial interests of the state. In this case, the real work being done by the criminal law is that of consolidating a provincial monopoly over expanding gambling revenues rather than controlling social harm. Indeed, the de-criminalization of gambling may have caused greater harm since gambling addicts feed their addiction through theft, embezzlement, and fraud and leave their dependants to fend for themselves. While the state's interest in profit by no means exhausts – indeed barely begins, as Bertrand's Afterword makes clear – an examination of the rationales underlying the choice of whether to label conduct as "crime," let us shift to the second strand of criminalization and then return to this question of rationales.

Criminalization through Law in Action

The case studies also reveal that the legislative categorization of behaviour provides only a partial account of who and what are, in fact, subject to being positioned within the realms of "crime" and the criminal being. Criminalization understood in the narrow sense described earlier – as categorization – is grounded in a view of the state in which the state commands and individuals obey (or are punished). It presupposes the unidirectional exercise of power between state and subject, which is, of course, an incredibly important component of criminalization. As Laureen Snider (2000, 172) has clearly shown in her work on corporate crime, the very survival of corporate crime "as an object of study is contingent on the passage and enforcement of 'command and control' legislation."

However, the markedly different enforcement practices uncovered by the studies of fraud in two different sites – the receipt of social assistance by low-income persons and the billing practices of health care professionals – make clear that to understand criminalization we need to move beyond the examination of categorization alone. What we see in the contrast between these two sites is that, while the categorization of a particular behaviour – fraud, in this case – as "crime" remains constant, the striking differences in surveillance, in the opportunities to "filter out" misconduct, in the punishment, and in the accompanying discourses that signify the moral character of the conduct – or perhaps, more aptly, the persons – suggest that whether the behaviour is in fact labelled and/or processed as "crime" is, like the choice of categorization itself, contingent. Understood in this further sense, the concept of criminalization expands beyond the definitional to capture law in action – the actual deployment of "crime" and crime control as they permeate daily life and selectively entangle citizens in their embrace. What, then, do these particular sites reveal about *who* is selectively entangled?

In Chapter 1, "Welfare Fraud: The Constitution of Social Assistance as Crime," Janet Mosher and Joe Hermer draw upon interviews with legal representatives in Ontario's community clinic system as well as an extensive review of case law to examine welfare fraud in Ontario, particularly in the post-1995 period when major reforms to social assistance ("welfare") were initiated. Led at the time by a Conservative government, major reforms to welfare legislation included a sharp reduction in benefit levels, a dramatic narrowing of entitlement, and the expansion of webs of surveillance and verification. Mosher and Hermer argue that "welfare fraud" was employed as a central device in transforming social assistance from an entitlement-based program to one of contractual obligation in which recipients were mandated to participate in employment-readiness activities as a precondition of limited eligibility for significantly reduced benefits.

Like the problem gambler, the recipients of social assistance were (and continue to be) portrayed as flawed neo-liberal citizens, having failed to ensure their own self-sufficiency. As the then responsible minister made explicit, "people have got to learn again to take responsibility for themselves and their families and not to leave it to everyone else to do."[5] As "flawed" or "partial" citizens, those claiming state assistance were clearly marked as deficient, deviant, and undeserving (Mosher 2007). However, welfare recipients were cast not only as flawed citizens but also as risky and dangerous citizens, threatening the values of individual responsibility, self-sufficiency, and the work ethic (Bauman 2005; Mosher 2007). The view of welfare recipients as slothful, rudderless souls seeking sustenance from the state without being prepared to do anything in return (thus, the need for mandated work activities) has leant itself readily to a depiction of recipients as "fraudsters."

Mosher and Hermer's detailed account of Ontario's welfare system reveals the active participation of the state in the construction of the problem of "welfare fraud" and the proliferation of a new battery of weapons to battle it: enhanced verification; snitch lines; eligibility enforcement officers with additional investigative powers; and harsh new forms of punishment. An extraordinarily large number of fraud investigations are undertaken every year, and, while relatively few are prosecuted through to conviction in criminal courts, a great many more end with administrative sanctions. In addition, the political discourse surrounding welfare and welfare recipients, particularly during the period the Conservative government remained in power (1995-2003), was peppered with language that was evocative of criminality. "Thieves," "fraudsters," and "cheats" comprised the vocabulary used to describe welfare recipients.

The second study on fraud by Joan Brockman, in Chapter 2, "Fraud against the Public Purse by Health Care Professionals: The Privilege of Location," which is based on a review of cases from 1990 to 2003 and interviews with key informants, analyzes the controls exercised over health care professionals suspected of pilfering public funds in Ontario and British Columbia and contrasts these controls with those governing welfare recipients. The fraud examined consists of over-billing by health care professionals, primarily physicians. For instance, physicians claimed fees for services that were not delivered or for more complicated and costly procedures than those provided, or they billed for more visits than actually took place. Unlike the welfare context, where "fraud" is the terminology invoked to describe virtually all rule transgressions by welfare recipients (irrespective of whether those transgressions have arisen as a result of the unintentional violation of one of the 800 rules that constitute the welfare system), non-criminal language – "up-coding," "over-billing," and "inappropriate billing" – are the terms commonly employed in the health care setting. And, again, while "fraud" lacks precision here, just as it does in the welfare context, this imprecision works in decidedly the opposite direction, and criminal fraud is described in innocuous terms – "fudging" or "padding" – or is dismissed altogether as being merely an oversight or misunderstanding.

Surveillance of physicians' billing practices is significantly less intense than the surveillance of Ontario's welfare recipients. In British Columbia, for the most part, the systems regulating physicians rely upon trust, and there is relatively little monitoring and few routine checks. Moreover, physicians are regulated by a great number of bodies – health insurance boards, colleges of physicians, medical boards, and health care joint committees – which often act to funnel or filter out accusations against deviant professionals. When accusations stand, the physicians can appeal to their professional committees and joint organizations, which may consider the complex rules of the system as an adequate justification for billing mistakes (unlike the treatment of mistakes made within the welfare system). Thus, physicians who commit fraud are treated relatively leniently. In the rare eventuality that a criminal accusation is brought, the physician can call upon a lawyer for assistance. Compared to the physician, the welfare recipient suspected of fraud appears to be in a much more serious predicament.

Rather than sounding a call to "get tough" on white-collar crime (which is engaged in by some health professionals), Brockman invites us to consider whether we could "reduce the use of the criminal law against crimes of the less powerful by transferring to their misconduct some of the attitudes and approaches that we presently have towards the crimes of the powerful." She warns that a call for a heavier hand on white-collar crime may propel us into a game of increased criminalization and fuel the engine of the crime control industry, giving it yet more power and manufacturing yet more needs for crime control professionals to address.

As Snider (2000, 170) notes in the context of corporate crime, increased punitiveness seems to be reserved for the impoverished – the gentle art of persuasive, positive incentives and tax breaks for the grave social harms perpetrated by corporations. Similarly, the comparison of fraud between the context of welfare receipt and that of health care billing suggests that aggressive enforcement is reserved for the "real criminal," the welfare recipient (*ibid.*, 184). In contrast to the physician – who is assumed to be a virtuous neo-liberal citizen and, as such, capable of self-correction and self-regulation – the welfare recipient poses a significant risk.

A similar observation can be made with regard to gambling. As Campbell, Hartnagel, and Smith point out, the regulatory practices of particular provinces in relation to gambling actually violate provisions of the *Criminal Code,* yet the provinces' vested interest in the profits of gambling creates a strong incentive to construe and apply the criminal law in ways that are most favourable to those interests. The case study of gambling in Canada also reveals the emergence of different regulatory models across the country and of different roles delegated to private sector companies. While some of these arrangements arguably contravene the provisions of the *Criminal Code,* as do some of the particular forms of gambling introduced in some provincial jurisdictions, these practices go largely unchallenged. The state's enforcement of its own laws is decidedly weak when its financial interests are at stake.

In sum, the case studies suggest that the law on the ground is interpreted, enforced, and applied in a manner that is consistent with the interests of dominant actors. While enforcement will often mirror the interests of the state, it is also the case that powerful interest groups (physicians, for example) are emboldened and empowered to resist and reshape state interests. The case studies also reveal that the construct of "crime" is infused as much by enforcement practices and the interests of criminal justice and related professionals – those responsible for detecting, processing, and reforming the carriers of "crime" – as by the definitional categorization. As Brockman concludes, "what we do about a law is perhaps as important as, or more important than, what the law says and has a major impact on the ultimate compositions of 'what is a crime?'"

Criminalization as Governing through "Crime"

David Garland (1997, 188 [emphasis in original]) helpfully distinguishes "three practicable objects and three forms of exercising power in respect of them: the *legal subject* governed by sovereign command and obliged to obey or be punished; the *criminal delinquent,* governed by discipline and required to conform or be corrected; and the *criminogenic* situation, governed by the manipulation of interests and the promotion of mechanisms of self-regulation." In our current neo-liberal society wherein hierarchy, order, and self-responsibilization are integral features, governing through crime is centred upon the attempt to identify or predict risky situations or risky populations. Put differently, these are the situations or sub-populations that pose a risk – not necessarily of a violent sort, but a risk to the values and practices integral to neo-liberalism. In what Ulrich Beck (2006, 335) describes as an exquisite irony, promises of security propel the production of risk itself. The more frequently we are assured that steps are being taken to secure us, the more likely it is that we anticipate danger and call for more law and regulation. Moreover, "in the face of the production of insuperable manufactured uncertainties society more than ever relies and insists on security and control."

To make good on its promise of security, the state must make visible its efforts to manage situations and populations in order to minimize risk. The criminogenic situation (or sub-population) is that which, if left unchecked, will breed "crime" – it and they are carriers of risk. In turn, these criminogenic situations or sub-populations become new sites of intervention and action by the state (Garland 1997). Who – or what – becomes defined as risky? The threat – or risk – is often located in those individuals ascribed with difference – the "other" whose observed "otherness" signals a form of deviance that if not checked and contained will bring in tow incalculable damage. Otherness is signalled in many ways but, most importantly, by reference to departures from the attributes of the neo-liberal citizen – that is, those who are not self-sufficient, not fully responsible for themselves, and inadequate in the role of consumers. As noted in the previous section, it is the failed neo-liberal citizen – the flawed consumer, the dependent or irresponsible citizen – standing as he or she does outside the normative boundaries of neo-liberal citizenship who constitutes a threat and, as such, is to be feared.

Consistent with neo-liberalism's focus on individual responsibility, risk discourse is focused squarely on individuals – not social, economic, and political structures or ideologies – as the source of social problems. As R.C. Schehr (2005, 51) notes, the "discourse of risk complements our dehumanizing and individualizing consumer culture in that it stimulates mistrust and suspicion ... [It] leads to divisions among people based on certain ascribed characteristics of difference. The poor, ethnic minorities, homosexuals and youth each find themselves marginalized by a discourse of fear." While discourses of fear will, inevitably, shape the categorization of behaviour as "crime" and, as we have seen, powerfully influence who is entangled in the actual enforcement of "crime," they also lend themselves not only to the governance of crime but also to governance through crime. In this latter instance, "crime" operates as a modality of governance in a manner only loosely connected with the formal criminal law and criminal justice system. It is the idea of "crime" and the risk it presents rather than a particular proscribed behaviour that is central to this technique of governance. The case studies of welfare fraud and Aboriginal harvesting make visible the form of criminalization that occurs in governing through crime – where "crime" is not constituted solely by defined individual conduct that is interrogated with a burden of proof but, rather, as an assembly of legal and normative practices and authorities that is severely moralized and thus arbitrary.

Mosher and Hermer trace the government's role in the construction of the menace of "welfare fraud." As described earlier, the characterization of rule breaches as "fraud" – conduct that is prohibited by the *Criminal Code* – the use of evocatively criminal terms in describing welfare recipients (thieves, cheats, and fraudsters), and the ramping up of both surveillance strategies and penalties served to position all welfare recipients as actual or potential criminals. Under the constant gaze of suspicious regard, the looming threat of fraud charges, and the insistent repetition of terminology associating welfare receipt with criminality, recipients feel demeaned, dehumanized, criminalized, and constantly fearful that they will be accused of fraud. They struggle – within a system, one might argue, that has been intentionally constructed to generate rule violations – to avoid accusations and investigations of fraud. The now ready association drawn between welfare receipt, social disorder, and crime effectively regulates the behaviour not only of those in receipt of welfare but, equally as important, of those in low-wage and/or exploitative employment who seek – at almost all costs – to avoid the welfare rolls. The authors conclude that "fighting welfare fraud has little to do with governing crime but more with a systematic attempt to disenfranchise and punish a highly vulnerable and easily stigmatized population who dare to seek assistance from the state." Bauman's (2005, 82) observation of the American context resonates with the conclusions drawn by Mosher and Hermer:

> When, however, the image of the idle poor is overlaid with the alarming news of rising criminality and violence against the lives and property of the decent majority, disapproval is topped up by fear; non-obedience to the work ethic becomes a fearful act, in addition to being morally odious and repulsive.
>
> Poverty turns then from the subject matter of social policy into a problem for penology and criminal law. The poor are no longer the rejects of consumer society, defeated in the all-out competitive wars; they are the outright enemies of society ...
>
> Linking poverty with criminality has another effect: it helps to banish the poor from the universe of moral obligation ... As actual or potential criminals, the poor cease to be an ethical problem – they are exempt from our moral responsibility.

As Peck (2001) has observed, the neo-liberal state, while "rolling back" its provisioning of social welfare, simultaneously "rolled out" vigorous and punitive "law and order" policies and practices. In the context of those in receipt of welfare benefits in Ontario, the "zero tolerance" of welfare fraud and other aggressive law and order policies have worked in tandem with the retrenchment of the welfare state to govern the socially marginalized – not only those in receipt of welfare but also those who dare not quit dead-end, low-paid, and/or dangerous employment (Beckett and Western 2001). In other words, the socially marginalized are governed through crime.

The study of Aboriginal harvesting by Chartrand and Weber-Pillwax reveals, like the study of welfare fraud, a form of governing through crime. Here, too, it is the language of crime and criminality – fraud, criminals, and cheats – and the constant and looming threat of possible charges and the loss of critical access to food that operate to discipline and control Aboriginal harvesters. What we see at play again is *not* the invocation of formal criminal justice processes to detect and punish specific harmful deeds but, rather, the use of the construct – the idea – of "crime" to stigmatize and disentitle a vulnerable social group. As is the case with welfare fraud, often the rules governing harvesting are complex and counter-intuitive, making it difficult to comply. Similarly, the stark choice is all too frequently between regulatory compliance and survival (in both its physical and cultural senses). A hunter, for example, who shares moose meat with elderly family members commits an infraction but chooses his obligation to provide for family over compliance with the law of others.

While quasi-criminal processes around hunting and fishing are often resorted to by enforcement officials, resulting in readily recognized forms of criminalization, it is also the case that, as with welfare fraud, other more subtle processes of criminalization are deeply entrenched. Participants in the various workshops that formed part of Chartrand and Weber-Pillwax's study often referred to the conduct and language of enforcement officials that clearly signalled that all Aboriginal peoples were suspected criminals. As participants explained, "they have a job to do, but I think they could do it in such a way that they don't make you feel like such a criminal"; "the way the undercover cop talked, we were outlaws, we were thieves." The authors explain that "abusive interrogations by enforcement officers often leave harvesters and their families with a general sense of apprehension of authority figures. As a result of these interactions, people begin to feel that, simply by walking on their traditional lands, they are guilty of some illegal act – in essence, that they are criminals." And what emerges poignantly from the study is the impact upon future generations where traditional practices and their practitioners are widely treated as "criminal" and the social and physical limitation on First Nations' space, created by law and policies, "places the whole people in a state of constant mental, physical, and emotional distress." As such, an entire group of people – and, in this context, also a way of living – become criminally suspect, subject to surveillance and demeaning treatment, and made to feel like they are criminals and widely regarded as such by others. As the authors suggest, "the cumulative effect of these situations in the long term is the broad criminalization of Aboriginal cultures and peoples."

In other words, these two case studies reveal a form of governance through "crime." In the case of welfare fraud, the disentitlement of vulnerable people to social assistance and, in the case of Aboriginal harvesting, the assimilation of Aboriginal peoples both emerge as the political projects accomplished through criminalization. Both projects reaffirm the neo-liberal citizen and the values she or he embraces and, as such, render him or her more secure. The deepening insecurity for low-income and Aboriginal peoples that is the consequence of these projects is rarely acknowledged.

Conclusion

These case studies illustrate, in multiple ways, the complex web of power relations at play in relation to "crime." An over-arching theme of these studies is that the state is not the sole purveyor of regulation that is often rationalized as a "public good" but, rather, that regulation is effectuated by the roles of private companies that profit from gambling, by citizens engaged in the surveillance of those they suspect are in receipt of welfare, and by industries that profit from natural resources and development. Conversely, the study of fraud by health care professionals also reveals, as does the gambling study, that those who already enjoy considerable power can push back and resist criminalization processes, often successfully relocating their conduct not only outside the criminal law paradigm but also outside the boundaries of negative moral judgment.

We conclude then by citing what seemed to be the LCC's hope for the future – an aspiration anchored in democratic ideals of equality and inclusive citizenship:

> The reflex to criminal law and punishment is a dangerous strategy. We should strive for a society that is not governed by fear and criminal law but by the values of participation and trust. We hope for society and its governments to develop response strategies that are rooted in an understanding of the limits of a criminal law approach and recognize the benefits of alternative response techniques. (LCC 2003b, 47)

It is our hope that this collection advances these goals by contributing to an understanding of criminalization as a primary and sophisticated resource of political power – one that is dependent on constantly shifting legal and moral boundaries around that which constitutes "crime." Bertrand's Afterword challenges us to go yet further, to move beyond the concept of "crime" in order to meaningfully tackle the truly harmful social conduct of our time.

Acknowledgment
We are indebted to Diana Morokhovets for her excellent research assistance and her thoughtful suggestions.

Notes

1 Also see Macdonald's statement prior to his appointment as the first president of the Law Commission of Canada (LCC) (Macdonald 1997). See Nathalie Des Rosiers (2007) for some of the methodological and ethical challenges the LCC faced in working with interdisciplinary and community-based scholarship.

2 The LCC launched a series of Legal Dimension Initiatives with the Canadian Association of Law Teachers, the Canadian Law and Society Association, and the Canadian Council of Law Deans. The "what is a crime?" project was its fourth research initiative.

3 *Criminal Code*, R.S.C. 1985, c. C-46, s. 264.

4 The most common historical example is alcohol prohibition. Recently, the prohibition of marijuana has come under siege with the reclassification of the substance outside the narcotics schedule, the recognition of the therapeutic properties of the drug, and the amendments allowing for its medical use and private "production" (cultivation) to counter the state's failure to provide the substance to authorized patients.

5 Ontario, Legislative Assembly, 28 September 1995, http://hansardindex.ontla.on.ca/hansardeissue/36-1/l003.htm.

References

Bauman, Z. 2005. *Work, Consumerism and the New Poor.* New York: Open University Press.

Beck, U. 2006. "Living in the World Risk Society." *Economy and Society* 35, 3: 329-45.

Beckett, K., and B. Western. 2001. "Governing Social Marginality: Welfare, Incarceration, and the Transformation of State Policy." *Punishment and Society* 3, 1: 43-59.

Coleman, R. 2003. "Images from a Neoliberal City: The State, Surveillance, and Social Control." *Critical Criminology* 12, 1: 21-42.

Des Rosiers, N. 2007. "In Memoriam: La Commission du droit du Canada / The Law Commission of Canada, 1997-2006." *Canadian Journal of Law and Society* 22, 2: 145-75.

Des Rosiers, N., and S. Bittle. 2004. "Introduction." In *What Is a Crime? Defining Criminal Conduct in Contemporary Society,* ed. Law Commission of Canada, vii-xxv. Vancouver and Toronto: UBC Press.

Garland, D. 1997. "'Governmentality' and the Problem of Crime: Foucault, Criminology, Sociology." *Theoretical Criminology* 1, 2: 173-214.

Hulsman, L.H.C. 1986. "Critical Criminology and the Concept of Crime." *Contemporary Crises* 10, 1: 63-80.

Le Bouthillier, Y. 2007. "The Law Commission of Canada / La Commission du droit du Canada." *Canadian Journal of Law and Society* 22, 2: 113-16.

Law Commission of Canada, ed. 2003a. *What Is a Crime?* Background Paper. Ottawa: Canada.

–. 2003b. *What Is a Crime? Challenges and Alternatives.* Discussion Paper. Ottawa: Law Commission of Canada.

–. 2004. *What Is a Crime? Defining Criminal Conduct in Contemporary Society.* Vancouver and Toronto: UBC Press.

Macdonald, R.A. 1997. "Recommissioning Law Reform." *Alberta Law Review* 35, 4: 831-79.

–. 2007. "Jamais deux sans trois ... Once Reform, Twice Commission, Thrice Law." *Canadian Journal of Law and Society* 22, 2: 117-43.

Mosher, J. 2007. "Welfare Reform and the Re-Making of the Model Citizen." In *Poverty: Rights, Social Citizenship, Legal Activism,* ed. M. Young, S.B. Boyd, G. Brodsky, and S. Day, 119-38. Vancouver and Toronto: UBC Press.

Ontario. Legislative Assembly. 1995. *Official Report of Debates (Hansard).* 36th Leg., 1st Sess. (28 September).

Peck, J. 2001. "Neoliberalizing States: Thin Policies/Hard Outcomes." *Progress in Human Geography* 25, 3: 445-55.

Schehr, R.C. 2005. "Conventional Risk Discourse and the Proliferation of Fear." *Criminal Justice Policy Review* 16, 1: 38-58.

Snider, L. 2000. "The Sociology of Corporate Crime: An Obituary (Or: Whose Knowledge Claims Have Legs?)." *Theoretical Criminology* 4, 2: 169-206.

1
Welfare Fraud: The Constitution of Social Assistance as Crime
Janet Mosher and Joe Hermer

The past two decades have witnessed a profound and complex shift in how the state is positioned in relation to the ideals of welfare and citizenship. These changes are, in a very broad way, encompassed by two related movements. The first is how the realm of crime and disorder as a legitimate object of state intervention has expanded and dispersed across a broad array of government activity that has traditionally been viewed under the rubric of public policy. Areas of public policy, such as immigration, education, and social welfare, are now increasingly viewed and acted upon as problems of safety, security, and crime. This expansion of social and legal regulation, often through means that are only loosely connected to the typical instruments of criminal justice, has seen the re-entrenchment of state power in a complicated and often invisible way. In tandem with this movement has been a basic reconfiguration of the collective ways in which we are responsible for one another through the instalment of the neo-liberal citizen. Idealized in a wide array of reforms, this ideal citizen is made flexible to labour market conditions (which are viewed as naturally desirable and involving little state intervention), responsible for his/her own particular circumstances under the preferences of "freedom" and "choice," and positioned narrowly as a consumer who must manage individual risk. The result has been that those who are the most socially and economically vulnerable have been widely disenfranchised in terms of making any claim for assistance and support based on social and economic need. This pincer of neo-liberalism – the expansion of a net of social regulation and state authority in the social sphere and a significant withdrawal of state commitment to the welfare of vulnerable people – is an overarching feature of the politics of early-twenty-first-century life.

This chapter examines one area where both of these movements have dramatically transformed a significant area of government policy – the re-ordering of social assistance programs through the policing of welfare fraud. In the past decade, welfare fraud has attracted substantial political and public attention. The language of "fraud" has been widely invoked in political discourse, together with such terms as "cheats," "liars," and "criminals" to describe social assistance recipients, and accompanied by promises to "crack down" and "get tough." The message that criminal misconduct is widespread within the social assistance system has certainly not been ambivalent. The obvious and logical deduction is that welfare recipients are morally suspect persons, criminals in waiting who are poised to abuse a public trust.[1] These changes in relation to welfare fraud have been occurring within a broader context of fundamental transformation to social assistance regimes not only in Ontario but also throughout North America. A shift away from state provision for those in need, the adoption of workfare programs, reductions in benefit levels, and a sharp winnowing of the categories of the "deserving poor" have been among the most significant features of this transformed landscape.

To better understand the nature and impact of these changes, we undertook a detailed examination of the new legislation, regulations, and policy directives in the province of Ontario. Although our focus was upon fraud, we wanted to locate and understand fraud within the broader constellation of changes that were under way within social assistance regimes. We conducted twenty-three semi-structured interviews with lawyers and community legal workers in Ontario's community legal clinic system between July and October 2004 and interviewed the director of the Ontario Disability Support Program. We also conducted an extensive review of reported criminal cases involving welfare fraud.[2]

Our study reveals "welfare fraud" to be a problem that has been constructed and deployed to disentitle and punish welfare recipients. Much of the behaviour commonly described as "welfare fraud" bears scant resemblance to actual criminal fraud and, instead, arises as a result of errors and misunderstandings made in the context of an astoundingly complex bureaucratic system composed of some 800 rules. The study also details the ambiguity, vagueness, and capriciousness of the system within which recipients struggle to survive on inadequate incomes and examines how behaviour that may seem innocuous or even socially valued – having dinner at a friend's or forming an intimate relationship – becomes the object of criminal suspicion and intense scrutiny.

While few cases are actually prosecuted as fraud in criminal courts, we argue that an intense form of criminalization of those in receipt of social assistance occurs through other processes that exist outside the criminal justice system: the construction of the menace of welfare fraud; the inadequacy of benefits; and the sweep and depth of surveillance measures. Thus, we view criminalization to be anchored in both a legal and moral field of labelling, condemnation, and punishment that is not limited to criminal justice processes. By broadening our analysis to capture a network of regulation beyond the category of criminal law, we draw attention to a prominent example of how poor people are positioned within the current political conditions of the "welfare state."

Constructing the Problem of Welfare Fraud

Welfare fraud has long been misunderstood and misrepresented (Social Assistance Review Committee 1988). Between 1995 and 2003, under the leadership of a Conservative government, these misrepresentations were amplified. The construction of the problem of welfare fraud was undertaken with a renewed political energy, and measures to combat fraud were central to the reforms introduced in 1997 through the *Social Assistance Reform Act (SARA)* and beyond.[3] The government employed a variety of strategies to construct welfare fraud as a serious problem – indeed, as one that was out of control and requiring more and increasingly harsh measures to curb its proliferation. In constructing welfare fraud as a significant problem, rhetorical claims about its magnitude and harms abounded. In her affidavit in support of the government's defence of the constitutionality of a lifetime ban on the receipt of welfare benefits for those convicted of welfare fraud, the director of the Ontario Disability Support Program, Debbie Moretta, detailed several initiatives undertaken by governments over the years to curb the problem. She concluded that, "despite initiatives to combat welfare fraud, it has remained a serious problem and was seen by the public to be insufficiently addressed by government. The zero tolerance policy is intended to deter welfare fraud, to ensure effective management of public funds and to restore public confidence in the welfare system" (Moretta 2003). In other words, despite valiant attempts, the problem of welfare fraud still needed to be contained, and harsher measures were required. The resort to additional forms of harsh punishment (a lifetime ban) and the introduction of a "zero tolerance" policy signalled the seriousness of welfare fraud as a crime.

The invocation of explicitly criminal terms – "fraud," "cheats," " liars," "theft," and "crackdowns" – in a host of government publications and news releases served to further construct the problem as a criminal menace and, thus, all the more serious and threatening. Welfare fraud "cheat sheets" posted on the government's website and accounts of complex fraud involving multiple fabricated identities that appeared in local news media strengthened the perception of serious and widespread criminality. By declaring the "fight" against fraud to be one of the three objectives of welfare reform, Ontario's welfare system demonstrated how critical fraud had become and also announced the government's intention to battle it.

However, it was the government's use of "official statistics" that provided perhaps the clearest evidence of its role in constructing the problem of welfare fraud. In the period from 1997 to 2002, the government released its annual *Welfare Fraud Control Reports,* which purported to document the extent and severity of the welfare fraud problem. The reports were permeated with the language of "fraud" and other references to forms of crime and criminality. The 2001-2 report, for example, makes reference to the Welfare Fraud Hotline, to the fraud control database for tracking fraud investigations, to "anti-fraud measures [that] help catch welfare cheats and deter others from thinking about cheating," and to welfare fraud as a crime that the government is cracking down on through the introduction of a zero tolerance policy (Ministry of Community, Family and Children's Services 2003). The report claims that "over $49 million was identified in social assistance payments that people were not entitled to receive and an estimated $12 million in avoided future costs." Given the general thrust of the report and its title, one might be forgiven for concluding that these dollars are directly attributable to welfare fraud. Indeed, this is the very message that the government seems to be intending to convey.[4] However, a closer examination reveals a different picture. For instance, in 2001-2, there were 38,452 fraud investigations, resulting in only 393 convictions for welfare fraud, but in 12,816 cases the assistance was reduced or terminated as a result of eligibility re-assessments. Although it is not entirely clear whether the 393 convictions (where benefits are also likely to have been reduced or terminated) are included among these 12,816 cases where benefits were reduced or terminated, it *is* clear that in more than 12,000 cases criminal "fraud" was not established, no crime was proven, and any dollars saved were not the result of "fraud" detection. Even though a certain number of the 12,000 cases may be instances where prosecution was not recommended even though there existed a strong case, the vast majority are likely to be instances where a rule was broken, but without the requisite *mens rea* or *actus reus* to constitute criminal fraud – in other words, as a result of client misunderstanding, error, or oversight. By referring to all of the errors as fraud and using terms such as "cheats," "cracking down on crime," and "zero tolerance," the report portrays a picture of criminal fraud as rampant and, correspondingly, of beneficiaries being actual or potential criminals. Tellingly, the report does not include instances of rule violations that have resulted in underpayments to recipients.

The only evidence that exists pertaining to the incidence of fraud in Ontario is the number of convictions for fraud, and even this evidence must be viewed with some skepticism given the lack of adequate or any legal representation as well as the tremendous pressures to plead guilty and get it over with.[5] The first year for which province-wide statistics are available is 1997-98, and the most recent year available is 2001-2 (Moretta 2004). All of the statistics in Table 1.1 show the cumulative data from the Ontario Works and Ontario Disability Support Program systems (Ministry of Community, Family and Children's Services 2003). In addition to the number of

Table 1.1

Fraud investigations and outcomes

Year	2001-2	2000-1	1999-2000	1998-99	1997-98
Convictions	393	430	557	747	1,123
Total fraud investigations	38,452	52,582	43,900	49,987	53,452
Social assistance reduced or terminated	12,816	17,734	15,680	16,946	14,771
No eligibility problems found	25,636	34,848	28,220	33,041	38,681

convictions, it is important to observe the very substantial numbers of fraud investigations.

The number of convictions for 2001-2 (393 convictions) is roughly equivalent to 0.1 percent of the combined social assistance caseload and 1 percent of the total number of allegations. Yet it is the broad sweep of "fraud" described earlier, to encompass rule infractions and not criminal fraud, that supports the characterization of welfare fraud as rampant and that no doubt fuels the widespread misconception held by the general public about its incidence.

Responding to Welfare Fraud
In Ontario, fighting welfare fraud was expressly identified as one of three central objectives of the *SARA*, which was introduced in the late 1990s and ushered in the most significant reforms to social assistance in decades.[6] The *SARA* contained two schedules, the *Ontario Works Act, 1997 (OWA)* and the *Ontario Disability Support Program Act, 1997 (ODSPA)*, the former governing the able-bodied and the latter governing those with statutorily recognized "disabilities."[7] Both the *OWA* and the *ODSPA* included a vast array of new measures to arm the government in its battle against welfare fraud. While neither the concern regarding welfare fraud nor the ready association of poverty and criminality were new features of the social assistance landscape, clearly they were substantially reinvigorated through these and subsequent legislative reforms.

The Conservative government introduced a broad array of measures, ranging from a controlling fraud protocol to a lifetime ban on eligibility for benefits if convicted of welfare fraud, in order to respond to the serious problem that welfare fraud was portrayed to be. In turn, the extent, breadth, and severity of these measures reinforced the view of the severity of the "fraud" problem. *Policy Directive 45 on Controlling Fraud* provides the framework in which delivery agents of Ontario Works are to develop local fraud control protocols and practices.[8] Every administrator is required, under the

Table 1.2

Source of welfare fraud complaint

Year	2001-2	2000-1	1999-2000	1998-99	1997-98
Welfare fraud hotline	6,527	9,348	8,825	8,327	7,910
Information-sharing agreements	9,988	10,447	12,502	11,577	12,514
Local provincial/ municipal offices	19,078	33,028	33,714	39,158	41,229
Total	35,593	53,823	55,041	59,062	61,653

directive, to "consult with the local police services and the Crown Attorney's Office to develop a written protocol for the effective investigation and prosecution of cases of suspected social assistance fraud." The local protocols are to spell out respective responsibilities for various stages of the investigation, including the collection of information, the securing of evidence, and the preparation of a Crown brief.[9]

The directive requires that all allegations of fraud, from both internal and external sources, be assessed in a timely manner. This assessment is undertaken by an eligibility review officer (ERO), who is to conduct a "comprehensive investigation" and prepare a written report for an ERO supervisor, including a recommendation regarding ongoing eligibility, any overpayment, and whether to refer the matter to the police. In January 2004, this directive was revised to provide that, "where sufficient evidence exists to suspect intent to commit fraud, the case *must* [bolded in original] be referred to police for possible criminal prosecution." A very substantial number of allegations of welfare fraud are communicated to the ministry each year from a variety of sources. Table 1.2, which was prepared by the ministry, notes these various sources and the numbers of complaints generated by source (Ministry of Community, Family and Children's Services 2003).

While the ministry's position is that the directive provides the framework in which local delivery agents are to operate, the picture that emerged during our interviews suggests that this is not invariably the case. Most significantly, the policy contemplates that the only consideration in deciding whether the matter should be referred to the police is whether sufficient evidence exists to suspect an intent to commit fraud. In practice, however, a range of additional factors is considered. Several municipalities apply a dollar threshold and do not refer cases below $5,000.[10] Variations also exist regarding the types of circumstances that may give rise to a referral to police. Thus, for example, student loans, casual gifts of small value, and spouses are treated differently in various parts of the province. Respondents reported variations among individual caseworkers that often depend upon who the recipient is and how she responds to the allegation – whether the recipient is sufficiently contrite; whether she is able to explain what is happening in a way that the worker can understand and empathize with; what the reputation of the recipient's family is in the community; how the recipient looks and talks; and what stereotypes inform how she is judged. These are all factors that were identified as influencing the decision whether to refer the matter to the police or not.[11]

Regions also vary in the significance, if any, that is given to the consideration of personal circumstances. This was an issue that was very much at play during the inquest into the death of Kimberly Rogers, who died in August 2001 while serving a period of house arrest upon a conviction of welfare fraud. She was eight months pregnant with a history of depression and was living under a three-month ban on eligibility (an injunction to lift the ban was granted prior to her death, but, even then, Rogers had only eighteen dollars per month to live on). Pursuant to a recommendation of the coroner's jury, the Fraud Referral Task Force was struck by the Ontario Municipal Services Association. As recommended by the jury, the task force prepared a detailed set of guidelines to ensure the "full appreciation of the person's life circumstances and the impact of the consequences of a fraud conviction," prior to a referral being made to the police (Ontario Municipal Social Services Association 2003). However, the ministry expressly did not endorse these guidelines and specifically declined to participate in the process that generated them (Moretta 2004). In fact, the recommendations of the task force stand in stark contrast to the revision of the ministry's *Policy Directive 45 on Controlling Fraud* that did occur – a revision that made mandatory the referral to the police of all cases where there is reason to suspect intent to commit fraud.[12] Unlike the task force guidelines wherein personal factors such as health, domestic violence, and the adequacy of benefits would be considered, the only consideration permissible within the framework of the policy directive is suspicion of the intent to commit fraud.

The *OWA* and regulations thereto also expanded the powers available to EROs to undertake their investigations of welfare fraud. As we discuss later in this chapter, this ramping up of police-type power and authority was not accompanied by commensurate safeguards in terms of protecting the legal rights of those under investigation. EROs have the power to enter any place other than a dwelling if there are reasonable grounds to believe that evidence relevant to eligibility may be found there, to require the production of records, to obtain a warrant to enter a dwelling place,[13] and to "require information or material from a person who is the subject of an investigation ... or from any person who the officer has reason to believe can provide information or material relevant to the investigation."[14] These powers are reinforced by subsection 79(3) of the *OWA*, which makes it an offence to obstruct or knowingly give false information to a person engaged in an investigation.

In the course of their investigations, EROs will often seek information from landlords, neighbours, teachers, and others who may know something of the circumstances of the recipient under investigation. A copy of a routine form letter, which was being mailed out to make inquiries about a neighbour, was provided to us. The letter explains, "we are conducting inquiries relating to an Ontario Works recipient and require information with respect to the above address. If you have any information regarding the tenants of the above address i.e.: number of occupants, sexes, names, employment, length of residence, or any other relevant information please do not hesitate to contact me. Your anonymity can be assured in responding to this inquiry." It is hard to imagine that a person receiving such a letter would not suspect wrongdoing on the part of the neighbour about whom the information is requested.

A fraud investigation will often include a meeting with the person who is the subject of the investigation. As noted earlier, an ERO has the power to compel information and material from the person who is the subject of the investigation. Our research indicates that those under investigation are not warned that statements they provide may be used against them in a criminal proceeding, notwithstanding that evidence so gathered is regularly used against recipients in subsequent criminal prosecutions. Certainly, one characterization of these meetings is that they are solely for the purpose of determining eligibility and are thus integrally connected to the enforcement of a regulatory regime. However, a competing – and compelling – characterization is that they often take the form of *de facto* criminal investigations and, as such, require *Charter* warnings and limitations on the use of evidence so gathered.[15] While the issue of when a regulatory investigation becomes a *de facto* criminal investigation has received significant attention in the income tax context, it has received very little critical interrogation within the welfare context.[16] This omission is troubling because it appears to be not at all uncommon for police and Crown attorneys to rely upon nothing but the investigations undertaken by EROs in their prosecution of persons accused of welfare fraud. Indeed, there was evidence given at the Kimberly Rogers inquest about police officers training EROs on how to put together their investigative files so that additional investigative work by the police would be minimized should the files be referred to the police.[17] Given the number of fraud investigations and the statutory power of EROs to compel information, there is a very good argument that the *Charter* rights of recipients – particularly the right in section 7 to life, liberty, and security of the person and the right not to be deprived thereof except in accordance with the principles of fundamental justice (among these principles, the right against self-incrimination) and the recipients' reasonable expectation of privacy protected by section 8 – are regularly being violated.

A related concern articulated by respondents in our interviews was that recipients under investigation who are called in for a meeting with an ERO frequently do not fully understand the import of the interview, nor do they comprehend that their statements may subsequently be used against them in a fraud prosecution. In the experience of our respondents, the fear of a possible criminal charge, especially within a broad context where "fraud" language is pervasive and recipients are constantly dehumanized, forces recipients to agree all too readily to administrative sanctions such as termina-tions or overpayments in hopes of avoiding a criminal charge when they are accused (even inferentially) of fraud. Respondents in our interviews also expressed concern that the threat of the government withholding monthly benefit cheques is sometimes used to extract admissions, particularly of overpayments. They described instances where their clients, desperate for their monthly cheques, simply signed documents – including statutory declarations – without understanding the content of the document or the implications of signing it. As Grainne McKeever (1999, 268) suggests in rela-tion to proposed British social security reforms, suspicion of fraud can be readily "played off against a fear of court proceedings" and against a fear of the termination of benefits. Recipients are also understandably reluctant to complain about mistreatment during investigations. They are, after all, in a position of extreme vulnerability in their interactions with agents of the administrative regime, who can cut them off benefits, assess overpayments, and refer matters to the police. Rocking the boat almost always promises to be more trouble than it is worth.

A further significant development in the arsenal of measures to combat welfare fraud was the introduction of "enhanced verification" and later "consolidated verification procedures" (CVPs). CVPs have changed both the frequency and nature of file reviews (Herd and Mitchell 2002). Previously, reviews were time based, with a review occurring usually every twelve months. In the CVP environment, priority-ranking factors, based upon an assumed risk of fraud, are used to determine when a review will occur. High-risk factors include high accommodation costs (equal to or greater than 80 percent of the recipient's net revenue, a common occurrence for those in receipt of assistance) and the receipt of social assistance for more than thirty-six months. Medium-risk factors include a social insurance number beginning with a "9" (thus indicating a non-citizen who has yet to secure permanent residence status but who has a work permit), accommodation costs equal to 75-79 percent of net revenue, and the receipt of social assist-ance for between twenty-four and thirty-five months (*ibid.*, 34-37).

The amount of information required to be provided at the time of apply-ing and during regular or risk-determined reviews can be overwhelming. Among other things, applicants are required to provide documentation to verify birth and marital status, child or spousal support obligations, immigration status, and any immigration sponsorship, income, property, debts, receivables, funds in trust, boarder(s), accommodation, school attendance for dependent children, employment, and education status (*ibid.,* 38-39). Information must be provided not only at the time of applying but also on an ongoing basis. The sweeping consent to the collection and release of information that must be signed as a pre-condition to the receipt of benefits, the extensive and ongoing reporting requirements, together with a host of information-sharing agreements negotiated with a range of provincial and federal departments (including the Ontario Ministry of Training, Colleges and Universities, social services ministries in other provinces and territories, and the federal Ministry of Immigration and Citizenship), permit the ministry to gather and share vast amounts of information about those in receipt of social assistance. As the earlier statistics reveal, these information-sharing arrangements generate a substantial number of fraud investigations.

Regulation 134/98 also authorizes random "home visits," with or without notice, to verify eligibility. Although consent is required before entering the home, the withholding of consent may result in termination of benefits or denial of eligibility unless the director is satisfied that there was a reasonable basis to withhold the consent. Given the coercive power of the state, backed by the threat of the denial of benefits, it is hard to imagine that consent is being volitionally given. Home visits are restricted to observing what is in "plain view" and, according to the policy directive on home visits, are not to be used for the purpose of investigating a specific participant because of a fraud suspicion.[18] *Policy Directive 12 on Home Visits* does provide, however, that CVP criteria may be "helpful in determining where random home visits are required" and goes on to note that a home visit can be made with a participant because she or he randomly falls within a specific group.[19] Given that CVP criteria are red flags for fraud and that these may be used to identify "groups" where home visits may be required, there is surely a good argument that home visits are linked through the policy to fraud investigations and are not, in fact, purely random.

In addition to EROs, the public is also charged with a responsibility – a civic duty – to engage in the project of monitoring and scrutinizing welfare recipients. As noted earlier, the public has been told that welfare fraud is rampant and that people not genuinely in need are taking money from those genuinely in need. One way to discharge this civic duty is to call a toll-free welfare fraud hotline (6,527 people called this number in 2001-2, down from 9,348 in 2000-1), and the toll-free line continues to be in operation (Ministry of Community, Family and Children's Services 2003; Ministry of Community and Social Services 2009). Introducing the welfare fraud hotline on 2 October 1995, then minister of community and social services, David Tsubouchi, proclaimed in the House of Commons that "welfare fraud is a problem that hurts the most vulnerable people in our society. Every cent that is paid to the wrong person through fraud is help taken from the needy." He noted that experience had shown hotlines to be an effective device for ensuring that this does not happen and that they would provide a projected savings of $25 million per year, and he invited the people of Ontario to call 1-800-394-STOP to help "stop fraud and to protect the system for people who really need help."[20] With respect to virtually no other crime that we can identify has there been such a vigorous effort to bring the public so actively into the task of surveillance and denunciation.

A very significant development in the welfare fraud control regime was the introduction of additional penalties upon conviction. The government first introduced a three-month ban on the receipt of welfare for a first conviction, six months for subsequent convictions, and, later, a lifetime ban (for crimes committed after 1 April 2000).[21] Thus, upon conviction for welfare fraud, one was automatically banned for life from the receipt of social assistance. As noted earlier, these additional and severe penalties were justified by the government as being essential in its battle against welfare fraud. While the sentencing options available under the *Criminal Code* were adequate for other crimes, harsher penalties were necessary to deter welfare fraud.[22] In this manner, welfare fraud was constructed as a particularly intransigent and harmful crime. The constitutionality of the lifetime ban was under challenge when the newly elected Liberal government announced its repeal in December 2003. Yet accompanying the repeal of the lifetime ban was a promise to get tough on welfare fraud and the introduction of the revised policy directive noted earlier, mandating referrals to the police whenever there was reason to suspect the intent to commit fraud.[23]

Other Features of the Reformed Character of Ontario's Social Assistance System

In order to fully understand how welfare fraud is presently constituted, it is useful to locate it within a much wider shift that has occurred in how poor people and poverty are positioned within the character of the reformed welfare state and how citizenship has been reconfigured. Our review of welfare reform in Ontario reveals that the ideal of the poor having an entitlement to assistance based on need and by virtue of their citizenship has now been widely diminished and has been replaced with a construction of poor people as a public burden who should themselves be held responsible, and personally blamed, for their circumstances. While the provision of social assistance has always been a contested role of the state, there has been a significant hardening of the view that receiving social assistance amounts to getting "something for nothing" by people who are lazy and simply do not want to be responsible for themselves and their families. Far too many employable men and women are being paid to "sit home and do nothing" (in the words of former Ontario premier Mike Harris), and the honest, hard-working taxpayer who is footing the bill has every right to resent this use of his hard-earned dollars.[24]

In the place of need-based entitlement, or any principle stating the importance of providing an adequate level of support to the disadvantaged, is a narrow view of the entrepreneurial citizen, who, as defined by the *OWA*, is self-reliant, responsible, and accountable to the taxpayers of Ontario. The act's purpose is expressly identified as the establishment of a program that (1) recognizes individual responsibility and promotes self-reliance through employment; (2) provides temporary financial assistance to those most in need while they satisfy obligations to become and stay employed; (3) effectively serves people needing assistance; and (4) is accountable to the taxpayers of Ontario. This emphasis upon self-reliance and employment obligations reflects a profound departure from the principle of entitlement to state support that, while never fully realized in practice, nevertheless formed an articulated basis for both provincial and federal legislation. Indeed, only a decade earlier, a report on social assistance commissioned by the government of Ontario identified a rights-based approach as the defining feature of a social assistance regime and affirmed that "all members of the community have a presumptive right to social assistance based on need ... The support that society provides is not to be understood as a gift or privilege, nor as charity to the disadvantaged. Rather, it represents a right to which all members of society are entitled" (Social Assistance Review Committee 1988, 10-11). In stark contrast, Janet Ecker, then minister of community and social services, when introducing the *SARA* in 1997, identified "self-sufficiency [as] the overriding goal of social assistance" (Ontario, Legislative Assembly, 26 November 1997). What had long been regarded as a crucial safety net for citizens temporarily or permanently cast off by a market economy was being methodically unravelled.

With the principle of entitlement removed, the reforms constructed a form of contractualism between those on social assistance and the "honest taxpayer," one enforced through the logic of a narrow economic rationalism. Beyond the statement of purpose itself, the introduction of "workfare" (a term that tellingly signals *neither* employment nor social assistance) is the most dramatic tool that enforces this contractualism between the taxpayer and those on social assistance, one that ensures that no one will get "something for nothing." Adult beneficiaries are required to enter into a "participation agreement" with the ministry, spelling out the employment assistance activities that they will undertake. These activities may include anything from job searches, to literacy or substance addiction screening, to job skills training. In addition, every recipient has the obligation to make reasonable efforts to accept and maintain any employment "for which he or she is physically capable"; if employed part-time, to find full-time employment; and if employed and still eligible for assistance, to seek, accept, and maintain employment that would increase his or her income.[25] The failure to comply or to make reasonable efforts will result in the cancellation of benefits, first for a three-month period and subsequently for six months.

Workfare has been justified by a discourse that portrays the poor as lacking a proper work ethic and who, for their own good, must be mandated to work as a condition of receiving benefits. The explanation for poverty in this conceptualization is purely individualistic: individuals are poor because they are lazy, dependent, undisciplined, and lack a work ethic. From a neo-liberal vantage point, welfare benefits undermine performance by blunting incentives to work. People choose welfare over work or are so embedded in a culture of dependency that they cannot even appreciate that paid employment is an option. From this perspective, welfare represents a moral hazard, enticing people away from paid employment rather than being a moral opportunity enabling some to escape exploitative work or abusive husbands or to survive with some modicum of dignity when rejected by the market economy.

Consistent with this shift from entitlement to contractualism, and the delimited role of the state reflected therein, benefit rates were dramatically cut and eligibility criteria tightened. Almost immediately upon its election, the Conservative government cut benefit rates by 21.6 percent in October 1995, and no increases were introduced during its term in office. Subsequently, a Liberal government instituted a *de minimus* 3 percent increase in 2004 and a further 2 percent increase in 2006. Current benefit levels are manifestly inadequate: a single person receives 34 percent of the Statistics Canada low-income cut-off; a single parent with one child receives 56 percent (National Council of Welfare 2006).[26] The diminishment of welfare rates to a level that places recipients (many of them single mothers with children) in conditions of abject poverty is, as with workfare, justified by a political discourse that portrays individuals on social assistance as free-riders, pathologically dependent upon government handouts, and lacking the motivation to work. This logic maintains that lowering benefit rates sharpens the spur of poverty and propels people into the labour market.

In addition to the cuts in benefit levels, categories of the "deserving poor" were substantially redrawn. The definition of "disability" within the *ODSPA* has made it more difficult to qualify for disability benefits, which are somewhat more generous (although still inadequate) and which are not attached to mandated employment readiness activities (Fraser, Wilkey, and Frenschkowski 2003). While the prior legislation had grouped single parents (overwhelmingly mothers) with those with disabilities – demarcating them from the able-bodied and temporarily unemployed – the reforms shifted single mothers into the broad category of the temporarily unemployed and able-bodied. In other words, single mothers were recast as workers, not mothers/parents.[27] Presently in Ontario, single mothers are exempted from the workfare requirements until their youngest child reaches school age. In some jurisdictions, the age is as young as three months (Smith et al. 2000). The very substantial numbers of single parents rearing children on social assistance (in 2003, 59 percent of Ontario Works recipients were women, and women constituted 94 percent of single parents on Ontario Works benefits) are, in the words of the former premier of Ontario, "doing nothing." The messages are very clear: a job, any job, is a more important contribution than rearing children; raising children with an income substantially below the poverty line is a cakewalk; and child rearing is not a socially valued activity.[28]

This shift away from state responsibility has simultaneously encompassed a renewed emphasis upon the obligations of family. In the context of the reforms to welfare, this shift has been propelled primarily through the introduction of an expansive definition of "spouse." The impact of this definition has been to disqualify very significant numbers of women, largely single mothers, from eligibility for state economic support and has forced them into relationships of economic dependence upon men who frequently have, at law, no corresponding obligation to support them.

These various reforms have fundamentally restructured the experience of living day in and day out on social assistance benefits. While few recipients are actually convicted of criminal fraud, our research makes clear that the reforms have, through a variety of processes, criminalized virtually all those in receipt of social assistance or, put differently, effectively criminalized the receipt of social assistance itself. It is to an examination of these processes that we now turn by exploring how the social assistance regime structures, orders, and regulates the lives of those dependent upon it.

Processes of Criminalization: Manufacturing Fraud

As our earlier discussion indicated, government statistics released in the *Welfare Fraud Control Reports* during the period the Conservative government was in office characterized rule violations as "fraud." While the current Liberal government has not, to our knowledge, released publicly any statistics on welfare fraud, it is abundantly clear from our research that the characterization of rule violations as fraud continues to pervade the administration of the social assistance system. Moreover, we have found significant evidence of the conflation of rule violation and fraud even within the criminal justice system.

The system upon which recipients must rely to meet their needs is extraordinarily complex. It has been variously described as "Kafkaesque" or "fiendishly difficult" (both of these descriptors from judges) and "mired in a labyrinth of rules" (*R. v. Maldonado* 1998; Matthews 2004). It is extremely difficult to access timely, accurate information about the roughly 800 statutory and regulatory provisions (or the rules of the system) that create both obligations and entitlements. Indeed, it can be difficult on some matters to get a consistent answer from a single welfare office. The rules are not only voluminous but also often counter-intuitive and in constant flux – what may be permissible today may not be tomorrow. Moreover, as noted earlier, the rules themselves are not consistently applied, and significant variations exist from one municipality to another.

In the following discussion, we consider several of the particular rules governing the two areas of social conduct that are most scrupulously policed by the welfare system: the acquisition of income and the formation of an intimate relationship. This examination illustrates the complexity of the system and the near impossibility of absolute compliance. Indeed, it reveals rule violations as a structured and endemic feature of the system itself. When these rule violations are routinely and incorrectly characterized as "fraud" – as in the *Welfare Fraud Control Reports* and, more broadly, in the day-to-day operation of the welfare system – "fraud" is institutionally manufactured as an endemic feature of the social assistance regime. The misapplication of the term "fraud" is not, however, simply a bureaucratic by-product of a poorly administered system. Rather, the sleight of hand that has created "welfare fraud" has been, we argue, strategically deployed to help construct a phenomenon of widespread criminality to facilitate the state's retreat from social provision.

We begin with a consideration of the criminal construct of fraud before turning to the structures that regulate "income" and "spouses," precisely because an examination of the criminal construct of fraud helps to make evident the significant gap between criminal fraud and "welfare fraud" as commonly invoked. "Fraud" is defined by section 380 of the *Criminal Code,* which prohibits the defrauding of the public or any person of any property, money, or valuable security or any service by deceit, falsehood, or other fraudulent means.[29] The Supreme Court of Canada has identified the *actus reus* of fraud as containing two elements: the prohibited act (of "deceit, falsehood or other fraudulent means") and deprivation caused by the prohibited act. While "deceit, falsehood and fraudulent means" encompass three separate heads, the real core or nub of the offence of fraud is dishonesty (Ewart 1986; Nightingale 1996). Whether an act is appropriately characterized as dishonest is to be determined not by reference to the accused's subjective mental state (whether the accused subjectively believed the act in question to be dishonest) but, rather, whether the reasonable person would stigmatize the act in question as such. While "dishonesty" is difficult to define with precision, it connotes an underhanded design, or behaviour, that is discreditable and perhaps unscrupulous. Mere negligence will not suffice (*R. v. Olan* 1978).

In 1993, the Supreme Court of Canada released two significant decisions on the *mens rea* of fraud, namely *R. v. Théroux* (1993) and *R. v. Zlatic* (1993). The Court carefully delineated two elements of the *mens rea* of the offence of "fraud:" subjective knowledge of the prohibited act (the act that is appropriately stigmatized as dishonest, based upon a reasonableness standard) and subjective knowledge that the prohibited act could have the consequence of depriving another. There must be a subjective awareness that undertaking the prohibited act (of deceit, falsehood, or other dishonest means) could cause deprivation. In *Théroux*, Justice John Sopinka and then Chief Justice Antonio Lamer, while concurring with the majority in the outcome, penned a separate judgment to draw attention to an important distinction relevant to the legal assessment of fraud. In particular, their decision underlines the difference between an accused who honestly, but mistakenly, believes her act to be honest (that is, where viewed objectively the act would be characterized as dishonest, although the accused believes the act in question not to be dishonest) and an accused who believes in a set of facts (and this belief is accepted by the trier of fact) that would deprive the act of its dishonest character (in other words, where viewed objectively the act would not be objectively characterized as dishonest given the belief in these facts). The importance of this distinction is clearly illustrated by the case of *R. v. Maldonado* (1998) discussed in the next section.

Regulating Income

Various provisions of the *OWA* and regulations require beneficiaries to provide ongoing information with respect to the "receipt or anticipated receipt of income." The failure to do so shall, administratively, result in the termination of benefits as well as in the possible assessment of an overpayment.[30] It may also give rise to an allegation of fraud. However, what is "income," and when might the failure to report it give rise to an allegation of fraud? Pursuant to the regulations, "income" is determined by adding "all payments of any nature paid to or on behalf of or for the benefit of every member of the benefit unit." This calculation is to include the "monetary value of items and services" as well as "amounts deemed available" (such as income from boarders and from support obligations assumed when a family class member is sponsored for immigration).[31] The regulations then provide a list of payments that are to be exempted. This list includes donations from religious or charitable organizations, portions of loans approved by the administrator for very specific purposes, certain provincial and federal payments, and casual gifts or casual payments of small value. Loans – except those exempted for limited purposes – and cash advances (as bizarre as it might seem) from a credit card or line of credit are considered income and, as such, result in a dollar-for-dollar deduction in the amount of benefits payable.

The rules regulating "income" are complex, voluminous, and frequently counter-intuitive. Not surprisingly, situations will arise where "income" (as defined by the governing legislation) is not reported simply because the recipient, although aware of the general obligation to report income, has no inkling that, for example, a food basket from her mother would be included in the definition of income. In an analysis of fraud, these are cases where, if the testimony of the accused is accepted, the *mens rea* for fraud has not been made out because there has been no intent to deprive (her lack of disclosure arises not from her intention to deprive the ministry but, rather, from the reality that she has no idea that a food basket is considered income and is thus to be disclosed). Moreover, as Justices Sopinka and Lamer highlighted in *Théroux*, if we accept the accused's testimony – her belief that the food basket does not constitute income – then we are also driven to the conclusion that, viewed objectively, the act in question is not dishonest. Thus, the *actus reus* for fraud is also not made out.

The case of *R. v. Maldonado* (1998), as suggested earlier, is a case in point.[32] Mr. Maldonado was in receipt of General Welfare Assistance (the precursor to Ontario Works benefits). He had been told that he must report any change in income. When his wife obtained part-time employment, it was dutifully reported. However, when he began attending school and obtained a student loan, he did not report the loan. Subsequently, when the ministry learned that Mr. Maldonado was in receipt of a loan, he was charged with fraud. His evidence at trial was that he had not considered a loan to be income, so he had never contemplated that the student loan needed to be reported. He did not know that the regulations, in defining "income," include loans and that, therefore, the loan ought to have been reported. Nor did he know that, had it been reported, a reduction in his benefits would have followed. In light of the Supreme Court of Canada's jurisprudence, it will not matter if Mr. Maldonado subjectively believed his actions to be honest. Rather, the question is can his actions be appropriately stigmatized as being dishonest – not merely negligent but of an underhanded or unscrupulous design? To invoke the query of Justices Sopinka and Lamer, is there a belief by the accused in a set of facts (a loan is not income and need not be reported) that would deprive the act of its dishonest character, such that the *actus reus* for fraud is thereby absent? The answer given by Justice Brian Weagant in *Maldonado* is affirmative. Indeed, he is loath to characterize Mr. Maldonado's actions as even negligent. When one considers Mr. Maldonado's state of mind, while he did have knowledge of the prohibited act (the non-disclosure of the loan), his belief that a loan is not income and, hence, not reportable deprived the act of its dishonest character. Moreover, given his belief in this set of facts, he lacked the subjective knowledge that the non-reporting could have as a consequence the deprivation of another. Justice Weagant concludes:

Not only do I have a doubt that Mr. Maldonado did not have the subjective knowledge of the possibility of deprivation, I am quite sure he did not ... I would not be surprised if Mr. Maldonado, even if given a copy of the Regulations to read for himself, were unable to glean the true meaning of "income" or "change of circumstances." The Regulations are extremely complicated and difficult to read ... My own experience of wading through the Regulations leads me to believe their inaccessibility plays a major role in the scenario under consideration. The Regulations governing the question of entitlement are fiendishly difficult to understand ... The sense or structure of the policy which might help a person on welfare to determine when he or she is breaking the law, is not apparent on the face of the Regulation. Why would a student loan be income, but a grant not? At first blush, one would think the opposite would be true ... If during a one month period a welfare recipient took a loan from a friend on a grocery shopping trip and repaid the loan to the friend when they reach the recipient's place of residence the very same day, the welfare benefit for that month should be proportionately less to reflect the amount of the loan. Yet no person with an ounce of sense would think that he or she would be obligated to report the amount of the loan. What is Kafkaesque about this scheme, to use Justice Campbell's word, is that the person who does not report the short-term loan from a friend might very well be prosecuted for fraud in the Province of Ontario ... Surely this is an example of something that Madame Justice McLachlin would put in the category of behaviour that does not warrant criminalization. (*Ibid.*, paras. 40, 41, and 43)[33]

Our research suggests, however, that the careful reasoning employed by Justice Weagant is very much the exception and that "fraud" is routinely the characterization given to rule violations by caseworkers, EROs, police, and, indeed, judges, irrespective of whether the necessary intent is present and, on occasion, irrespective of whether the *actus reus* is present (in addition to the *Maldonado* situation, there are also instances of alleged fraud where there has been no deprivation as defined by the Supreme Court of Canada in *R. v. Olan* [1978]).[34] Pervasively within the social assistance system, the assertion is made that the accused's lack of knowledge of the "fiendishly difficult" requirements of welfare law and regulations is irrelevant to the question of whether a "fraud" has been committed, and the principle of "ignorance of the law is no defence" is invoked in support. The line of reasoning employed is that one is assumed to know the law and that ignorance of the law is no excuse: hence, a lack of knowledge of the detailed requirements of the social assistance regime is irrelevant to the determination of criminal liability. One respondent in our interviews described to us how Ontario Works caseworkers in his district always rely on this line of reasoning: "You're required to disclose everything (the regulations require, for example, the reporting of changes in circumstances and of income), and if you don't you're guilty of fraud; ignorance of the law is no excuse – everyone is deemed to know the law, therefore you are guilty." This respondent went on to observe that "if anyone was genuinely trying to assess if this person intended to defraud the government that would be a very different case than the ones we see presented." Another respondent noted that even within the criminal justice system "the fact that the accused couldn't understand the tome [the complex regulations] doesn't get you to first base."

However, this reasoning reflects a profound distortion of the principle being invoked. One is not claiming that ignorance of the law of fraud is a defence but, rather, that a mistake of fact – in this case, the lack of knowledge or understanding of the underlying rules of the administrative regime – negates *mens rea* (one did not intend deprivation as a consequence of one's actions) and potentially the *actus reus,* since the quality of the act in issue is one that is not appropriately stigmatized as dishonest. By contrast, in our review of the literature on income tax evasion – which is also a complex administrative regime – we found not a single instance where this principle was distorted. To the contrary, it is routinely accepted within both the case law and the secondary literature that a lack of knowledge of the requirements of the income tax regime will negate *mens rea.*[35] Sophisticated business people who often have access to a panoply of expert advisors are regularly forgiven for not understanding the complexities of the income-reporting requirements for tax purposes. Yet, by contrast, welfare recipients – most of whom have absolutely no access to expert advice – are held to an impossibly high standard – perfect knowledge of a Kafkaesque labyrinth of rules.

Another very problematic dimension of the income rules relates to "casual gifts or casual payments of small value." *Policy Directive 16 on Income* provides that

applicants or participants may receive occasional financial help from relatives and friends while in receipt of assistance. Casual gifts and payments of small value are normally exempt from income. However, any income from a person who has an obligation to support the applicant or participant will be deducted at 100 percent unless the gift or payment is tied to a special occasion such as Christmas or a birthday.

Delivery agents may exercise their discretion when determining whether or not gifts or casual payments are chargeable as income. There are occasions where an applicant or participant may be faced with an immediate financial crisis. Help may be obtained from family, friends, or another third party. When making a determination, the delivery agent must consider the source, amount and frequency of the gift or casual payment and the opportunity to resolve the crisis. Exercising discretion should be in favour of applicants or participants to assist them to manage their financial circumstances ...

Examples of casual gifts and payments of small value may include items such as clothing, meals at family members' homes and the occasional purchase of items such as food. Gifts tied to a special occasion are generally exempt. Casual payments are considered infrequent payments. Continuous payments of small value are non-chargeable up to six months. After six months they are no longer considered casual and therefore are considered income to be charged at 100 percent.[36]

One respondent described the case of a client on Ontario Works who, during a home visit, opened her refrigerator to show her Ontario Works caseworker that her son had given her food. Her worker advised her, kindly, that in the future she should not open the refrigerator to reveal the contents and source of the food.[37] The respondent who shared this story noted that this was a compassionate worker and that other workers in the region would, as she described it, "pounce" on this, possibly assigning a dollar value, assessing an overpayment, terminating benefits for failure to disclose "income," and/or launching an investigation for fraud.

Member of the legislature Deb Matthews (2004, 28) reports a case described to her where this regulation was used to assign a value to the leftovers from Sunday dinner at a parent's house and deducted from the social assistance cheque. In addition, one of the persons interviewed by Herd and Mitchell (2002, 48) described the following situation:

[I had] a form of what was considered a gift that had to be reported. Shoes, and various items like that, you were supposed to report at dollar value. You were allowed a birthday gift and a gift at Christmas. One of the things that I always remembered on that list was that if you were invited to somebody's house on a regular basis for a meal, that meal is a reportable item. Like if every Sunday you went to your Mom's for dinner, you were supposed to say to them, "I had dinner at my Mother's 3 Sundays this month and the value of the meal was $8.95 or whatever." If you got taken to a restaurant on a regular basis, that was a reportable item ... One of the few things that was excluded was gifts from the church, like from the food bank, but you were allowed one visit a month and no more than a certain dollar value.

One of the respondents we interviewed described a situation where parents of a social assistance recipient, after reading about some welfare fraud cases in the newspaper, came into the office to inquire whether they had committed fraud because they had been giving their daughter money each month to help her get by.

The complexity of this regulation, together with its invocation to assign a dollar value to leftovers, meals, groceries, or other needed items (often provided compassionately by caring friends and family), means that many recipients simply have no idea that the reporting obligation is triggered because they are in receipt of "income" as defined by the regulations. One respondent described a client, struggling to survive, who undertook odd jobs in exchange for meals or a small supply of groceries. This respondent suggested that it would never have crossed her client's mind that the meals or groceries he received may have been characterized as a "casual gift or payment of small value" that was reportable and that could potentially have been deducted from his cheque or have led to the termination of benefits or to a fraud investigation.

Our respondents indicated that in their experience casual gifts or payments of small value generally do not give rise to fraud charges but, rather, more commonly lead to the assessment of overpayment charges and to the termination of benefits. However, one respondent reported that since the change to *Policy Directive 45 on Controlling Fraud* in January 2004, which requires referrals to the police where sufficient evidence exists to suspect intent to commit fraud, casual gifts or small payments are being referred to the police. Others observed that such cases may be referred, particularly where the payments or gifts continue beyond the six-month time period and become automatically deductible.

Regulating Intimate Relationships

The second arena of intense surveillance and regulation is the formation of intimate relationships. A cursory historical overview reveals that the intimate relationships of single women in receipt of social assistance have long been subject to intense moral scrutiny, and the failure to report the details of such relationships is a common ground for fraud charges. In Ontario, in the period preceding 1987, a single recipient risked having her benefits (the regime impacts almost exclusively upon women) terminated and a possible charge of fraud if a conclusion was made that she was living in a "marriage-like" relationship that she had not disclosed. Needless to say, the concept of a marriage-like relationship was ambiguous, and determinations of the nature of the relationship in issue frequently turned on evidence of sexual intimacy (Little 1998). The practices of welfare officials in enforcing the man-in-the-house rules were vigorously and thoroughly critiqued by feminists and equality activists because such practices not only ignored women's privacy interests but also forced women into relationships of economic dependence with men who had, at law, no obligation to support them. In 1987, Ontario dramatically altered the definition of "spouse" for welfare purposes so that it would largely track the definition in provincial family law legislation (the *Family Law Act*).[38] Importantly, this change meant that couples could live together for three years before they would be deemed to be spouses for social assistance purposes and before legal obligations of support would arise. This change was incredibly important for women because it meant that they could continue to receive welfare benefits in their own right as "singles" or as "sole support parents." Significantly, it also meant that, for this period of time, they could enter into intimate relationships without the fear that the formation of the relationship could give rise to a fraud investigation and a possible criminal charge.

Even prior to the introduction of the *SARA*, the Conservative government acted in October 1995 to amend the regulatory definition of "spouse" for social assistance purposes. This definition (a definition that has been modified on a handful of occasions subsequently) treated persons of the opposite sex presumptively as spouses if they shared a common residence. As such, the definition tracked much more closely the pre-1987 definition. The new definition resulted in 10,013 people being cut off social assistance. Of these, 89 percent were women, and 76 percent were single mothers, presuming that the men in their lives, who had no legal obligation to support them, would in fact do so (*Falkiner et al. v. Ontario (Ministry of Community and Social Services)* 2002, para. 77; *Falkiner et al. v. Ontario (Ministry of Community and Social Services)* 2000, para. 82).

The definition of "spouse" that was introduced in 1995 was constitutionally challenged in the case of *Falkiner et al. v. Ontario (Ministry of Community and Social Services)* (2000 and 2002). Significantly, on appeal the Ontario Court of Appeal found the definition to be overly broad – capturing relationships that do not resemble marriage-like relationships – and deeply ambiguous (since adjudicative boards had come to different findings regarding whether the degree of financial interdependence had to be more than trivial). The government of Ontario (then a Liberal government) abandoned its appeal to the Supreme Court of Canada in October 2004 and introduced a new definition, which apart from the introduction of a three-month "grace period" (a far cry from the earlier three-year period) largely mirrored its predecessor. Currently, "spouses," for social assistance purposes, are any two persons who reside in the same dwelling (for three months), if "the extent of the social and familial aspects of the relationship between the two persons is consistent with cohabitation" and "the extent of the financial support provided by one person to the other or the degree of financial interdependence between the two persons is consistent with cohabitation."[39]

The expanded definition of "spouse" – namely, the circumstances in which it is assumed that financial support is being provided – has shifted public responsibility to the private realm, and, in so doing, deepened women's vulnerability not only to economic marginalization but also to domestic violence, by limiting their options to exit abusive relationships (Mosher, Evans, and Little 2004). The message to women is clear: get a man, any man, and keep him or get a job, any job, and keep it. While Ontario has yet to adopt the same extremes of marriage promotion as many American jurisdictions, there is no doubt that within Ontario's welfare regime the formation of spousal relationships is valued and encouraged.[40]

Yet, while valued and encouraged, the formation of spousal relationships simultaneously plays a significant role in the deployment of the welfare fraud regime. It is telling to observe that, in 1981-82, 84 percent of welfare fraud charges were based upon an allegation of an undeclared spouse, resulting in 200 charges, 161 convictions, and incarceration in 42 percent of those cases. Both Anne Marie Gutierrez (1987, 17 and 28) and the Canadian Research Institute for Law and the Family (1987, 17), in their background reports for the Social Assistance Review Committee, observed that the definition of "spouse" introduced in 1987 (tracking the *Family Law Act*) resulted in dramatic reductions to these very high rates. The creation of a presumption of spousal status upon co-residency in 1995 signalled a renewed state interest in monitoring and criminalizing poor women's relationships with men.

Policy Directive 19 on Co-Residency lists a variety of factors to consider when determining whether co-residency exists, among them a statement from a landlord that the recipient lives with another person or that another person is listed on the lease, driver's licence history, employment records, or credit checks.[41] There is no formula that weighs these various factors to determine whether a recipient is "co-residing." Not surprisingly, then, there is little consistency – even at the appeal level before the Social Benefits Tribunal – as to what combination of factors will lead to a determination of co-residency. Respondents pointed out to us that in some cases a determination of co-residency is made on very little evidence. One respondent told us of a case in which a finding of co-residency was made, and upheld by the tribunal, on the basis of a common address on their respective drivers' licences. Respondents also observed that many of the factors relied upon as indicative of co-residency are not properly evaluated in the context of the lives of persons who are living in poverty. For example, frequently low-income persons are unable to secure a lease or obtain credit unless a second person co-signs the legal document. A friend, a neighbour, or a current or former boyfriend are among those to whom a recipient might turn to take on this role. So, too, low-income people without a fixed address may use the address of a friend or acquaintance when applying for employment, a licence, or any number of other things for which an address is required. These reflect survival strategies for low-income people but are often interpreted out of context and assumed to be evidence of co-residency.

In addition to the consideration of co-residency, a determination also must be made as to whether the persons in issue are "spouses."[42] In some instances, this question is answered readily if, for example, there is an existing obligation of support under the *Family Law Act*. However, in other cases, the determination will turn on a consideration of financial, social, and familial factors. While here too the policy lists a host of factors to be considered, there is again no formula that permits any predictability as to the circumstances in which a "spousal" determination will be made. And, as with determinations of co-residency, decisions regarding spousal status are, as one respondent described, "all over the map." Indeed, as noted earlier, the vagueness and ambiguity of the definition were bases on which the Ontario Court of Appeal struck the definition down as being unconstitutional (*Falkiner et al. v. Ontario (Ministry of Community and Social Services)* 2002). Understandably, then, recipients are frequently uncertain as to when and whether they may be "spouses" or "co-residing."

Imagine, for a moment, the circumstances of a single mother forming a new, heterosexual relationship within this regime where it is difficult, if not impossible, for her – or anyone else for that matter – to predict when she becomes a "co-residing spouse." She agrees to go out on the occasional date. Over the next several months, he begins to spend a great deal of time at her home and shares in many of the household tasks. They now regularly go out together, and, consequently, many people in their neighbourhood see them together. He may move some of his clothing into her place, and he spends a few nights each week there. At what point is she no longer a single person but "co-residing" with her "spouse"? And when does her obligation under the regulations to report a "change in circumstances" arise – with each and every turn of the relationship – and in what circumstances is she guilty of fraud? When can it be established, beyond a reasonable doubt, that she has engaged in the prohibited act of deceiving Ontario Works about the "true" nature of the relationship – that she is co-residing with a spouse – and that she has done so with the intent to deprive?

One common response to the first two questions (the third is almost never asked since the failure to report a detail of the relationship is assumed to constitute fraud) is to say that she does not have to make the determination of whether she is co-residing with a spouse but, rather, leave it up to Ontario Works to decide. Her only obligation is to report any change in circumstances, and then Ontario Works will decide if the change in circumstances renders her a co-residing spouse.[43] Indeed, this approach seems to underlie many cases where fraud charges are prosecuted, based again on the fundamental misunderstanding that the failure to report any information that Ontario Works now says it ought to have constitutes fraud. However, neither the statute nor the regulations require the reporting of all changes in circumstances but, rather, only the reporting of changes in circumstances *relevant to eligibility*. The rights and responsibilities form, for example, states that "you are responsible for following the rules of the Ontario Works program, including honest reporting of all circumstances that *affect eligibility*" (emphasis added). Similarly, in the application form, the applicant acknowledges that

I/we will notify the Administrator, the Director, or his/her representative as the case may be, of any change of relevant circumstances of any beneficiary of the allowance/assistance to be provided, including any change in circumstances pertaining to assets, income, living arrangements and my/our participation in Ontario Works activity as set out in the participation agreement. (Emphasis added)

However, we have come full circle and must now ask what is relevant to eligibility? Moreover, consider the implications for women's privacy, dignity, and autonomy if the requirement was that a recipient had to report every imaginable change in circumstance. Is a woman required to report each time her boyfriend visits, each time they go out together, each time he cares for her children, each time they have sex, each time he buys her coffee, each time he helps out around the house, and each time he spends a night? And what are the implications for women in receipt of assistance when the mere failure to report any of these circumstances may lead to an allegation of fraud and the termination of benefits? The obvious implication is that the formation of an intimate relationship – something that society generally, and the welfare system specifically, encourages if not valorizes – becomes an object of surveillance for potential criminal charges. The inquisitiveness of front line workers, the policing powers of EROs, and the wide net of intrusive surveillance cast by measures such as the snitch lines are deployed to scrutinize the intimate lives of women in the search of "criminal" misconduct. The stereotyping of poor, single, and especially racialized women makes them particularly vulnerable to this kind of scrutiny. As Dee Cook (1987) argues, single mothers on benefits are seen to have transgressed the borders of acceptable behaviour – they are neither good mothers, good wives, good workers, nor good consumers. Their intimate relationships are regarded with acute interest, suspicion, and often open hostility. They are, in fact, everybody's business. And it is an astoundingly treacherous business. Behaviour that is encouraged and socially valorized simultaneously attracts intense surveillance and criminal suspicion. On a flimsy evidential basis, one might be found to be residing with a spouse and also accused of fraud for not having disclosed this detail. For women on welfare, the border between positively valued social actor doing the right thing by finding a man and criminal transgressor is often extremely difficult to discern with any precision.

A close examination of the concepts of "income" and "spouses" as deployed within the welfare regime reveals how the very complexity and ambiguity of the regulatory regime structure an environment in which rule breaches are endemic. Yet the concepts reveal something even more troubling. Where the nature of the breaches commonly alleged takes the form of a "failure" to disclose information, and where it is often difficult to know in advance just what information must be disclosed, compliance becomes not merely difficult but virtually impossible. Recipients struggle to get by within a regime that will accuse them of fraud, cut them off, and toss them out for failing to disclose a detail of their lives. It may be that they had no idea of the "obligation" to disclose this detail, and it may be that there was in fact no legal obligation to disclose the detail or that the detail's intimacy and privacy were more important to protect. All too often, however, none of this will matter. The mere fact that the system now says it ought to have been informed will be sufficient to ground an allegation of fraud, an assessment of an overpayment, and/or a termination. Often this failure to inform, and nothing more, is the "fraudulent" behaviour of which recipients are guilty.

It is also deeply troubling that valued forms of social conduct – forms of conduct that are frequently constitutive, positive, and affirming – take on a highly ambiguous character for social assistance recipients. The compassionate gestures of friends and family and the details of one's intimate and private life are suspiciously monitored. Indeed, for some recipients, these forms of conduct are so fraught that they are avoided altogether – food baskets from family are halted and intimate relationships avoided (Mosher, Evans, and Little 2004).

The complex and counter-intuitive rules and the impossibility of compliance in a regime that may characterize the "failure" to share a detail of one's life as a rule violation – when what one is required to disclose is often impossibly difficult to determine in advance – are structural features of the social assistance regime, which, by nature if not by design, will generate significant numbers of rule violations. Accordingly, when these violations are routinely labelled as "fraud," fraud is structurally manufactured by the welfare system itself.

Processes of Criminalization

Benefit Inadequacy
Beyond the mischaracterization of rule breaches as criminal fraud, the welfare system, by its structure and design, generates actual criminal fraud. One of the central ways in which fraud is produced is through the inadequacy of benefits. By far the majority of cases of actual criminal fraud arise as a result of desperate need, a reality acknowledged by the Social Assistance Review Committee (1988, 384) in its review of Ontario's social assistance system. In the committee's view – a view borne out by our interviews and our review of criminal cases of welfare fraud – the single most important measure to prevent actual fraud is the provision of adequate welfare rates. Indeed, the correlation between criminal fraud and the inadequacy of rates is implicitly

acknowledged by the system's own red flags for fraud – among them, the length of time on benefits and the percentage of benefits paid for shelter.

The cuts introduced in 1995, the impact of inflation, and the extremely modest increases over the past dozen years have put some recipients in the untenable position of having to choose between feeding their children and complying with the rules.[44] Social assistance recipients struggle to make ends meet, often going without adequate food, shelter, and/or clothing. The challenge of meeting basic needs for themselves and their children often places recipients in the grips of difficult moral binds, where none of the choices is a good choice. Consider, for example, the single mother who receives $100 from her former boyfriend and father of her child to help her get through to the end of the month. Even with this $100, she does not have enough to adequately feed and clothe herself and her child. If she discloses the $100, it will be deducted dollar for dollar from her welfare cheque because the father is a person with a support obligation. If she does not disclose it and it is later discovered (perhaps because he, in fact, reports it to welfare), what action will follow?[45] Section 14 of the general regulation (134/98) of the *OWA* indicates that she shall be found to be ineligible for financial assistance since she has failed to disclose income. She may well be cut off, and, while she can re-apply, there will likely be a period of time when she will be without assistance. She will probably be assessed with an overpayment of $100. The possibility of being charged with fraud has likely been implied if not explicitly stated, and, depending upon which municipality she resides in and her relationship with the staff of the office, the matter may or may not be referred to the police. And what if the money – or the food or the diapers – were to come from a person without a support obligation? The discretionary and complex nature of the rule regarding casual gifts or casual payments of small value makes it exceedingly difficult to know if and when the amount of money (or desperately needed goods) would be treated as "income" and deducted from the cheque.

One respondent described a client who was receiving $520 per month. His rent was $500. Paying more than 80 percent of his income on rent, he was identified as a high priority for risk of fraud through the consolidation verification process (CVP). He was called in and asked to explain how he survived on $20 per month. He explained that he received some food from his grandmother as well as friends and other family members. He was required to itemize exactly what he received. The items were assigned a cost based on local grocery flyers and assessed a total value of $70. He was then deemed to be in receipt of $70 income per month, and this amount was deducted from his benefits, and, as a result, he was no longer able to pay his rent. What are his choices now? Will he ask family and friends not to provide food, and, if he does, will he then have adequate nutritious food? Significantly, the dramatic reductions in benefit levels in Ontario occurred in tandem with the increased focus upon welfare fraud, deepening the horrendous "Catch-22" for recipients.

Surveillance

The *Welfare Fraud Control Reports* reveal that a staggering number of social assistance recipients suspected of fraud are reported by a variety of sources to welfare authorities, and an equally staggering number are formally investigated. Landlords, neighbours, and concerned citizens are encouraged to utilize the toll-free welfare fraud hotline. Ongoing reporting/disclosure obligations, sweeping consents to the disclosure and sharing of information, information-sharing agreements with other provincial and federal departments, and extensive powers vested in the eligibility review officers all contribute to an environment of near-total surveillance. It is an environment that recipients experience as profoundly hostile, disrespectful, and demeaning and one that recipients commonly describe as treating them like "criminals." Virtually everyone on welfare struggles to survive and comply within this intense and unrelenting web of surveillance, experiencing ongoing and profound violations of privacy and living in constant fear of a "fraud" allegation.

Several of those we interviewed described the CVP environment as analogous to "living under a microscope"; to having "one's life gone through with a fine-tooth comb"; and to having one's "life micro-managed." In addition, because the CVP flags recipients for fraud risk factors, persons who are summoned for a meeting are often put in the position of explaining how they are managing to survive on so little money without breaching the rules, again something that is experienced as profoundly demoralizing. One respondent described how recipients sometimes feel ambushed, having to account for every single entry in their bank books, months after the fact and without warning. As one respondent explained, "it is made clear to people that you're in our scopes because we know you're doing something ... This leaves people on tenterhooks all the time."

Herd and Mitchell (2002, 48) report a concrete example of this occurring to "K," a recipient interviewed for their study. "K" asks rhetorically, "Do you know what my worker told me? She is not giving me enough money to make it on a monthly basis so she knows that I'm defrauding them, but just hasn't figured out how yet. I get $1,106 a month and between my rent, heat and hydro which is all in one, it's $950. So she knows I'm defrauding them, she just hasn't figured out how and because of that, and because of the new government standards, they can actually call me in every month for an update." Tellingly, this worker explicitly confirms that the welfare system, by its very design, will inevitably and unavoidably produce fraud.

Herd and Mitchell's finding that the climate is permeated with suspicion and hostility is consistent with what respondents reported to us. As Herd and Mitchell (*ibid.*, 8, 9, and 33) describe, "the new system is more concerned with surveillance and deterrence, than it is with assisting people to find employment. What is new is the intensity of surveillance and the technologies employed, the importation of private sector methods and standardized business practices ... Overall the mood of the focus groups was that the new system was inspiring a greater degree of suspicion and hostility ... more concerned with constant surveillance and treating 'everybody like they're cheating the system.'" One of our respondents summed it up very effectively with the observation that hardly any of her clients now refer to their welfare workers as their social workers as they did formerly. Rather, welfare workers have become much more closely associated with police officers. Fraud is now *the* focus of the system, explained another of our respondents.

Respondents also described how intensely scrutinized their clients' lives are by non-state agents: present or current abusive boyfriends or spouses, landlords, and neighbours appear to have all taken up the government's invitation to participate in the surveillance project. As noted earlier, in some instances the state actively solicits information from persons acquainted in some way with those "in their scopes." In others, unsolicited reports are made to the welfare fraud hotline or directly to a local Ontario Works office. Respondents pointed out that when these calls form the basis of the allegation of fraud it is usually difficult to respond because the subject of the allegation is not told who made the allegation and often not told precisely what the allegation is. We also heard of many instances where allegations were reported to welfare for purposes completely extraneous to the prevention or detection of fraud. Abusive men make false reports to Ontario Works to further their power and control over women; landlords make false reports to facilitate the eviction of a tenant; and vindictive neighbours or other acquaintances make false or misleading reports simply out of spite (Mosher, Evans, and Little 2004). Two of our respondents also noted how the snitch lines, in particular, encourage gossip that is very destructive in smaller rural and First Nations communities. And yet none of these abuses and potential harms created by the policing welfare fraud has entered into political discourse as matters of serious public concern, despite the recommendations made by the inquest investigating the death of Kimberly Rogers.

Several respondents also observed how stereotyping plays into the calls that are made. For example, class and race stereotypes of racialized women portray them as bad and potentially dangerous – as likely criminals. Dominant stereotypes also caricature Aboriginal people as "living off the system" and being too lazy to get a job, and single mothers – especially those with children by more than one father – are portrayed as promiscuous, having children to increase welfare dollars, and likely to be hiding men in their homes. Under the gaze of surveillance by concerned citizens who harbour these stereotypes, virtually any racialized woman, any single mother, or any

Aboriginal person is a person suspected of fraud, who ought to be investigated. Thus, not surprisingly, many respondents expressed the view that the sweep and impact of surveillance by non-state actors impact differentially on particular groups of recipients: racialized peoples, women, and racialized women, in particular, are subject to the most intensive surveillance.

When neighbours, landlords, teachers, local shopkeepers, and others in the community are encouraged (through active solicitations from state officials or through devices such as snitch lines) to suspect, watch, and report on social assistance recipients, social relations within communities are transformed. Rather than being regarded as neighbours, customers, or the mothers of children in the classrooms, social assistance recipients become the objects of surveillance – as persons possibly deceiving the social assistance system. In such an environment, recipients find it exceedingly difficult to trust anyone, and the fear of being suspected and reported is for many a constant feature of day-to-day life. In this climate, positive social interactions become extremely difficult to maintain, and recipients feel acutely that they are not welcomed and included.

It is important to emphasize how pervasively fear permeates the lives of those in receipt of Ontario Works. Such fear has multiple sources: fear of not being able to meet the basic needs of one's children; fear of losing custody; fear of declining health; fear of social exclusion and discrimination; and fear, as one respondent put it, "that no matter what choice you make it will be the wrong choice, and the axe will fall." The constant surveillance not only by the state but also by neighbours, landlords, shopkeepers, and so on generates fear as well – fear that virtually whatever one does might lead to an allegation that one has broken a rule and is guilty of fraud. Underlying and integral to this pervasive, constant surveillance is a view of recipients as suspected fraudsters – potential criminals waiting to abuse a public trust. Recipients are effectively criminalized – suspected by others, made to feel like they are criminal, dehumanized, demonized, and intensely surveilled – with only the occasional resort to actual criminal law processes.

Conclusion: The Crime of Social Assistance
There is nothing new about the nexus between poverty and criminality, an intersection that we have explored in the context of social assistance. The poor have historically been subjected to some of the most violent and sweeping criminal laws that, at their core, enforce status offences or "crimes of character" against the morally loose, economically idle, and socially disorderly (Chambliss 1964). While the bodies of poor people are no longer imprisoned in workhouses or subjected to the brutal punishments of the vagrancy statutes, the poor today are nonetheless subjected to exclusionary prejudices and stereotypes that are centuries old. While the letter of the criminal law has, in theory, withdrawn from explicitly targeting the character

crime of being poor and disorderly, what we see today instead is an extra-ordinary net of regulation that is constituted by a mesh of legal, adminis-trative, and informal practices that are highly intrusive, retributive, and punitive.

Is "welfare fraud," as it is now constituted and policed, really the crime that it has been portrayed as? As we have discussed, only a very small frac-tion of what the government includes as successful policing of "welfare fraud" involves criminal prosecution. Indeed, the actual level of criminal fraud detected across the thousands of cases investigated is remarkably low – and this is particularly notable given the intense level of surveillance and investigation that recipients find themselves under. By far the majority of conduct that is described and promoted as the menace of "welfare fraud" stems from often highly informal and capricious practices of disentitlement that flow from the breaches of any of a mass of complex, often contradictory, and frequently counter-intuitive rules that now govern social assistance administration. Many of these almost 800 rules and regulations are so vague and confusing that they seem intentionally designed to make receiving social assistance an ungovernable activity that inherently involves rule breaking and thus the committing of "welfare fraud."

As should be clear from our discussion, regulation that revolves around "income" and "spouses," in particular, is so capricious and vague that no reasonable person could conduct herself in a way that would not put her in jeopardy of an accusation of "fraud" in receiving social assistance. This is particularly so when one considers the extensive and often arbitrary powers of EROs, the ambiguity of how officials apply rules and regulations in local settings, and the use of the welfare fraud hotline, which translates what can often be malicious gossip into official action. It is the highly informal poli-cing of this network, fuelled by prejudicial stereotypes of those on social assistance, that results in the termination of benefits, assessments of over-payments, accusations of fraud, and, very infrequently, formal fraud charges. Based on the extensive evidence that we have reviewed, one is left to draw the conclusion that there is little actual criminal conduct of fraud in social assistance administration. The constitution of social assistance as a crime itself presents a striking paradox: welfare fraud policing is located primarily outside of criminal law yet in a way that locates social assistance recipients as criminalized objects worthy of being socially disentitled through intense forms of exclusionary regulation.

Two aspects of the criminalization of social assistance can be viewed as particularly troubling. The first is how the largely informal mechanisms that are deployed to fight welfare fraud do not attend very closely to legal prin-ciples, including *Charter* obligations. Even basic legal requirements in inves-tigating a criminal offence, such as the element of *mens rea* or the *Charter* right of being cautioned once a criminal investigation is commenced, seem to be widely viewed as safeguards that should not be extended to poor people. Sweeping informational demands and broad, generic consent forms authorizing disclosure of information about oneself and lifetime bans on benefits are practices reminiscent of the 1834 *Poor Law,* pursuant to which the needs of the poor would be met only if the claimant forfeited his civil and political liberties – that is, if he ceased to be a citizen. As T.H. Marshall (cited in McCluskey 2003, 789n23) himself noted, the *Poor Law* "treated the claims of the poor, not as an integral part of the rights of the citizen, but as an alternative to them – as claims which could be met only if the claimants ceased to be citizens in any true sense of the word."

The second aspect revolves around how this criminalization is gendered in a prejudicial and insidious way. The facts that the majority of people on social assistance are women and that the majority of them are single parents have enabled prejudicial, historically embedded views of single women and single mothers – views that they are irresponsible, sexually loose, lazy, and ought to find men to support them. The regulation of women through the re-introduction of the man-in-the-house rule explicitly re-enforces this view. And it is not only the intimate aspect of women's lives that is utilized as an area of control in social assistance regulation but also the sphere of everyday life. Despite a rhetoric of "community responsibility" in government discourse, it is the very people that might constitute a support network in their communities – neighbours, family, boyfriends, landlords, school officials – that are either re-responsibilized as agents to snitch on any perceived "fraud" or possibly complicit in rule breaking by being supportive by buying food for a mother and her child, for example, who have exhausted what is a completely inadequate benefit for that month. It is no wonder that being on social assistance has been characterized by an experience of fear, retribution, and isolation – qualities that "cracking down" on welfare fraud intentionally generate. The constitution of social assistance as crime through the policing of "welfare fraud" stands as an acute and dramatic example of how the neo-liberal reform of the welfare state has expanded its regulatory reach and authority while, at the same time, vastly diminishing a collective response to caring for the poor and vulnerable. The centuries-old vagrancy stereotype has been given new life – those on social assistance are morally suspect in being too lazy and shiftless to take responsibility for themselves and are thus a threat to public order. And, in turn, the shift away from state responsibility has enabled a perverse logic of responsibility to be put in place, where poor women in particular are subject to a sphere of blame, admonishment, and stigmatization. The findings of our study suggest that fighting welfare fraud has little to do with governing crime and more to do with a systematic attempt to disenfranchise and punish a highly vulnerable and easily stigmatized population who dare to seek assistance from the state.

Acknowledgments

We would like to acknowledge the very able research assistance provided by Aida Abraha, Vanessa Iafolla, and Shannon Slattery and the support of the Law Commission of Canada. We are also grateful to the anonymous reviewers for their insightful suggestions.

Notes

1 We use the terms "welfare" and "social assistance" interchangeably to describe public benefit programs of last resort.

2 Our focus in this chapter is on the regulation of welfare fraud. The research for the Law Commission of Canada that forms the basis of this chapter also formed the basis for two earlier publications, each of which contrasted the treatment of welfare fraud with another area of regulation. Mosher (2008) compares and contrasts the treatment of welfare fraud and income tax evasion, and Mosher (2006) considers welfare fraud and employment standards violations.

3 *Social Assistance Reform Act, 1997,* S.O. 1997, c. 25 [*SARA*].

4 The government's press releases regarding its various *Welfare Fraud Control Reports* and more broadly on the fight against fraud also support this conclusion.

5 One of the community clinic lawyers interviewed for our project described the quality of legal representation as "tragic."

6 The other two objectives were to make self-sufficiency the overriding goal of social assistance and to meet the unique needs of persons with disabilities. See the closing comments on the third reading of Bill 142 (*SARA, supra* note 3) of then minister of community and social services, the Honourable Janet Ecker (1997).

7 *Ontario Works Act, 1997,* S.O. 1997, c. 25, Sched. A. [*OWA*]; *Ontario Disability Support Program Act,* S.O. 1997, c. 25, Sched. B. [*ODSPA*].

8 *Policy Directive 45 on Controlling Fraud,* Ontario Works, Ministry of Community, Family and Children's Services, 2001. Ontario Works is delivered by "delivery agents," most of which are municipalities, while others are First Nations. There are forty-seven consolidated municipal service managers and First Nations delivery agents. The Ontario Disability Support Program, by contrast, is delivered by the province. In the discussion that follows, we focus primarily on the Ontario Works system, but much of what we discuss is equally applicable to the Ontario Disability Support Program. Note that the directive was further revised in July 2008, well after the completion of the research. It is now *Policy Directive 9.7, Controlling Fraud,* Ontario Works, Ministry of Community and Social Services, 2008. While the wording has changed, the development of local protocols continues as a requirement in the revised directive.

9 While we understand from the ministry that all delivery agents have negotiated such local agreements, we were unable to secure copies of any. The ministry does not have copies of these agreements, none of the legal advocates we spoke with had ever seen a local agreement, and time did not permit us to try to track these down through the various municipalities.

10 Dianne Martin (1992) found similar variations in her work on welfare fraud in the late 1980s.

11 These regional variations suggest that particular municipal governments may not accept the provincial rhetoric regarding the scope of the fraud problem. In fact, several municipal councils passed motions formally disapproving the implementation of the lifetime ban.

12 Note that this requirement continues in the revised *Policy Directive 9.7, supra* note 8, of July 2008.

13 Although the power to apply for a search warrant exists, we have been told by the ministry that this power has, to date, never been utilized (Moretta 2004).

14 O. Reg. 134/98, s. 65, amended to O. Reg. 231/04.

15 *Canadian Charter of Rights and Freedoms,* Part 1 of the *Constitution Act, 1982,* being Schedule B to the *Canada Act 1982* (U.K.), 1982, c. 11.

16 In the income tax context, see *R. v. Jarvis* (2002). In the welfare context, this issue has been considered, although not adequately, in *R. v. Coulter* (1995) and *R. v. D'Amour* (2002).

17 *Inquest into the Death of Kimberly Rogers,* transcript of the evidence of Constable Sheldon Roberts, 28 October 2002.

18 O. Reg. 34/08, s. 12(3).
19 *Policy Directive 12 on Home Visits,* Ontario Works, Ministry of Community and Social Services, 2001. The policy directive on home visits was revised in July 2008 and is now *Policy Directive 2.8.* In large measure, it continues unchanged.
20 Ontario, Legislative Assembly, 2 October 1995, *Official Report of Debates (Hansard),* 36th Leg., 1st Sess., http://hansardindex.ontla.on.ca/hansardeissue/36-1/l004.htm.
21 See O. Reg. 134/98, s. 36, as amended by O. Reg. 227/98; O. Reg. 48/00; O. Reg. 314/01; and O. Reg. 456/03.
22 *Criminal Code,* R.S.C. 1985, c. C-46, s. 264.
23 The constitutional challenge was mounted in the case of *Broomer et al. v. Ontario (A.G.)* (2002).
24 Ontario, Legislative Assembly, 28 September 1995, *Official Report of Debates (Hansard),* 36th Leg., 1st Sess., http://hansardindex.ontla.on.ca/hansardeissue/36-1/l003.htm.
25 O. Reg. 134/98, s. 28.
26 Canada does not have any officially recognized "poverty lines." The Statistics Canada low-income cut-offs are the most commonly used measure of relative deprivation and are in-tended to convey the income level at which an individual or family is living in "straitened circumstances," spending a greater portion of income on the basic necessities than the average family of similar size within a particular community.
27 For an interesting discussion of how workfare in the United States is enforcing a masculine worker-citizen subject through the deployment of various discursive strategies, see Korteweg (2003).
28 For a discussion of the privatization and devaluation of the tasks of caring for dependents, see Fineman (1999).
29 If the value of the subject matter exceeds $5,000, it is an indictable offence, carrying a maximum penalty of imprisonment not exceeding fourteen years. Below $5,000, the Crown may proceed by indictment (maximum term of two years) or by summary conviction. Until the provisions of C-13 came into effect in September 2004, the maximum penalty was ten years.
30 O. Reg. 134/98, s. 14(1); *Policy Directive 9.3,* Ontario Works, Ministry of Community and Social Services, 2008.
31 O. Reg. 134/98, s. 48; *Policy Directive 16 on Income,* Ontario Works, Ministry of Community, Family and Children's Services, 2001.
32 See also an important Supreme Court of Canada decision, *R. v. Parisé* (1996), and from the Ontario Court of Appeal, *R. v. Wakil* (2001).
33 Justice Weagant's reference to Justice McLachlin arises from her caution that because the Supreme Court of Canada had cast the net of "fraud" rather widely it was important to ensure that fraud was not interpreted so widely as to capture behaviour that does not war-rant criminalization.
34 Among this category of cases are those where, had the information been disclosed, no deduction of benefits would have resulted. Also included, arguably, are some of the cases discussed later in this chapter regarding the failure to disclose a spouse. In many of these cases, a single woman in receipt of benefits who is accused of fraud for failing to disclose a "spouse" would be eligible for greater benefits were she to apply jointly with her "spouse."
35 See, for example, Innes (2003).
36 *Policy Directive 16 on Income, supra* note 31. Note that, as with other policy directives, this directive was amended as of July 2008. The directive now also provides that a casual gift or payment of large value is considered exempt as income if it is "clear that it will be used to meet an extraordinary need to maintain the health and well-being of a benefit unit, and there are no other financial resources that are accessible." *Policy Directive 5.7,* Ontario Works, Ministry of Community and Social Services, 2008.
37 Note that because a home visit is limited to what is in plain view there is no legislative authority for a worker to open a refrigerator.
38 *Family Law Act,* R.S.O. 1990, c. F.3.
39 O. Reg. 134/98, s. 1, as amended. The category of "same-sex partner" was introduced as a result of the Supreme Court of Canada's decision in *M. v. H.* (1995). The Ontario government

.responded to the Supreme Court of Canada's ruling by introducing an omnibus piece of legislation to add the category of "same-sex partner" to several pieces of legislation, including the *OWA* and the *ODSPA*. A further amendment eliminated the distinction between spouses and same-sex partners to include both same-sex and heterosexual couples within the definition of "spouse." O. Reg. 294/05, s. 1.

40 For a review of American initiatives to promote marriage within the context of welfare reform, see Smith (2002).

41 *Policy Directive 19 on Co-Residency,* Ontario Works, Ministry of Community, Family and Children's Services, 2001. This directive was renumbered in July 2008 and is now *Policy Directive 3.3,* Ontario Works, Ministry of Community and Social Services, 2008.

42 The interplay of the welfare fraud regime, the definition of "spouses," and the practices of investigating and determining spousal status are developed more fully in Mosher (2010).

43 During our interview with Debbie Moretta, the director of the Ontario Disability Support Program, in 2004, she suggested to us that, while the rules may be complex, what is asked of recipients is really quite simple: report changes in their circumstances. Similarly, in her affidavit in the *Broomer* case (2002), Moretta (2003, para. 54) observes that "the system is designed so that recipients make full disclosure of any changes in their circumstances to the program; individuals are not required to make any self-assessment of eligibility."

44 For a discussion of this dilemma in the American context, see Gilliom (2001).

45 As discussed later in this chapter, we heard throughout our interviews that abusive past and current boyfriends/spouses frequently call welfare snitch lines or welfare offices to report their partners for "fraud" as a means of furthering their power and control. See also Mosher, Evans, and Little (2004).

References

Canadian Research Institute for Law and the Family. 1987. *A Literature Review of Welfare Fraud: Nature, Extent, and Control,* prepared for the Social Assistance Review Committee. Toronto: Canadian Research Institute for Law and the Family.

Chambliss, W.J. 1964. "A Sociological Analysis of the Law of Vagrancy." *Social Problems* 12: 67-77.

Cook, D. 1987. "Women on Welfare: In Crime or Injustice?" In *Gender, Crime, and Justice,* ed. P. Carlen and A. Worral, 28-42. Milton Keynes, UK: Open University Press.

Ewart, J.D. 1986. *Criminal Fraud.* Toronto, ON: Carswell Legal Publications.

Fineman, M. 1999. "Cracking the Foundational Myths: Independence, Autonomy, and Self-Sufficiency." *American University Journal of Gender, Social Policy, and Law* 8: 13-29.

Fraser, J., C. Wilkey, and J. Frenschkowski. 2003. *Denial by Design ... The Ontario Disability Support Program,* Income Security Advocacy Centre, http://www.incomesecurity.org.

Gilliom, J. 2001. *Overseers of the Poor: Surveillance, Resistance, and the Limits of Privacy.* Chicago: University of Chicago Press.

Gutierrez, A.M. 1987. *The Interaction of the Criminal Law and the Income Maintenance System in Ontario,* research report prepared for the Social Assistance Review Committee, Toronto.

Herd, D., and A. Mitchell. 2002. *Discouraged, Diverted, and Disentitled: Ontario Works' New Service Delivery Model.* Toronto: Community Social Planning Council of Toronto and Ontario Social Safety Network.

Innes, W.I. 2003. *Tax Evasion.* Toronto: Carswell.

Korteweg, A.C. 2003. "Welfare Reform and the Subject of the Working Mother: 'Get a Job, a Better Job, Then a Career.'" *Theory and Society* 32: 445-80.

Little, M.J.H. 1998. *"No Car, No Radio, No Liquor Permit": The Moral Regulation of Single Mothers in Ontario, 1920-1997.* Toronto: Oxford University Press.

Martin, D.L. 1992. "Passing the Buck: Prosecution of Welfare Fraud; Preservation of Stereotypes." *Windsor Yearbook of Access to Justice* 12: 52-97.

Matthews, D. 2004. *Review of Employment Assistance Programs in Ontario Works and Ontario Disability Support Program.* Toronto: Ministry of Community and Social Services.

McCluskey, M.T. 2003. "Efficiency and Social Citizenship: Challenging the Neoliberal Attack on the Welfare State." *Indiana Law Journal* 78: 783-878.

McKeever, G. 1999. "Detecting, Prosecuting, and Punishing Benefit Fraud: The Social Security Administration (Fraud) Act 1997." *Modern Law Review* 62, 2: 261-70.

Ministry of Community, Family and Children's Services. 2003. *Welfare Fraud Control Report 2001-2002.* Toronto: Ministry of Community, Family and Children's Services.

Ministry of Community and Social Services. July 2009. "Who to Contact If You Suspect Fraud?" Ministry of Community and Social Services, http://www.mcss.gov.on.ca/mcss/english/pillars/social/fraud.htm.

Moretta, D. 2003. Affidavit sworn 29 August 2003, submitted in *Broomer v. Ontario (A.G.)* (5 June 2002), Toronto 02-CV-229203CM3, Ontario Superior Court.

–. 2004. Director of the Ontario Disability Support Program. Interview by Janet Mosher, Toronto, 22 December.

Mosher, J. 2006. "The Construction of 'Welfare Fraud' and the Wielding of the State's Iron Fist." In *Locating Law, Race/Class/Gender/Sexuality Connections,* ed. E. Comack, 2nd edition, 207-29. Halifax: Fernwood Press.

–. 2008. "Welfare Fraudsters and Tax Evaders: The State's Selective Invocation of Criminality." In *Marginality and Condemnation: An Introduction to Criminology,* ed. B. Schissel and C. Brooks, 2nd edition, 287-309. Halifax: Fernwood Press.

–. 2010. "Intimate Intrusions – Welfare Regulation and Women's Personal Lives." In *The Legal Tender of Gender,* ed. M. Ajzenstadt, D. Chunn, and S. Gavigan, 165-88. Oxford: Hart Publishing.

Mosher, J., P. Evans, and M. Little. 2004. *Walking on Eggshells: Abused Women's Experiences of Ontario's Welfare System.* Toronto: Woman and Abuse Welfare Research Project, http://www.yorku.ca/yorkweb/special/Welfare_Report_walking_on_eggshells_final_report.pdf.

National Council of Welfare. 2006. *Welfare Incomes 2005* (as revised). Ottawa: National Council of Welfare.

Nightingale, B.L. 1996. *The Law of Fraud and Related Offences.* Toronto: Thomson Carswell.

Ontario Municipal Social Services Association. November 2003. *Fraud Referral Task Force Report.*

Smith, A.M. 2002. "The Sexual Regulation Dimension of Contemporary Welfare Law: A Fifty State Overview." *Michigan Journal of Gender and Law* 8: 121-218.

Smith, L., P. Wise, W. Chavkin, D. Romero, and B. Zuckerman. 2000. "Implications of Welfare Reform for Child Health: Emerging Challenges for Clinical Practice and Policy." *Pediatrics* 106, 5: 1117-25.

Social Assistance Review Committee. 1988. *Report of the Social Assistance Review Committee: Transitions.* Toronto: Queen's Printer.

List of Cases

Broomer et al. v. Ontario (A.G.) (5 June 2002), Toronto 02-CV-229203CM3 (Ont. Sup. Ct.).

Falkiner et al. v. Ontario (Ministry of Community and Social Services) (2002), 213 D.L.R. (4th) 633 (Ont. C.A.).

Falkiner et al. v. Ontario (Ministry of Community and Social Services) (2000), 188 D.L.R. (4th) 52 (Div. Ct.).

M. v. H., [1995] 2 S.C.R. 3.

R. v. Coulter, [1995] O.J. No. 645 (Prov. Div.) (QL).

R. v. D'Amour, [2000] O.J. No. 5122 (Sup. Ct.) (QL) and 2002 CanLII 45015 (ON C.A.).

R. v. Jarvis, [2002] 3 S.C.R. 757.

R. v. Maldonado, [1998] O.J. No. 3209 (Prov. Div.) (QL).

R. v. Olan, [1978] 2 S.C.R. 1175.

R. v. Parisé, [1996] 3 S.C.R. 408.

R. v. Théroux, [1993] 2 S.C.R. 5.

R. v. Wakil (2001), 150 O.A.C. 194.

R. v. Zlatic, [1993] 2 S.C.R. 29.

2
Fraud against the Public Purse by Health Care Professionals: The Privilege of Location
Joan Brockman

The debate over "what is (a) crime?" has a long history and continues today (see Henry and Lanier 2001; Law Commission of Canada 2003, 2004). In answering this question, it is important to acknowledge that our reactions to crime are as important as our definitions of crime. Some crimes are dealt with privately; some are not dealt with at all. Some offenders are "over-policed," while others are "under-policed" (see Mosher and Hermer, Chapter 1 in this volume; Chartrand and Weber-Pillwax, Chapter 3 in this volume). This blatant inequality, often based on social and economic location, led the Law Commission of Canada (2003, 20) to ask: "Why do we treat some people as criminal and not others?" In 2004, the commission called for "a more equitable and accountable process for defining crime and enforcing criminal law" (Des Rosiers and Bittle 2004, xxiii).

In reality, we use the criminal law to enforce some laws that are ungrounded in social consensus and that cause little harm.[1] Sometimes the enforcement of our criminal law causes more harm than it prevents.[2] The differential application of the criminal law to white-collar[3] or suite crime (crimes of the powerful) and street crime (crimes of the less powerful) can undermine law's legitimacy. When people question whether there is one law for the rich and another for the poor, it is generally a question about the application of the law – law in practice or law in action, not definitions of "crime."[4] Inequality of treatment between the powerful and less powerful can result in demands to include activities of the powerful in the definitions and applications of the criminal law, juxtaposed with a call for the reduction in the use of criminal law.[5]

As such, those who enforce the law are engaged in defining it. What they do in terms of enforcing the law is as important as the law itself. For example, if fraud by health care providers is discovered, it can be ignored or tolerated. The government agency in charge of monitoring the payment of bills can react informally or formally. The police may or may not be called upon to investigate. Professionals can be prosecuted under the *Criminal Code* or provincial legislation (for example, section 46 of the *Medicare Protection Act*) and be brought before their self-regulating organization (SRO) for a disciplinary hearing (see Brockman and Rose 2010, 1-2; Murdoch and Brockman 2001).[6]

Although historically there has been some question as to whether fraudulent practices should be considered criminal,[7] today there seems to be a general consensus that fraud should be prohibited. At least there is no widespread support to decriminalize fraud, as there is, for example, with the offence of possession of marijuana. Under section 380 of the *Criminal Code*, anyone "who, by deceit, falsehood or other fraudulent means ... defrauds the public or any person ... of any property, money or valuable security or any service" commits the offence of fraud.[8] Fraud is a crime that spans through the socio-economic classes. It ranges from welfare and unemployment fraud to health care fraud by doctors, legal aid fraud by lawyers, and corporate fraud by officers and directors of corporations. The crime of fraud allows us to examine how we deal with one crime that occurs in a variety of different social and economic spheres. What we do about a law is perhaps as important as, or more important than, what the law says, and it has a major impact on the ultimate compositions of "what is a crime?"[9]

This chapter is about law in action. The first part briefly provides some background information on the range of health care fraud that exists and then narrows the discussion to a specific form of health care fraud. Namely, it focuses on professional misconduct in Canada during fee-for-service billing. Most of these professionals are physicians because they are the most likely, and in the greatest number, to be billing the state in the fee-for-service billing system. The second part of the chapter also briefly outlines how deviant billings are monitored and processed in British Columbia and Ontario. In order to piece these processes together, I canvassed the legislation, regulations, and publications by the government agencies that monitor fee-for-service billing. I searched newspapers as well as the websites and bulletins/newsletters of government agencies and the colleges of physicians and surgeons. I also conducted interviews with ten lawyers, doctors, and administrators who worked in the health care system in British Columbia in order to better understand how the system worked. A number of written submissions to Justice Peter Cory (available through his website), whose review of the Ontario audit system was ongoing as I conducted my research, were of great assistance in understanding the system in that province.

The third part of the chapter then describes administrative, self-regulating, criminal, and quasi-criminal actions against health care professionals for fraud, commenced between 1990 and 2003 across Canada, which were available in the public domain through court and Quicklaw databases, newspaper coverage, and court transcript services. This part then focuses in greater detail on cases arising in British Columbia and Ontario and examines the similarities and differences between the two provinces. The conclusions, which are outlined in the fourth part of the chapter, identify a number of issues that arise out of the differences in social and economic location between professional health care fraud and welfare fraud. I then address the question of how the compassion, or perhaps the tolerance, that we show to white-collar criminals can be transferred to so-called "street" criminals. Could we reduce the use of criminal law against crimes of the less powerful by transferring to their misconduct some of the attitudes and approaches that we presently have towards the crimes of the powerful?

Background to Health Care Fraud

Health care fraud can be perpetrated by individual patients (using someone else's card or a fraudulent health card), hospitals, extended care facilities, suppliers, laboratories, health care providers, and fictitious companies. The victims can be a publicly funded system or private insurance as well as all those who are required to pay higher premiums or go without service because of a lack of funds. Malcolm Sparrow (2000, 19) provides numerous examples of health care fraud in the United States and suggests that organized crime has turned from drugs to heath care fraud because it is "safer and more lucrative, and the risk of being caught is smaller. Moreover, if they are unlucky enough to get caught, these criminals know the punishments for health care fraud are likely to be much less severe than those for drug dealing."

As noted earlier, this chapter deals with one aspect of health care fraud – fraudulent over-billing carried out by health care professionals (mostly physicians) who bill on a fee-for-service basis. The fee-for-service system is based on trust, and without serious monitoring it provides easy opportunities to engage in inappropriate or fraudulent billing. Health care professionals may bill for services when none has been provided, charge for a more expensive procedure than the one that was performed (known as up-coding), carry out unnecessary or inappropriate services, or even conduct themselves unethically. In addition to the financial cost of health care fraud, unnecessary diagnostic techniques and surgeries may cause serious harm or death to patients.[10] Since there is some discretion in how doctors might bill certain services, so-called "aggressive billing" or "fudging and padding" might be tolerated or viewed more as business-oriented behaviour than as fraud. Even the terminology ("up-coding," "over-billing," or "inappropriate billing") leaves the impression that this type of behaviour might not be considered "fraud." Nevertheless, according to a number of academics, a fee-for-service health care system is criminogenic or crime facilitative in that it "subtly corrupts its own practitioners [and is] a major contributor to the disintegration of standards among physicians" (Jesilow, Pontell, and Geis 1993, 8). It allows doctors to "increase income illegally with little risk of apprehension" (*ibid.*, 3-5).

For instance, there appears to be an element of "group think" in health care fraud as well as a reliance on techniques of neutralization, which allow health care professionals to engage in fraud without being overly concerned about the criminal nature of their behaviour.[11] This notion is reinforced by the fact that physicians who are charged with misconduct may bring in other physicians to testify that the alleged misconduct is common practice in their field and therefore justified. Paul Jesilow, Henry Pontell, and Gilbert Geis (1993, 186) suggest that the conditions that facilitate health care fraud include "(1) the perpetrator's ability to redefine the violation, both in private and to others, in benign terms; (2) the perpetrator's feeling that insensitive external forces are interfering with his or her just deserts; (3) the availability of opportunities to violate the law easily; and (4) the perpetrator's belief that the violations are unlikely to be discovered, or, if found out, are unlikely to result in serious penalties."[12]

In Canada, unlike in the United States, there appeared to be little concern over health care fraud until recently (see, for example, Jesilow, Pontell, and Geis 1993; Sparrow 2000).[13] In 1993, the United States attorney general declared that health care fraud would be the Department of Justice's second priority (violent crime was first) and announced several initiatives to "crack down" on it. Legislative changes in 1996 and 1997 were designed to assist anti-fraud initiatives (Sparrow 2000, 56-69). The United States also subjected Medicare and Medicaid fraud to *qui tam* actions[14] under the *False Claims Act*.[15] This legislation allows whistleblowers (formally referred to as relators) to receive between 15 and 30 percent of the amount recovered, which in some cases can amount to millions of dollars.[16]

There were a number of cases in the mid-1990s that the media used to bring the issue of health care fraud to the public's attention in two Canadian provinces. In 1994, the British Columbia Medical Services Plan (MSP) released the names of seven doctors who were required to repay between $50,000 and $750,000 to the plan. While these doctors received some media attention, it was not until 1996 that the system encountered serious criticism after the provincial cabinet approved settlements that excused two doctors from repaying $216,164 and $400,000 to the plan. More specifically, the government was criticized for its "deferential coddling of the doctors" (Editorial 1996).

In 1996, a number of newspapers covered a story about Dr. Ara Artinian, a Toronto doctor, who was alleged to have over-billed the Ontario Health Insurance Plan (OHIP) by $4.7 million for services that were never provided. It was reported that he left the country in 1994. It is unclear whether OHIP ever recovered the money. However, Dr. Artinian and his mother had moved $5.5 million in liquid assets to the Bahamas. It was later reported that the criminal charges were stayed because of delay. This was not Dr. Artinian's first encounter with over-billing. In an earlier discipline decision, the College of Physicians and Surgeons wrote: "By his dishonest and persistent billing to both OHIP and Workers Compensation, Dr. Artinian showed total disregard for the trust which is essential for the operation of [a] publicly funded health care system" (Oziewicz 1996).

Although changes to managing health care fraud occurred in both provinces following these incidents, it was Ontario that introduced harsher measures. In 1997, the Ontario health minister, Jim Wilson, stated in a news conference that his "government has zero tolerance for fraud. Every healthcare dollar lost to fraud is a dollar stolen from a patient in need" (Armstrong 1997).[17] The historical solution for dealing with fraud by increasing premiums or adding to/increasing the money available for health care appeared to be coming to an end.[18] The focus on rising health care costs may have triggered the Ontario government's interest in health care fraud since a shortage of funds was bringing fraud to the attention of budget-conscious governments. Jesilow, Pontell, and Geis (1993, 35-36) suggest that the focus on Medicaid fraud in the United States may also have been a tactic to distract the public from another major issue – namely, the under-funding and unavailability of health care for many individuals. In Canada, John Ralston Saul (1999, 6-8) suggested that fear-mongering and elected representatives' focus on fraud comprised a tactic to make the privatization of health care more acceptable to the public.

The untimely death of Dr. Anthony Hsu in 2003 (an Ontario pediatrician who committed suicide following an order to reimburse OHIP for $108,000) and the subsequent appointment of former Supreme Court of Canada Justice Peter Cory to conduct a review of Ontario's medical audit system brought the issue of health care fraud to the public's attention in Canada (Canadian Medical Protective Association 2004). This time public sympathy appeared to be with the Ontario doctors who had been complaining that the Medical Review Committee (MRC) was too aggressive and unfair in its approach to over-billing. The terms of reference for the review stated that "the initiative shall be undertaken in a manner which does not affect or impede the ongoing statutory and operational duties and functions of the MRC and the General Manager of the Ontario Health Insurance Plan."[19] Despite this proviso, the Ontario legislature passed the *Transitional Physician Payment Review Act* on 24 June 2004, which halted all audits conducted by the MRC until after Justice Cory's report was considered.[20] Later the Ontario auditor general estimated that the province may have lost about $13 million in claims recoveries between June 2004 and March 2006 (Auditor General of Ontario 2006, 194).

The Cory report (2005) was delivered to the government on 21 April 2005, and, on 12 December 2006, the Ontario government introduced legislation (Bill 171) based on the report. The president of the Ontario Medical Association (OMA) was pleased with the results (Bach 2007). However, the OMA's detailed analysis as to how Bill 171 corresponded with the 118 recommendations in the Cory report was only available to its members (Anonymous 2007). A lawyer who works in the area concluded that "almost all" of Justice Cory's recommendations were adopted. She summarized his recommendations saying they "included a redirected focus on education (rather than recovery), the opportunity for cost awards in favour of physicians, the removal of an often crippling publication threat, a repayment stay pending appeal, restricted audit periods and ... the application of the rules of natural justice to all audit hearings" (Tremayne-Lloyd 2007). This approach was confirmed by the 2008 annual report of the auditor general of Ontario (2008, 428): "The new process places primary emphasis on educating medical practitioners to follow correct billing practices in the first place, and provides new mechanisms for practitioners to respond to ministry concerns about their billings." The current audit process can be found in the Education and Prevention Committee's *Interpretative Bulletin* (Ontario Health Insurance Plan 2008).

How Extensive Is Health Care Fraud?
Guesstimates of health care fraud come largely from other countries. Jesilow, Pontell, and Geis (1993, 12-13) suggest that estimates of Medicaid fraud by physicians in the United States ranged from 10 to 25 percent of the total budget, which in 1989 was $61 billion. They provide some extreme examples of fraud and associated offences such as the psychiatrist who billed Medicaid for 4,800 hours a year (almost twenty-four hours per work day) and physicians who billed for services on the dead and unnecessary eye operations that resulted in impaired vision. Others charged Medicaid for sexual liaisons, abortions on women who were not pregnant, and the extraction of thirty-eight teeth from one person (when there are only thirty-two teeth in a human mouth).

Sparrow (2000, 71) suggests that health care fraud in the United States was somewhere between 10 and 40 percent of the costs in 2000. He points out that evaluations of efforts to reduce health care fraud can be very misleading. One study showed that overpayments were reduced in 1997, 1998, and 1999 from 14 percent, to 11 percent, to 7.1 percent, respectively. However, the auditing procedures, which simply compared incoming claims with the documentation that the providers were later asked to submit for verification, did not include contact with patients. Providers simply had to lie twice in order to verify any phantom services (*ibid.*, 90-93). Accordingly, the system, which is based on trust, is set up for thieves: "Bill your lies correctly [and you] can rely on the payment systems to process [your] lies correctly, and pay them" (*ibid.*, 39).[21] A more modest estimate of health care fraud comes from the Blue Cross and Blue Shield Association – $85 billion was lost to health care fraud in the United States in 2003 – a mere 5 percent of the $1.7 trillion spent on health care in that year (Matlin 2004).[22]

In Canada, newspaper articles cite the Inkster report, completed in 1997 for the Ministry of Health in Ontario, as stating that there is up to $60 million in fraud each year in the province of Ontario. However, the report merely states that, as an example, "Provider Services' analysis of one billing code, intermediate medical examinations, indicates that the abuse of this code could be as high as $60 million per year" (Inkster 1997, 9). The Ontario government has estimated that health care fraud runs between $60 and $300 million a year in this province (Canadian Press 2001). However, another source puts the Ontario government's estimate as high as $650 million per year (Borsellino 2001). The results of a survey of public and private health care providers in 2004 estimated that the cost of health care fraud in Canada ranged from $3 billion to $10 billion a year (Blackwell 2005). Saul (1999, 6) suggests that there are probably no more cheating doctors than there are cheating patients and chief executive officers – between .5 percent and 5 percent.[23] This would amount to between 186 and 1,860 doctors in Ontario and between 49 and 490 doctors in British Columbia.

The Control of Professional Work

Eliot Freidson (2001, 179) elaborates on three logics or ideal ways to control professionals: (1) professionalism (self-regulation by the occupation); (2) managerialism (control through bureaucracy); and (3) the free labour market (control through consumerism or commercialism). He believes that the monitoring of service delivery and fraud is moving from professional control to bureaucratic control and that there is increasing pressure for labour market control (through privatization). Saul (1999, 15) reminds us that, although managerialism is often associated with government bureaucracy, "the private sector is also managerially-driven and suffers to an equal if not greater extent from the negative consequences of corporatism."[24] In practice, Freidson (2001, 216) thinks there should be a policy-driven mix of the three logics, but he also believes that managerialism and consumerism have invaded the medical profession.[25] He believes that the professions could regain public trust and control over medical services through better self-regulation and the enforcement of ethical codes.

One of the defining characteristics of a profession is that it is self-regulating.[26] The professions argue that they are in a better position to monitor their colleagues' behaviour because they have the expertise to do so. They can "funnel in" to their own self-regulatory system unethical and inappropriate behaviour that would not easily be subjected to the criminal justice system or other means of government control.[27] Critics of the professions say that professional self-regulating organizations (SROs) are too easy on their members and, in effect, "funnel out" deviant professionals by not imposing any, or any significant, penalties for professional misconduct. SROs are also criticized for taking professional misconduct out of the criminal justice system – that is, "funnelling [it] away" (Brockman 2004, 55-57). In addition, harsh treatment by SROs against selected "scapegoats" in their communities may result in unfairness to some of the more marginal members of a profession (see, for example, Daniel 1998).

In addition to self-regulation, bureaucracy, and consumerism, there are other systems that control professional work – the criminal justice system and the common law tort system.[28] For example, health care professionals can face criminal charges for fraudulent billing and civil lawsuits for unnecessary surgery. In the United States, the civil law system is also used to impose harsh financial penalties on health care fraud without the protections of the criminal justice system (Jost and Davies 1999, 247).[29] These various systems raise the questions of which is the best way to control the billing practices of health care professionals and under what circumstances is each system appropriate? When is it appropriate to use more than one system?[30] Is there a particular policy-driven mix that should prevail?

One of the issues raised by Edwin Sutherland's challenge to criminology to pay attention to white-collar crime, which is also echoed by the Law Commission of Canada (2003, 2004) and Stuart Henry and Mark Lanier (2001), is the role of equality in the application of the criminal law. Does the application of criminal law to street criminals and white-collar criminals result in inequality based on socio-economic status? Does the existence of self-regulating professions and other administrative alternatives for dealing with white-collar crime allow professionals who commit crimes to be "funnelled away" from the criminal justice system? If white-collar criminals are treated more leniently, can we apply this leniency to street criminals in order to even out the playing field? Can the lessons we learn from the application of the criminal law to white-collar crime be used to decrease its application in other areas of enforcement? I will return to some of these questions in the conclusions.

The Billing Systems in British Columbia and Ontario at the Time of This Study

In British Columbia, the MSP is managed by the Medical Services Commission (MSC), comprising one-third British Columbia Medical Association (BCMA) appointees (that is, physicians), one-third government, and one-third public members (jointly nominated by the BCMA and the government). In 1998, structural changes occurred in the monitoring of Medicare bills when the government created the Billing Integrity Program (BIP) to scrutinize inappropriate billing. At the same time, the professional SRO (in this case, the College of Physicians and Surgeons of British Columbia) withdrew from monitoring Medicare fraud by physicians and limited itself, through its Patterns of Practice Committee, to educating or warning doctors whose billing patterns were exceeding those of their colleagues. The college believed the BIP to be in a better position to enforce billing rules since the college could not order repayment. The SRO was still able to discipline a doctor who was criminally convicted of Medicare fraud. However, criminal and quasi-criminal prosecutions have been very rare in British Columbia.

The billing process in British Columbia also offers a number of informal avenues for health care professionals to challenge any assessment done by the BIP. Practitioners who are unhappy with a decision by MSP staff can first resubmit their bill for reassessment and then take their complaint to the MSP's Claims Billing Support Unit for another assessment by adjudication staff. The complaint may be resolved through an alternative dispute resolution process. Where settlement does not occur, an audit hearing panel will hear from the practitioner before any recovery order is made. Essentially, the British Columbia model is based on education, warnings, reconciliation, and assistance. If this process does not work, however, the priority appears to be the recovery of money rather than prosecution or punishment. This culture of non-criminalization appears to permeate the government, professional, and criminal justice systems in British Columbia when it comes to health care abuse and fraud.

In Ontario, at the time of my study, OHIP, a government agency that is part of the Ministry of Health and Long-Term Care, monitored claims and referred inappropriate billing cases to the MRC, which was a committee of the College of Physicians and Surgeons of Ontario. OHIP could also refer cases to the police or (since 1996) recover money directly from the health care professional.

The process of enforcing accurate billing by physicians in Ontario, prior to being halted in June 2004, was far less forgiving. Professionals were responsible for accurate billing and were not provided with billing profiles of their colleagues so they could adjust their billing practices to avoid an audit based on comparative patterns of practice. In addition, zero tolerance to fraud was introduced in 1997, along with the creation of a special police unit to investigate health care fraud (see discussion in Mosher and Hermer, Chapter 1 in this volume). The Ontario Provincial Police's (OPP) Health Fraud Investigation Unit, which was created in April 1998, doubled in size from nine to twenty in the first year. From 1998 to 2000, 500 cases were referred to the unit, including sixty cases of alleged fraudulent billing by health care professionals. In 2000, the unit was "pursuing 10 cases of alleged fraud by physicians and pharmacists in the courts; the fraud involve[d] an average of about $800,000 per case" (Sibbald 2000, 591). The unit also had proceeds-of-crime investigators who would pursue property bought by a doctor's "ill-gotten gains" (Sibbald 2000, 591). By 2001, the OPP had twenty-eight members in its OHIP fraud squad, and thirteen of them were assigned to investigating physicians' billings (Editorial 2001b). As noted earlier, in January 2003, a more informal settlement process was introduced (the OHIP Payment Review Program) together with the Education and Prevention Committee, following an outcry by physicians that they were the victims of enforcement actions.[31] The MRC's enforcement activities against physicians were put on hold until after the Cory report was completed and considered.

Although there was a move away from professional oversight of billings to a government managerial model with the introduction of the BIP in British Columbia, physicians still permeated the entire process, including the MSC, the BIP investigations, and audit decision making. The system certainly appeared to be under government bureaucratic control and responsibility; however, physicians were incorporated into all aspects of the decision making. In Ontario, while the physicians were overseen by a government bureaucracy (OHIP), the professional SRO (through the MRC) maintained decision-making powers over all billing disputes. As a consequence, the SRO took the heat when physicians violated public trust by fraudulent billing. The government agency (OHIP) and the newly created police unit have taken an active role in bringing health care fraud, including fraud by physicians, into the criminal justice system. Hence, the SRO has had little choice but to discipline physicians who have been criminally convicted for OHIP fraud.

Physicians in British Columbia have not appeared to have suffered greater enforcement because their SRO (the College of Physicians and Surgeons) has lost its power over billing misconduct to the government-run BIP. It could be argued that there would be greater capacity (and perhaps pressure) for enforcement had the enforcement powers been left with the SRO.[32] Physicians are now employed by the BIP to conduct much of the work that would have been conducted by physicians through their SRO. However, now when fraudulent cases in British Columbia are exposed in the media, the pressure is predominantly on the government agency and less on the SRO. In Ontario, the College of Physicians and Surgeons received criticism over the fact that its MRC was not controlling fraud, but the college was also blamed by the physicians for overly aggressive enforcement of the billing rules. To summarize, British Columbia physicians appear to have less conflict with the enforcement agency (physicians working for government) and are subject to less enforcement than physicians in Ontario, where pressure has been placed on the SRO to enforce the law and the government has set up a police force to monitor health care fraud. The political, economic, and social factors that might account for the differences between the two provinces, however, are beyond the scope of this chapter.

Cases of Health Care Fraud and Inappropriate Billing in Canada

Parameters of Data Collection

In order to examine how health care fraud is dealt with in Canada, I gathered cases of health care professionals abusing or defrauding the public health's fee-for-service system.[33] Included in my study are cases from all of the provinces and territories in the public domain (newspapers, court decisions, professional publications, websites, and decisions accessible by request) in which the health professional's name was mentioned at least once and one or more of the following occurred: (1) administrative investigation or action by a government branch or agency; (2) a professional SRO investigation or action (usually by the College of Physicians and Surgeons); or (3) a criminal or quasi-criminal charge. Cases where a tribunal or court did not uphold the allegations are also included, but there were very few of these.[34] In some cases, there is little information in the public domain – for example, only the professional's name and the amount he or she was required to return to the health care system. The time frame used was from 1990 to 2003. Cases that were commenced prior to 2003 were followed into 2004 and 2005 in order to record the results.

The Cases

The study's search resulted in eighty-seven cases: 36 percent from British Columbia, 39 percent from Ontario, 17 percent from Saskatchewan, 5 percent from Newfoundland/Labrador, and 3 percent from Quebec.[35] These eighty-seven cases resulted in at least 113 actions. Table 2.1 shows the types of actions in each province. For example, 16 percent of the actions in British Columbia were criminal or quasi-criminal, compared to 31 percent of the actions in Ontario. Most of the cases in Saskatchewan (81 percent) were administrative.

Table 2.1

Types and numbers of actions against health care professionals by province, 1990-2003

	BC		SK		ON		QC		NL	
	#	(%)	#	(%)	#	(%)	#	(%)	#	(%)
Administrative	20	(54)	13	(81)	12	(24)	3	(50)	4	(80)
SRO	11	(30)	3	(19)	22	(45)	1	(17)	0	(0)
Criminal/quasi-criminal	6	(16)	0	(0)	15	(31)	2	(33)	1	(20)
Total	37	(100)	16	(100)	49	(100)	6	(100)	5	(100)

Profession and Speciality
Most of the eighty-seven cases involved physicians (93 percent). This finding is to be expected because physicians bill on a fee-for-service basis in much greater numbers than other health care professionals. There were also two physiotherapists, two chiropractors, one dentist, and one optometrist. Some studies suggest that psychiatrists are more likely to be delinquent than other specialities.[36] Of the eighty-one physicians, 16 percent were psychiatrists. A rough indication of their proportion in the profession comes from a search of the College of Physicians and Surgeons of Ontario database for specialists. It indicates that 2,677 of the 37,214 physicians specialize in psychiatry (7 percent).[37] In this study, an additional 6 percent of the delinquent physicians practised psychotherapy, and 57 percent were general practitioners or family doctors.

Gender
As with most crimes, men appear in the health care fraud/misbehaviour statistics in greater proportion than women. Only 7 percent of the eighty-seven cases involved women, and 7 percent of the eighty-one physicians were women. In 2001, 33 percent of the 65,525 physicians in Canada were women (Statistics Canada 2001). A search of the College of Physicians and Surgeons of Ontario database for active physicians, including specialists, indicates that 11,636 of the 37,214 physicians in the database are female (31 percent).[38]

Age and Experience
For those health care professionals whose age and the year the behaviour commenced were available (N = 38), their ages ranged from twenty-nine to seventy-four, and the median age at the commencement of the misconduct was forty-four, and the mean was 45.3. The average age of physicians in Canada was 47.1 in 1998 and 47.7 in 2002 (Canadian Institute of Health Information 2002). The median number of years between graduation and when the fraudulent or inappropriate billing commenced (N = 42) was 16.5 years, and the number of years following their professional degree ranged from one to forty-five.

Cases of Fraudulent and Inappropriate Billing in British Columbia and Ontario
There were thirty-one cases and thirty-seven actions in British Columbia and thirty-four cases and forty-nine actions in Ontario. Table 2.2 shows how many of the cases resulted in a particular action. It should be remembered that this analysis was confined to cases in which the health care professional's name made it into the public domain. Given the sources of data available in the public domain, the most accurate information on the

Table 2.2

Actions taken in British Columbia and Ontario for health care fraud and inappropriate billing by the government administrative agency, the professional SRO, and the criminal justice system

	British Columbia		Ontario	
	#	(%)	#	(%)
Government administrative	20/31	(65)	12/34	(35)
Professional SRO	11/31	(35)	22/34	(65)
Criminal/quasi-criminal	6/31	(19)	15/34	(44)

three enforcement actions in Table 2.2 is probably for the criminal/quasi-criminal prosecution. Only 19 percent of the thirty-one cases in British Columbia, compared to 44 percent of the thirty-four cases in Ontario, resulted in criminal or quasi-criminal charges. This difference corresponds with the media coverage and the interviews that I conducted, which confirmed that British Columbia appears reluctant to prosecute these offenders, while Ontario has taken a "get tough" approach in dealing with them.

Only 35 percent of the cases in British Columbia resulted in an action by the professional SRO compared to 65 percent in Ontario. This finding too is consistent with media coverage and interview data. The British Columbia College of Physicians and Surgeons (which conducted nine of the eleven SRO proceedings in British Columbia) leaves these matters to the MSC because in their view the MSC is better equipped to recover inappropriately paid sums. The British Columbia college does not look at these cases unless they involve a quality-of-care issue or the doctor is convicted of a criminal offence. On the other hand, the Ontario college deals with fraudulent or inappropriate behaviour itself, even if it is not subject to criminal proceedings. However, if there are criminal proceedings, it usually waits for the outcome of these proceedings before it commences its own proceedings. In terms of multiple proceedings, five of the thirty-one cases in British Columbia (16 percent), as compared to twelve of the thirty-four cases (35 percent) in Ontario resulted in both an SRO and a criminal or quasi-criminal action. The data on government administrative actions are the sparsest. While data on the administrative actions by the British Columbia MSC are published in the news media and through their own news releases, OHIP only publishes amounts that are recovered and only seldom provides the names of the health care professionals.

Forms of Misconduct/Fraud

Table 2.3 shows the types of behaviour investigated by the government administrative agency and the professional SRO.

Table 2.3

Types of behaviour dealt with by the government administrative agency or professional SRO in British Columbia and Ontario				
	British Columbia		Ontario	
Type of behaviour	#	(%)	#	(%)
Billed but not provided	10	(24)	17	(38)
Up-coding	8	(19)	12	(27)
Over-servicing/unnecessary	8	(19)	4	(9)
False diagnosis	3	(7)	4	(9)
Inadequate records	8	(19)	7	(16)
Patterns of practice	5	(12)	1	(2)
Total	42	(100)·	45	(101)

Billing for Services Not Provided

The most frequent type of behaviour was a health care provider billing for services that were not provided (24 percent of the behaviour investigated in British Columbia and 38 percent of the behaviour in Ontario).[39]

An example of a case where services were not provided is that of Dr. Michael Bogart, who was ordered to pay back close to $1 million for fraud between 1990 and 1996. He billed for services conducted in his Toronto office while he was holidaying in Europe, Australia, and various other places. Bogart would regularly bill for seeing patients on Thursday and Friday, when he never saw patients on those days. Another example is Dr. Mario Halenar, who apparently charged the MSP in British Columbia for treating a seventy-eight-year-old woman for problems surrounding childbirth and menopause (Ouston 1998).

When interviewees were asked a general question about whether billing for services that did not occur was fraud, some suggested that such billings may be the result of clerical errors or carelessness and could therefore be explained away. Although one respondent recognized it as fraud, she stated that since the standard of proof is high in a criminal trial it may be hard to prove. One respondent indicated it was fraud, without any provisos. All respondents thought it would be fraudulent for doctors to bill for sexual encounters with their patients. One commented, "the college would be all over them. Most of that stuff is extracurricular – not billed for."

Up-Coding

The next most frequent activity was up-coding – simply charging for more than was performed (19 percent of the activities in British Columbia and 27 percent of the activities in Ontario).[40] For example, Dr. Michael Ing, a British Columbia optometrist, billed for extensive eye examinations when he had conducted only brief examinations. Some doctors billed for a complete physical examination when they did only a brief one. When interviewees were asked a general question about whether billing for more than was actually performed was fraud, some suggested that it may be difficult to prove intention – there are grey areas or sliding scale issues that are a matter of interpretation, and, in some cases, the physician's own judgment might come into play. Another respondent indicated that it was fraud, without any provisos. In response to whether it was fraud to bill for individual psychiatric therapy while conducting group sessions, some stated it depended on whether it was done knowingly. One thought it was deceptive and inappropriate but was not sure that it would meet a judge's standard of fraud.

In 1999, a British Columbia ministry official stated that only fifteen to twenty physicians are guilty of inappropriate billing each year: "It's a relatively small number, but there's probably a little bit of fudging or padding, which occurs in every practice, while fraudulent billing is in fact very rare" (Fayerman 1999). Some interviewees agreed that padding occurs and that it is unacceptable. It is a serious problem, "but most doctors are not fraudulent." One interviewee explained that some doctors are

antagonists towards government. They feel they are entitled to bill more than they are allowed to. It's a relationship issue; their perception at the microlevel is that they did so much work they're entitled to more.[41] A small percentage would bill fraudulently. Others would use greyness to justify their billing – rarely intentionally. In fairness to doctors, some believe what they're doing is OK.[42]

Some doctors maximize their revenue by "aggressive billing" or taking advantage of "good practice management." Others are poor managers, and "lots of services go un-billed."

Over-Servicing/Unnecessary Services
There were eight instances in British Columbia and four in Ontario of over-servicing or unnecessary services.[43] For example, Dr. Ara Artinian, who administered anabolic steroids to his patients, was found to have billed for medically unnecessary services (*College of Physicians and Surgeons of Ontario v. Artinian* 1992, para. 34). There were a number of cases (not included in this analysis) where physicians performed unnecessary services, but the billing aspect of the case was not discussed.

When interviewees were asked a general question about whether billing for medically unnecessary services or over-servicing was fraud, some said it was very difficult to determine or to see this situation as a criminal issue. In some cases, they felt it was just poor judgment on the part of the physicians and that they should repay the MSP. Some physicians were just pushing the envelope in terms of giving their patients maximum care. Another respondent indicated that it was fraud, without any provisos.

False Diagnosis

Billing for services that were not provided can result in a false diagnosis or false medical record. However, this item was coded only when the false diagnosis was an issue in the proceedings. As such, false diagnoses can create serious problems (three instances in British Columbia and four in Ontario).[44] In addition to being a fraud on the public purse, they create a medical record that may have negative consequences for the unsuspecting patient. For example, Dr. Alexander Victor Scott billed OHIP for "29 treatments for alcoholism, two treatments for a brain tumour, and five treatments for anxiety, hysteria and nervous exhaustion [on one patient] – none of which were ever requested or received" (Elliott 2001).[45] In another case, Dr. Ara Artinian was found by the college to have billed for sexual and psychological problems and assessments that his patients never had or discussed with him. He also billed for diagnoses such as asthma, dermatitis, vertigo, and low back pain – services that his patients denied receiving (*College of Physicians and Surgeons of Ontario v. Artinian* 1992). When interviewees were asked a general question about stating a false diagnosis in order to bill for something that was done, but not covered, all of them stated that this action was fraud. However, one had never seen such an event and added that physicians would simply get advanced approval to have such a procedure covered.

Patterns of Practice

Some legislation allows for recovery from doctors who exceed the patterns of practice in their cohort of doctors by a specified amount (five cases in British Columbia and one in Ontario). For example, Dr. Simon Wing Yip was found to have seen each of his patients on an average of eight times a year when the average doctor saw patients only four times a year. Dr. Yip was seeing patients at twice the normal rate, and his visits per patient were more than two standard deviations from the average. On appeal, the Supreme Court of British Columbia indicated that while the audit committee found "an unjustifiable departure from the patterns of practice of practitioners in the practitioner's class" there was no finding of wrongdoing. "Doctors can choose to give exceptional care to their patients and the purpose of clause (a) is simply to place a limit on the amount that the Medical Services Plan is obliged to pay" (*Yip v. Audit Committee, Medical Services Commission*, 1993, 13-14). Sometimes a pattern of practice audit will lead to the discovery of up-coding or billing for services that were not rendered.

Amount in Issue

Where the information was available, the median amount in issue in British Columbia (N = 19) was $216,164, and the median amount in Ontario (N = 22) was $104,000. The mean (average) amounts were $297,558 in British Columbia and $421,844 in Ontario. Although British Columbia had five cases over $500,000, while Ontario only had four, Ontario had three cases over $900,000, and British Columbia had none.

Government Administrative Proceedings

As shown in Table 2.2, information in the public domain indicated that government administrative proceedings were conducted in 65 percent of the thirty-one British Columbia cases and in 35 percent of the thirty-four Ontario cases. These findings probably reflect the fact that the administrative process in Ontario is more secretive than the process in British Columbia, which is possibly why I could not find information on the other cases in the public domain. Given Ontario's position of zero tolerance, it is very likely that administrative actions were taken in close to 100 percent of the Ontario cases. There was insufficient data to do any further quantitative analysis of these cases.

Professional SRO Proceedings

SRO proceedings were conducted in 35 percent of the British Columbia cases (N = 11) – nine by the College of Physicians and Surgeons, one by the College of Optometrists, and one by the College of Physical Therapists. SRO proceedings were conducted in 65 percent of the Ontario cases (N = 22) – all by the College of Physicians and Surgeons. Only two of the nine cases in British Columbia (22 percent) were by the College of Physicians and Surgeons in 2000 or later, compared to fifteen of the twenty-two cases in Ontario (68 percent). In British Columbia, the physiotherapist had his licence revoked. The optometrist was suspended for twenty months, fined $3,000, and ordered to pay costs of $110,000. The Board of Examiners in Optometry (2001, 1) later lifted the last eighteen months of the suspension if certain standards and monitoring demands were met. Both individuals faced criminal charges. On the other hand, four of the nine physicians resigned or had their licences revoked, four were suspended from between one and thirty-six months, and one was reprimanded.

Between 1990 and 1997 (when the government introduced the BIP, which took over the monitoring of Medicare fraud), the College of Physicians and Surgeons in British Columbia disciplined five doctors who were not prosecuted in the criminal justice system. These five cases were examined to determine whether any conclusions could be drawn on the question of whether the SRO was funnelling in and investigating behaviour that was not otherwise suitable for the criminal justice system or whether the SRO was instead funnelling criminal behaviour away from the criminal justice system. Dr. C.[46] made thirty-two "improper claims ... for fees with respect to patients who had not received the service claimed. In the majority of cases, he billed the plan for office attendances when he had not seen the patients. In some cases he billed for office attendances when he had only spoken to the patients by telephone."He promised to stop doing this after his staff confronted him. Thirteen of the thirty-two claims took place after his staff confronted him. According to newspaper reports, Dr. L. billed the MSP for sexual encounters with one of his patients but did not record all of her visits on her chart. The issue of billing disappeared in the physician's appeal to the Supreme Court of British Columbia and British Columbia Court of Appeal after the college made the finding of infamous and unprofessional conduct regarding the sexual encounters.

Dr. H. was found guilty by the college of entering into financial relationships with his patients when they were incapacitated by the drugs he was prescribing to them. He also billed the MSP for services that could not have been rendered – for example, removing tonsils from a person who had them removed twenty-five years earlier. Dr. T. billed the MSP for "approximately 150 instances where she had either performed no service or a service for which she was not entitled to bill the plan." Dr. F. billed the MSP for services to family members that violated the physicians' code of ethics, and he was required to repay the amounts. With the exception of the last case, it is difficult to see why these cases could not have been prosecuted in criminal or quasi-criminal proceedings. Even after the college withdrew from this enforcement arena in 1997, the criminal justice system did not pick up the slack.

Five of the twenty-two SRO cases in Ontario resulted in a resignation or licence revocation. Ten professionals were suspended for three to eighteen months (a mean of 7.5 months and a median of 5.5 months). However, six of these individuals had their suspensions reduced to one to twelve months if they fulfilled certain conditions (for example, paying the fine within a specified time). Seven professionals were fined from $3,000 to $10,000 (a median of $5,000). Additional conditions and penalties included the following: three physicians were required to take remedial courses; two were subjected to inspections or oversight; fifteen were reprimanded; and fifteen were ordered to pay costs ranging from $1,000 to $15,000 (a mean of $4,600 and a median of $2,500). Only three decisions were appealed, and, of these, the results were against the professional in two cases, and one was split as to which party was successful.

There were nine cases in Ontario where the College of Physicians and Surgeons disciplined doctors for inappropriate billing, but it appears as though no criminal charges were laid. In three cases, the college found various violations of practice standards but could not find sufficient evidence to establish that the physicians had billed OHIP for services that were not performed or that the bills were false or misleading. In another case, the physician had billed same-day visits on different days but had not billed for services that he did not perform. In the remaining cases, the inappropriate billings seemed to be of less concern since the physicians were involved in other matters such as sexual abuse or sexual relations with patients, violating professional boundaries, and the inappropriate prescription of drugs. In some cases, the witnesses may not have stood up under cross-examination in the criminal justice system. In these cases, the SRO was probably funnelling in inappropriate billing behaviour that would not have been dealt with elsewhere. Unlike the college in British Columbia prior to 1997, the Ontario College of Physicians and Surgeons does not appear to be funnelling fraud away from, or keeping it out of, the criminal justice system.

Criminal and Quasi-Criminal Proceedings

There were six criminal or quasi-criminal prosecutions and convictions in British Columbia between 1990 and 2003, compared to fifteen prosecutions and twelve convictions in Ontario. Only three of the six prosecutions in British Columbia, and fourteen of the fifteen in Ontario, were against physicians (4.7 times as many as in British Columbia).[47] All but one of the accused were men, and all pleaded guilty. Although there were only six prosecutions in British Columbia, there appeared to be a pattern of plea negotiations that resulted in facts before the court that were substantially less serious than what the media had reported as the original allegations. In two cases, the amounts that were repaid during civil proceedings were substantially higher than the amounts that were the subject of the criminal charges. The penalties imposed appear to be very lenient, and the judges' comments were, with one exception, quite sympathetic to the plight of the convicted health care providers. Plea negotiations were also a major factor in Ontario, but, overall, the professionals did not seem to fare as well as their British Columbia counterparts when it came to criminal sentencing.

Three of the twelve professionals convicted in Ontario served time in jail. In 1991, Dr. Louis Stephen O'Connell, a family physician, pleaded guilty to defrauding OHIP of $100,000. Apparently, his behaviour was discovered because he billed for more hours than there were in a day (Upton 1991). O'Connell was sentenced to reimburse OHIP, spend eighty-nine days in jail (to be served on weekends), complete 250 hours of community service, and serve two years probation (*College of Physicians and Surgeons of Ontario v. O'Connell* 1994). Dr. Alexander Victor Scott, a general practitioner in the Kingston area who made house calls to the elderly and those confined to their homes, pleaded guilty to defrauding OHIP of $586,924.59 between 1992 and 1999. Although there was an order of forfeiture for some of his retirement savings because they had been obtained as part of an enterprise crime offence, "charges of money laundering and profiting from the proceeds of crime were dropped as part of Scott's plea bargain" (Phillips 2002; *R. v. Scott* 2000, 8). Scott had billed for fictitious appointments with some patients and fabricated procedures on patients that he did see. On 8 May 2000, the judge followed a joint submission by Crown and defence counsel and sentenced Scott to thirty months in prison (*R. v. Scott* 2000, 8).

On 11 September 2000, Dr. Michael Charles Bogart pleaded guilty to defrauding OHIP of $923,780.53 over a period of seven years (see discussion earlier in this chapter). Although of the view that such a crime warranted a five-year penitentiary sentence, the trial judge considered "the accused's background, his present status, his remorse, his continued service to his patients and his guilty plea" and sentenced him to two years less a day to be served in the community, three years probation, and restitution (*College of Physicians and Surgeons of Ontario v. Bogart* 2001, paras. 16-18). On appeal by the Crown, the Ontario Court of Appeal found that the sentence was "demonstrably unfit." While such a crime ordinarily would call for a four-year penitentiary term, given the mitigating circumstances the court imposed an eighteen-month sentence in jail (*ibid.*, paras. 16-18). An application for leave to appeal to the Supreme Court of Canada was denied (*ibid.*).

Three of the twelve professionals served conditional sentences of imprisonment (this means the sentence of imprisonment was served in the community). Dr. Donald MacDiarmid, a general practitioner in Ajax, Ontario, pleaded guilty to defrauding OHIP of $155,675 and was sentenced to an eighteen-month conditional sentence, two years probation, a fine of $100,000, and 150 hours of community service. On appeal, the fine was deleted since sentencing an accused to imprisonment and both probation and a fine was found to be illegal (*R. v. MacDiarmid* 2001). In 2001, Dr. Miles Moore pleaded guilty to defrauding OHIP of $75,000 and was sentenced to a fifteen-month conditional sentence with a curfew from 9:00 p.m. until 6:00 a.m., followed by three years of probation, and he was ordered to pay $75,000 in restitution. Dr. Gustavo Tolentino pleaded guilty to defrauding OHIP of $58,120.40 on 25 October 1999. He was sentenced to a twelve-month conditional sentence and ordered to pay restitution. Of the remaining six professionals convicted of an offence, two were fined $5,000 each, three were placed on probation, and one was given a discharge.

The Privilege of Social and Economic Location: Professional Health Care Fraud and Welfare Fraud

In 1996, an editorial in the *Vancouver Sun* opined that "the contrast between government's deferential coddling of the doctors, and their handling of suspected welfare abuse is striking" and is "almost enough to make one believe there's one law for the rich and another for the poor" (Editorial 1996).[48] Academics have suggested that the nature of the offender (for example, welfare versus professional) often characterizes the offence more so than the offending behaviour.[49] Essentially, this notion confirms Sutherland's emphasis on the need to examine how our enforcement of the criminal law may be more important than our legal definitions of crime.

Table 2.4 provides a brief overview of my impressions of the differences between welfare fraud and fraud by health care professionals.[50] There is definitely a difference in terms of who these people are (impoverished women and men as compared to privileged men) and how the public perceives them (lazy, dependent, and "never deserving" as compared to hardworking, underpaid, and deserving). In terms of the law, complex rules work against welfare recipients who are assumed to know the law, whereas complex rules can serve as an excuse for health care professionals who commit fraud. Despite the individual responsibility that goes with the neo-liberal approach to welfare fraud (see Mosher and Hermer, Chapter 1 in this volume), physicians to some extent still get to blame the system.[51]

When it comes to law in practice, welfare recipients are subjected to surveillance, whereas health care professionals are subjected to education – more so in British Columbia than in Ontario, although in 2004 Ontario did introduce billing educational programs for physicians. In 2007, physicians in Ontario started to receive mini billing profiles so that they could compare their billings to the billings of other physicians (Education and Prevention Committee 2007). In contrast, welfare recipients are subject to harsh administrative actions with little education or leniency (for example, removal of entitlement to social assistance), and they have little power to resist (see Mosher and Hermer, Chapter 1 in this volume). Once in the criminal justice system, welfare recipients may be found guilty on evidence that is probed very little, or not at all, by defence counsel. The costs of using the criminal law against welfare recipients are minimal compared to the prosecution of professionals who can afford to hire the best lawyers to either test the prosecution's case to the fullest or negotiate a plea bargain to minimize the criminal law's impact. The high social and economic costs that criminal prosecutions have on welfare recipients appear to be ignored, whereas the high social and economic costs to professionals are recognized in sentencing decisions. Overall, welfare recipients are much less powerful than the professionals when it comes to influencing what the rules are and how they might be enforced.[52]

Conclusions: Lessons from Crimes of the Powerful
The wealthy often have advantages in the criminal justice system. Darryl K. Brown (2004) suggests that money buys privacy such that wealthier offenders can more readily avoid detection and investigation. Money also buys trust. The health care billing system is built on trust with very few controls. It is much easier to falsify bills in health care fraud than to commit welfare

Table 2.4

Comparing the treatment of welfare fraud with professional health care fraud

Welfare fraud	Health care fraud
• mostly impoverished women and men	• mostly privileged men
• publicly seen as "lazy, dependent, undisciplined, and lack work ethic"	• seen as hardworking and underpaid
• "never deserving"[a]	• deserving
• not entitled	• entitled
• criminal prosecution; pay it back • jail	• BC: pay it back, maybe • Ontario: criminal and pay it back
• complex rules work against offender • "technical" fraud = fraud	• complex rules work for offender • technical fraud = errors
• fraud defined broadly • overpayments; all infractions viewed as fraud	• fraud defined narrowly • strict application of the law
• surveillance / not trusted	• education on how to bill / relative lack of oversight / trusted
• low criminal enforcement costs to the system (high costs to the individual not recognized)	• high criminal enforcement costs (high costs to the individual recognized)
• payback difficult for accused	• payback may be used as alternative to criminal law; payback less difficult
• condemnation by community; no power to change public perception	• support from the community; power to change public perception
• welfare snitch line	• nothing equivalent
• "tragic" or no legal representation	• the best legal representation
• social context irrelevant • individual responsibility	• social context a factor • ability to blame the system
• no power to influence rules, enforcement, or public perception	• power to influence rules, enforcement, and public perception
• concern with moral condemnation	• concern with retaining physicians?
• "walking on eggshells"[b]	• walking on water?

Notes:
[a]   This phrase is borrowed from Chunn and Gavigan (2004).
[b]   This phrase is borrowed from Mosher *et al.* (2004).

fraud. If caught, white-collar criminals can often match or exceed the resources of prosecutors, unlike street criminals. Equality between the powerful
and less powerful might demand that such barriers become more equal. For
example, rather than prosecutors in British Columbia asking whether there
is a "substantial likelihood of conviction" before approving charges, they
might want to ask, "if this accused had the resources to litigate this criminal
charge, would there be a substantial likelihood of conviction?"[53]

The crime control industry runs into challenges when its professionals
direct their attention to their own kind – other professionals. In addition to
the legal tools and money that the powerful have to fight criminal allegations in the courtroom, heavy-handed enforcement against the powerful
leads to a backlash (Jost and Davies 1999). The backlash and resentment
that greet aggressive enforcement result in recommendations by many academics for a more co-operative approach to such crimes or unwanted behaviours.[54] What we probably are less likely to see, acknowledge, and do
something about is the fact that heavy-handed enforcement against the less
powerful also breeds anger, contempt, and defiance (see, for example, Snider
1998; Braithwaite 2002). Examining how professionals react to having the
criminal law applied to them and how we, as a society, react in return may
assist us in developing more empathy for the less powerful.

In order to introduce equality into the enforcement of fraud laws, the
backlash of the less powerful must be given the same weight as the backlash
of the more powerful. For example, when the government appointed Justice
Cory to review the Ontario MRC's auditing system, the terms of reference
stated that the MRC's auditing function would not be impeded. Shortly
thereafter, new legislation halted all audits until after Justice Cory's report.
How likely is it that reviews of welfare recipients' claims would be halted
while an inquiry determined their effectiveness for the purpose of rebuilding
the confidence of welfare recipients in the review process? In its submission
to the Cory review, the OMA stated that the audit process should focus on
education and prevention and that physicians should be given six months
to alter their billing behaviour if the ministry was not satisfied with the
physicians' explanations of their billings. How likely is it that we would
allow welfare recipients to continue violating the complex welfare rules for
six months after they were discovered to be in violation of them? According
to the OMA, physicians should have knowledge of the statistical norms
expected of them so they can bill accordingly. This system exists in British
Columbia. Do we give welfare recipients the same opportunity to self-correct
so as to avoid penalties or the disapproval of their supervisors? The OMA
suggested that there should be no recovery from a physician who is practising "in accordance with prevailing standards of care."[55] Again, are we prepared to translate this excuse to accommodate prevailing practices by welfare
recipients?

There is a common perception that white-collar criminals are treated more leniently than those engaged in street crime. One way to reduce this discrimination is to explore how our compassion for white-collar criminals can be transferred to so-called "street" criminals. There are good reasons to move in this direction rather than moving towards more heavily penalizing white-collar criminals. Anne Alvesalo and Steve Tombs (2002, 30) argue that the call for a heavier hand on white-collar crime may lead to "a game of spiralling criminalization" and a "fuelling [of] the engine of crime control." Such an approach may provide further legitimacy to a class-biased system "through the appearance that even the wealthiest and most powerful actors can be subject to state control." In addition, resources designated for such enforcement may be re-directed at more conventional offenders (ibid., 31). For example, in the context of this study, additional resources for health care fraud may be directed at consumers of health care rather than providers, since the former are easier targets for enforcement.

Alvesalo and Tombs suggest that changes to the present system to assist investigations and prosecutions of complex white-collar crimes, such as giving state agents novel and invasive powers or reversing the onus of proof, may then be used against lower-class offenders. Even within the sphere of economic or white-collar crime, social control measures may be directed at the less powerful rather than at the more elite offender (ibid., 32).[56] In addition, the increased focus on the use of criminal law obscures the need to find non-criminal solutions to harm.[57] Finally, Alvesalo and Tombs (ibid., 32-33) suggest that economic crime crusades may be "used as Trojan horses for expanding the totality of the repressive armoury of the state."[58] Criminalization of conduct can do more harm than good. Much like medical intervention, which can make patients worse (iatrogenesis), legal intervention can have its own negative consequences (the juridogenic effect).[59]

Once conduct is criminalized, it is extremely difficult to de-criminalize it, especially if the conduct criminalized is engaged in by the less powerful.[60] Societal consensus is often not sufficient. The strongest resistance comes from the crime control industry, which is "now a powerful force in its own right; it has a vested interest in defining events as crime" (Hillyard and Tombs 2004, 18). The crime industry includes public and private police and investigators, the prison industry, and the growing number of professionals who make their living off the crime control industry – psychiatrists, psychologists, profilers, lawyers, social workers, probation and parole officers, judges, and so on.

The crime industry problem is directly linked to what John McKnight (1995) refers to as the "professional problem." He provides numerous examples of what Ivan Illich (1976) referred to as "specific counterproductivity." Not only do some services not have the intended effect, they may also produce more of what they are trying to prevent. McKnight (ibid., 8), writes, "thus, one can imagine sickening medicine, stupidifying schools, and crime-making corrections systems."[61] He believes that, "through the propagation of belief in authoritative expertise, professionals cut through the social fabric of community and sow clienthood where citizenship once grew" (*ibid.*, 10). The effect is the essence of the professional problem – "poor people defined as deficient by those whose incomes depend upon the deficiency they define" (*ibid.*, 18). "Sick," "criminal," and "unfit" can be substituted for the various problems created by professionals who live off the backs of those they define as being in need of their services.

The growing number and variety of professionals being produced require that we manufacture needs to keep them employed. The professional problem in the criminal justice system is becoming more obvious. Psychology departments are turning out more and more graduates who will conduct questionable risk assessments on many people who will then be subjected to confinement or treatment for behaviour that should not have been criminalized. Criminology departments are turning out more graduates who expect jobs as criminal justice technicians (Brockman 2003, 288). According to Alan Young's (2003, 316) mantra, "too many soldiers and not enough peace. Too many cops and not enough liberty. Too many lawyers and not enough justice." One could add many more: too many doctors and not enough health; too many experts and not enough community. To the Law Commission of Canada's question "who benefits from labelling behaviour a crime?" one could list all of the occupations designed to control and, in some cases, nurture crime. Accordingly, problem definers are key to the question "what is a crime?" Critically examining the work of the "problem definers" may be the most effective means of reducing crime in our society. However, McKnight (1995, 22) warns us that this is not what politicians want to hear since "the more privileged of our society ... expect [professional employment and] the prestige accorded professional work." The crime control industry not only produces many professionals, it also keeps them employed and assists in the re-election of governments (Robinson 2001, 98).[62]

In conclusion, this study demonstrates the power of the powerful when it comes to defining and enforcing laws. If the less powerful could do the same, we would have a drastic reduction in the behaviour that we define and enforce as crime. The study of white-collar crime in the "what is a crime?" debate exposes the class-biased criminal justice system, the crime control industry, and the professional problem. We are warned that a harsher approach to white-collar crime will have the unintended consequences of fuelling the crime control industry against the less powerful. It may be time to seriously reconsider the inequality of the criminal law and restrain its use. This may be the only road to arriving at "a more equitable and accountable process for defining crime and enforcing criminal law" (Des Rosiers and Bittle 2004, xxiii).

Acknowledgments

I thank the Law Commission of Canada for the funding to expand my research on crimes and misconduct in the professions to health care fraud. I greatly benefited from meeting with the other researchers and attendees at the "what is a crime?" roundtables. Special thanks to Janet Mosher, Steven Bittle, Marcel Saulnier, and anonymous reviewers for their written comments on earlier drafts and to my researchers Dana Christensen and Caroline Murdoch.

Notes

1 For an exposé on how we waste criminal justice resources on activities that should not be criminalized because they do not cause serious harm to others, see Young (2003).

2 Although the typical examples that come to mind are the black markets and criminal activities built up by criminalizing drugs and prostitution, there are also unintended consequences that follow the enforcement of laws that have social consensus. Few would dispute that car theft should be prevented. However, one can only wonder if the highly publicized car-bait program used by the police in the Vancouver Lower Mainland (where bait cars are left in parking lots for the would-be thieves and some are caught on tape wondering out loud whether they might be stealing the bait) might itself incite these car thieves to engage in car-jackings, purse snatchings, park muggings, and home invasions to support themselves and perhaps their drug habits. An increase in the latter crimes, which are more personal than car theft, is likely to increase fear of crime and fuel support for the crime control industry.

3 In 1939, Sutherland (1983, 7) coined the phrase "white-collar crime" to draw attention to crimes committed by the upper class and the fact that they were "not ordinarily included within the scope of criminology." See Sutherland (1940) for his original speech. This lack of attention to white-collar crime continues today (see, for example, Friedrichs 2007; Lynch McGurrin, and Fenwick 2004; and Tombs and Whyte 2003).

4 A study by Ericson and Doyle (2004, 119-20) on how insurance companies define and regulate fraudulent insurance claims found that one insurance company, which catered to clients from a more desirable socio-economic background, serviced them through professional, in-house adjusters who were very accommodating to the claims. Another company, with clients from a lower socio-economic background, contracted ex-police officers as private investigators to reduce the amount the company had to pay on insurance claims, and the company more readily invoked the criminal justice system.

5 In 2003, the Law Commission of Canada (2003, 15) called for the criminal law to be limited to controlling or responding to serious threats of harm when other means of control were not appropriate.

6 *Criminal Code*, R.S.C. 1985, c. C-46; *Medicare Protection Act*, R.S.B.C. c. 286.

7 Nightingale (1996, 1-3) provides an example from 1703 where Chief Justice Holt questioned: "Shall we indict one man for making a fool of another?"

8 If the subject matter exceeds $5,000, it is an indictable offence punishable by a term of imprisonment not exceeding fourteen years. Prior to 2004, the maximum penalty was ten years. If the value of the subject matter does not exceed $5,000, the offence can be prosecuted by indictment (maximum term of imprisonment not to exceed two years) or by way of summary conviction. For more details on the elements of fraud, see Mosher and Hermer (Chapter 1 in this volume).

9 As the Law Reform Commission of Canada (1977, 1) said about theft and fraud in 1977, "a law, it's said, is what it does. Criminal law, for instance, isn't merely what the *Criminal Code* says but also what is done by judges, prosecutors, defence counsel, police, prison officials and all who operate our criminal justice system. What all these do is law reform's prime target."

10 Jesilow, Pontell, and Geis (1993, 19) refer to a study that found that 10 percent of medical operations in the United States were unwarranted. For some procedures, the estimate of inappropriate surgery was 44 percent. In Ontario, Dr. Wai-Ping was found to have exposed women to unnecessary and risky hysterectomies (*College of Physicians and Surgeons of Ontario*

v. Wai-Ping 2004). The lawyer who filed a lawsuit on behalf of his former patients alleged that financial gain may have been a motivating factor in these surgeries (Brean 2003, A5).

11 Techniques of neutralization were first proposed by Sykes and Matza (1957) to explain how juvenile delinquents rationalize or justify their delinquent behaviour. However, the authors were also of the view that techniques of neutralization could be used by other deviants to justify their behaviour. Glasbeek (2002, 141-42) makes similar arguments about the criminogenic nature of corporate culture.

12 These techniques of neutralization parallel those used by tax evaders (see Mosher 2008).

13 A study in the mid-1980s found that, "despite widespread public and government interest in medical fraud and overservicing in other industrial countries, little interest in this issue has been generated in Canada" (Wilson, Chappell, and Lincoln 1986, 236). It is possible, as one reviewer suggested, that some of this difference may be attributed to the public nature of health care in Canada.

14 *Qui tam* ("who as well") is an abbreviation of "*qui tam pro domino rege quam pro seipse*," which means "he who sues for the king as for himself." *Qui tam* suits are brought by plaintiffs for themselves and the government. In such actions, the plaintiff is entitled to a percentage of the recovered penalty "as a reward for exposing the wrong-doing and recovering funds for the government. Sometimes the federal or state government will intervene and become a party to the suit in order to guarantee success and be part of any negotiations and conduct of the case." See *Legal Dictionary*, http://legal-dictionary.thefreedictionary.com/qui+tam+action.

15 *False Claims Act*, 31 U.S.C., ss. 3729-33.

16 For example, Dr. Steven J. Bander was paid $56 million when the US government collected $350 million from Gambro Healthcare. The company set up a shell company, which allowed it to illegally collect almost $500 per patient per month for kidney dialysis, above the entitled amount. Dr. Bander had tried unsuccessfully to stop the fraud before bringing an action (Shinkle 2005). For further information on these actions, see "All about Qui Tam," http://www.all-about-qui-tam.org/.

17 This particular media report was more focused on users of Ontario Health Insurance Plan (OHIP) services than the providers of health care.

18 Ericson and Doyle (2004, 106-7), who studied private property and casualty insurance, suggest that the "fraud problem" in the insurance industry in the United States became a more prominent issue when legislation that restricted premium increases meant that money lost to fraud artists could no longer be recovered through increasing premiums.

19 Medical Audit Practice in Ontario, Terms of Reference, 30 April 2004, available at http://www.petercory.org/.

20 *Transitional Physician Payment Review Act*, S.O. 2004, c. 13.

21 The trust the system depends on is illustrated by an Ontario physician who decided to test the system by billing for a heart-lung transplant conducted in the patient's home with local anaesthetic. He was amazed to see that his bill was paid by OHIP (Anonymous 1996).

22 As one reviewer suggested, there may be differences in Canada and the United States based on the extent of private health care insurance in the United States.

23 Like all hidden figures of crime, it is impossible to know how accurate these estimates are.

24 According to Freidson (2001, 4), managerial control can occur in the public and private sphere. Saul (1999, 10) suggests that the more efficient a Medicare system becomes the more ineffective it will be. The growth of management over the past 100 years has been a "natural and necessary parasite of growing specialization among those who actually do something," and the resulting corporatism or corporatist technocracy has pushed the public interest out of a system now obsessed with self-interest (*ibid.*, 12-17). Similarly, Germov (1995, 60) suggests that the goals of efficiency in a health care system are not neutral, but, rather, they deflect attention away from "issues of equity, participation, minority rights and social justice." Later he suggests that "managerialism and its associated commercialism and consumerism may undermine the access, equity, and universalism of Medicare itself" (*ibid.*, 63).

25 This view is shared by Garland (2001, 151), who suggests that decision-making power has moved from practitioners to accountants and managers. It should be remembered, however,

that this movement is less invasive in Canada, where the professions have much stronger self-regulating powers. For a discussion of how the professional autonomy of doctors and nurses in Ontario has been eroded in favour of managerial control, see Beardwood (1999).

26   Self-regulation is one of the characteristics that the current author and others use to define a profession (Brockman 1998). Others disagree. For example, the Manitoba Law Reform Commission tallied ninety licensed occupations, only twenty-two of which were self-regulating, and sixty-six occupations that relied on certification, only fourteen of which were self-governing.

27   The funnel analogy is further defined in Brockman and McEwen (1990) and Brockman (2004).

28   One could argue that the criminal justice system is part of the bureaucratic-managerial system and that the civil law system is part of the free labour market, and, therefore, neither of these are additional to Freidson's three ideal types.

29   Jost and Davies (1999) discuss the federal civil *False Claims Act, supra* note 15, which allows for treble damages and civil penalties of $5,000-10,000 per claim. This can result in multi-million-dollar penalties. Such punitive/criminal sanctions in the civil law system in Canada would likely be unconstitutional.

30   Some of the issues of multiple proceedings are discussed in Murdoch and Brockman (2001).

31   A home page was created for Medical Review Committee (MRC) victims: MRC and OPRP Victims Home Page, http://www3.sympatico.ca/dindar/mrc/mrc.htm. The Ontario Physicians' Alliance also went on the attack, referring to the "grotesque harassment" of doctors by the MRC, a "kangaroo court," and calling for an "independent tribunal with the usual legal safeguards for those accused." See http://www.archive.org/index.php.

32   This effect would be in keeping with the "funnel-in" justification for self-regulation, referred to earlier in this chapter.

33   I excluded, for example, Stephen Chung, who impersonated a family practitioner for fifteen years in Hamilton, Ontario, defrauding OHIP of $4.4 million throughout his career. Chung was not recognized as a legitimate health professional in a system where the College of Physicians and Surgeons holds a monopoly on specified services. There are also a number of cases of unnecessary surgery, unnecessary prescribing of drugs, and "sex as therapy," in which the financial fraud side of the case was never developed (at least not in the public domain). Cases of defrauding patients (for example, charging up to $30,000 for ineffective cancer treatment), hospitals, workers' compensation (without a Medicare/OHIP angle), other private insurance companies/financial institutions, or drug plans were also excluded.

34   It is not clear whether this is because few were dismissed or because those that were dismissed were not in the public domain.

35   Given that I was accessing English newspaper sources, I am fairly certain that the number of cases I found in Quebec is fewer than those in the public domain. I also put most of my efforts into finding cases in British Columbia and Ontario, so there may be cases in other provinces that were in the public domain but were not discovered. In Saskatchewan, the lawyer for the College of Physicians and Surgeons confirmed that the college had dealt with only three doctors on this issue.

36   In the United States, "psychiatrists represent about 8 percent of all physicians but about 20 percent of all doctors suspended from Medicaid for fraudulent practices" (Rosoff, Pontell, and Tillman 2004, 463). The authors suggest that the nature of the service (time billed by the hour as opposed to specific services such as examinations, surgeries, and tests) makes it easier for psychiatrists to fraudulently bill and also easier for enforcement agents to apprehend and prosecute them. These authors state that it is unclear whether psychiatrists are more or less prone to bill fraudulently than other physicians.

37   Search conducted on 26 September 2004. Not all of these physicians would work on a fee-for-service basis, but it does give some indication of the percentage of psychiatrists in Ontario today.

38   Search conducted on 26 September 2004. Not all of these physicians would work on a fee-for-service basis, but it does give some indication of the percentage of women doctors today.

The British Columbia College of Physicians and Surgeons' database, which contained 9,799 doctors on 25 January 2005, cannot be tabulated by gender.

39 Billing for services not provided was also the most frequent fraud mode identified by a 2004 Canadian Health Care Fraud Survey of health care payors – 89.7 percent had identified this as the most common fraud they experienced in 2003 (Fraudbox 2004, 10). The respondents were registered delegates at the 2004 Canadian Health Care Anti Fraud Association in Richmond Hill, Ontario, and clients of Fraudbox who were directed to a web-based survey. The seventy-eight respondents included public sector payors (9.7 percent), private health and life insurer payors (35 percent), government agency (8.7 percent), and third-party payors (16.5 percent).

40 This was also the second most frequent fraud mode identified by a 2004 Canadian Health Care Fraud Survey of health care payors – identified by 67.9 percent of the respondents (Fraudbox 2004, 10).

41 Again, these justifications or techniques of neutralization parallel those found among tax evaders (see Mosher 2008).

42 Of course, such a belief does not negate fraud. As Justice McLachlin said in *R. v. Théroux* (1993, para. 22), "just as the pathological killer would not be acquitted on the mere ground that he failed to see his act as morally reprehensible, so the defrauder will not be acquitted because he believed that what he was doing was honest."

43 In the 2004 Canadian Health Care Fraud Survey of health care payors, 62.8 percent had experienced fraud in terms of providers performing unnecessary services (Fraudbox 2004, 10).

44 In the 2004 Canadian Health Care Fraud Survey of health care payors, 53.8 percent had experienced fraud in terms of billing for fictitious services (Fraudbox 2004, 10).

45 After much effort, the patient managed to obtain an order from the information and privacy commissioner ordering the ministry to remove the false medical records from his file (Order PO-1881-1, 2001). Ministry of Health and Long-Term Care, Interim Order PO-1881-I, Appeal PA-000286-1. See http://www.accessandprivacy.gov.on.ca/english/order/prov/po-1881.html.

46 I have used initials here because these doctors were not charged or convicted of a criminal offence, but I have assessed the facts as they appear in the college proceedings. Had these cases gone through the criminal justice system, the doctor may have been acquitted.

47 There were two prosecutions against physiotherapists and one against an optometrist in British Columbia and one prosecution against a chiropractor in Ontario.

48 The reference to one law for the rich and another for the poor was also made in reference to the sentencing of Dr. Bogart (Editorial 2001a; Editorial 2001c).

49 Chunn and Gavigan (2004, 219) suggest that the social images of welfare fraud have been transformed to welfare as fraud. See also Mosher and Hermer (Chapter 1 in this volume). Mirchandani and Chan (2007) also illustrate that the criminalization of poverty is also the criminalization of people of colour.

50 Information about how we treat welfare fraud comes from Martin (1992), Chunn and Gavigan (2004), Mirchandani and Chan (2007), Mosher and Hermer (Chapter 1 in this volume), and Mosher et al. (2004).

51 This is illustrated in the numerous submissions received by the Cory Medical Audit Practice Initiative, http://www.petercory.org/.

52 Although one reviewer stated that there is no profession to "educate" and funnel behaviour away from the criminal justice system, a review board composed of welfare recipients could assume such tasks.

53 For a discussion of pre-charge screening by prosecutors in British Columbia, Quebec, and New Brunswick and the standard used to approve charges, see Brockman and Rose (2010, 77-78).

54 See, for example, Brown (2001): "Command-and-control regulation ... engenders an adversarial resentment in regulated firms that leads to greater resistance [to] regulatory standards and less cooperative compliance by firms." Ayers and Braithwaite (1992, 25) suggest that punitive regulation "fosters an organized business subculture of resistance to regulation – a subculture that facilitates the sharing of knowledge about methods of legal resistance and counterattack."

55   The Ontario Medical Association (2004) was of the view that, given the record-keeping requirements, the current system "would mandate a recovery from virtually any Ontario physician reviewed by it."

56   Daniel (1998) points out that the excessive targeting or punishing of scapegoats happens in self-regulating professions.

57   For example, although a 1988 report on social assistance in Ontario identified the inadequacy of benefits as "the single most important weapon in the fight against fraud in the system," it went on to recommend a special fraud unit to deal with such "fraud" (Social Assistance Review Committee 1988). See Martin (1992) for her critique of this report.

58   Despite these misgivings, the authors argue for the criminalization of economic crimes.

59   Smart (1989), as cited in Comack and Balfour (2004, 176). A historical example of juridogenic effects (the law making a problem worse rather than better) is prohibition, and a present-day example is drug law enforcement. See also earlier examples in note 2 in this chapter.

60   Corporations more easily decriminalize and de-stigmatize behaviour. See Snider (2000, 2001, 2003).

61   McKnight (1995, 17) acknowledges the influences of Ivan Illich's discussion of the "iatrogenic capacities of professionals," Peter Berger and Richard Neuhaus' description of "the decay of primary social structures facilitated by modern professionalism," and others.

62   As pointed out by one of the reviewers, this observation ignores some of the macro-political and economic factors in operation that are beyond the scope of this chapter (see, for example, Garland 2001; Simon 2007).

References

Alvesalo, A., and S. Tombs. 2002. "Working for Criminalization of Economic Offending: Contradictions for Critical Criminology?" *Critical Criminology* 11: 21-40.

Anonymous. 1996. "Prank Billing by Ontario Doctor Proves OHIP Easy to Defraud: No One Questioned Bill for Transplant at Patient's Home." *Ottawa Citizen,* 24 January, A2.

–. 2007. "A New Medical Audit System for Ontario: Comparing Government's Proposed Bill with Justice Cory's Recommendations." *Ontario Medical Review* 74, 1: 7.

Armstrong, J. 1997. "Wilson to Slash Health Fraud: Province Hopes to Save Millions in Crackdown." *Toronto Star,* 24 September, A3.

Auditor General of Ontario. 2006. *Annual Report, 2006,* Ontario Health Insurance Plan, http://www.auditor.on.ca/en/reports_en/en06/308en06.pdf.

–. 2008. *Annual Report, 2008,* Ontario Health Insurance Plan, http://www.auditor.on.ca/en/reports_en/en08/408en08.pdf.

Ayers, I., and J. Braithwaite. 1992. *Responsive Regulation: Transcending the Deregulation Debate.* New York: Oxford University Press.

Bach, D. 2007. "Toward a New Medical Payment Audit System for Ontario." *Ontario Medical Review* 74, 1: 7.

Beardwood, B. 1999. "The Loosening of Professional Boundaries and Restructuring: The Implications for Nursing and Medicine in Ontario, Canada." *Law and Policy Quarterly* 21, 3: 315-43.

Blackwell, T. 2005. "Health Fraud Rampant." *National Post,* 23 September, A1.

Board of Examiners in Optometry (BC). 2001. "Discipline Hearing: Dr. Michael Ing." *The Examiner,* February, 1.

Borsellino, M. 2001. "Controversy Clouds MRC Auditing Process." *Medical Post* 37, 27: 50-51.

Braithwaite, J. 2002. *Restorative Justice and Responsive Regulation.* New York: Oxford University Press.

Brean, J. 2003. "MD Pressured Women into Unneeded Hysterectomies." *National Post,* 19 November, A5.

Brockman, J. 1998. "'Fortunate Enough to Obtain and Keep the Title of Profession': Self-Regulating Organizations and the Enforcement of Professional Monopolies." *Canadian Public Administration* 41, 4: 587-621.

–. 2003. "The Impact of Institutional Structures and Powers on Law and Society: Is It Time for Reawakening?" *Law and Society Review* 37, 2: 283-94.

–. 2004. "An Update on Self-Regulation in the Legal Profession (1989-2000): Funnel In and Funnel Out." *Canadian Journal of Law and Society* 19, 1: 55-84.
Brockman, J., and C. McEwen. 1990. "Self-Regulation in the Legal Profession: Funnel In, Funnel Out, or Funnel Away." *Canadian Journal of Law and Society* 5: 1-46.
Brockman, J., and V.G. Rose. 2010. *An Introduction to Canadian Criminal Procedure and Evidence*, 4th edition. Toronto: Thomson Nelson.
Brown, D.K. 2001. "Street Crime, Corporate Crime, and the Contingency of Criminal Liability." *University of Pennsylvania Law Review* 149, 5: 1295-1360.
–. 2004. "The Problematic and Faintly Promising Dynamics of Corporate Crime Enforcement." *Ohio State Journal of Criminal Law* 1: 521-49.
Canadian Institute of Health Information. 2002. "Average Age of Physicians by Physician Type and Province/Territory, Canada, 1998 and 2002," http://secure.cihi.ca/.
Canadian Medical Protective Association. 2004. *2004 Review of the Medical Audit Practice in Ontario: Canadian Medical Protective Association Submission to the Honourable Justice Peter Cory.* 3 August.
Canadian Press. 2001. "Doctors Who Falsely Billed Ontario Ordered to Pay Back $16 Million." *Canadian Press Newswire*, 23 January.
Chunn, D.E., and S.A.M. Gavigan. 2004. "Welfare Law, Welfare Fraud, and the Moral Regulation of the 'Never Deserving' Poor." *Social Legal Studies* 13, 2: 219-43.
Comack, E., and G. Balfour. 2004. *The Power to Criminalize: Violence, Inequality, and the Law.* Halifax: Fernwood Publishing.
Cory, The Honourable Peter deC. 21 April 2005. *Study, Conclusions, and Recommendations Pertaining to Medical Audit Practice in Ontario* (Submitted to the Hon. George Smitherman, Minister of Health and Long-Term Care, Government of Ontario). Available at www.health.gov.on.ca/english/public/pub/ministry_reports/cory05/rep_cory_05.pdf.
Daniel, A. 1998. *Scapegoats for a Profession: Uncovering Procedural Injustice.* Australia: Harwood Academic Publishers.
Des Rosiers, N., and S. Bittle. 2004. "Introduction." In *What Is a Crime?* ed. Law Commission of Canada, vii-xxv. Vancouver and Toronto: UBC Press.
Editorial. 1996. "Doctored Billing: With Little Check on the Payment Claims MDs Put in, the Possibility of Overpayments Runs Feverishly High." *Vancouver Sun*, 23 December, A10.
–. 2001a. "Doctor's Fraud Merited Jail Time." *Kingston Whig Standard*, 19 June, 6.
–. 2001b. "Policing Physician Fraud." *Ottawa Citizen*, 26 April, A17.
–. 2001c. "Uneven Scales of Justice." *Ottawa Citizen*, 18 June, A12.
Education and Prevention Committee. 2007. "OHIP to Distribute Confidential 'Mini Billing Profiles.'" *Ontario Medical Review* 74, 1: 14-19.
Elliott, L. 2001. "Ontario Needs Standards for Faulty Medical Files: Privacy Commissioner." *Canadian Press Newswire*, 21 March.
Ericson, R., and A. Doyle. 2004. "Criminalization in Private: The Case of Insurance Fraud." In *What Is Crime? Defining Criminal Conduct in Contemporary Society*, ed. Law Commission of Canada, 99-124. Vancouver and Toronto: UBC Press.
Fayerman, P. 1999. "Ministry to Caution Doctors about Double-Billing Fraud." *Vancouver Sun*, 15 September, B8.
Fraudbox. 2004. *Results of the 2004 Canadian Health Care Fraud Survey.* Markham, ON: Fraudbox.
Freidson, E. 2001. *Professionalism: The Third Logic.* Chicago: University of Chicago Press.
Friedrichs, D.O. 2007. *Trusted Criminals: White Collar Crime in Contemporary Society.* Belmont, CA: Thomson Wadsworth.
Garland, D. 2001. *The Culture of Control: Crime and Social Order in Contemporary Society.* Chicago: University of Chicago Press.
Germov, J. 1995. "Medi-Fraud, Managerialism, and the Decline of Medical Autonomy: DeProfessionalization and Proletarianisation Reconsidered." *Australian and New Zealand Journal of Statistics* 31, 3: 51-56.
Glasbeek, H. 2002. *Wealth by Stealth: Corporate Crime, Corporate Law, and the Perversion of Democracy.* Toronto: Between the Lines Press.

Henry, S., and M.M. Lanier. 2001."The Prism of Crime: Towards an Integrated Definition of Crime." In *What Is Crime? Controversies over the Nature of Crime and What to Do about It*, ed. S. Henry and M.M. Lanier, 227-42. Lanham, MD: Rowman and Littlefield.

Hillyard, P., and S. Tombs. 2004. "Beyond Criminology?" In *Beyond Criminology: Taking Harm Seriously*, ed. P. Hillyard, C. Pantazis, S. Tombs, and D. Gordon, 10-29. Blackpoint, NS: Pluto Press.

Illich, I. 1976. *Medical Nemesis*. New York: Pantheon.

Inkster, N.D. 10 September 1997. *Fraud and Abuse in the Ontario's Health Care System: A Preliminary Review*, prepared by KPMG Investigation and Security.

Jesilow, P., H.N. Pontell, and G. Geis. 1993. *Prescription for Profit: How Doctors Defraud Medicaid*. Berkeley: University of California Press.

Jost, T.S., and S.L. Davies. 1999. "The Empire Strikes Back: A Critique of the Backlash against Fraud and Abuse Enforcement." *Alabama Law Review* 51: 239-318.

Law Commission of Canada. 2003. *What Is a Crime? Challenges and Alternatives*. Discussion Paper. Ottawa: Law Commission of Canada.

–. 2004. *What Is a Crime?* Vancouver and Toronto: UBC Press.

Law Reform Commission of Canada. 1977. *Theft and Fraud Offences*. Working Paper 19. Ottawa: Law Reform Commission of Canada.

Lynch, M.J., D. McGurrin, and M. Fenwick. 2004. "Disappearing Act: The Representation of Corporate Crime Research in Criminological Research." *Journal of Criminal Justice* 32, 5: 389-98.

Martin, D.L. 1992. "Passing the Buck: Prosecution of Welfare Fraud; Preservation of Stereotypes." *Windsor Yearbook Access to Justice* 12: 52-97.

Matlin, V. 2004. "Fraud Plagues U.S. Health Care." *Knight-Ridder Tribune*, 14 July, http://findarticles.com/p/articles/mi_hb5553/is_200407/ai_n22202084/.

McKnight, J. 1995. *The Careless Society: Community and Its Counterfeits*. New York: Basic Books.

Medical Audit Practice in Ontario, Terms of Reference. 30 April 2004. Available at http://www.petercory.org/.

Mirchandani, K., and W. Chan. 2007. *Criminalizing Race, Criminalizing Poverty: Welfare Fraud Enforcement in Canada*. Halifax: Fernwood Publishing.

Mosher, J. 2008. "Welfare Fraudsters and Tax Evaders: The State's Selective Invocation of Criminality." In *Marginality and Condemnation: An Introduction to Criminology*, ed. C. Brooks and B. Schissel, 2nd edition, 287-309. Halifax: Fernwood Press.

Mosher, J., P. Evans, M. Little, E. Morrow, J. Boulding, and N. VanderPlaats. 2004. *Walking on Eggshells: Abused Women's Experiences of Ontario's Welfare System*, Final Report of Research Findings. Toronto: Woman and Abuse Welfare Research Project.

Murdoch, C., and J. Brockman. 2001. "Who's on First? Disciplinary Proceedings by Self-Regulating Professions and Other Agencies for 'Criminal' Behaviour." *Saskatchewan Law Review* 64, 1: 29-56.

Nightingale, B.L. 1996. *The Law of Fraud and Related Offences*. Toronto: Carswell.

Ontario Health Insurance Plan, Education and Prevention Committee. April 2008. "Revised Medical Audit Process." *Interpretive Bulletin* 6, 3, Ministry of Health and Long-Term Care, http://www.health.gov.on.ca/english/providers/program/ohip/bulletins/bulletin_mn.html.

Ontario Medical Association. July-August 2004. "OMA Submission to the Honourable Justice Cory – Review of the Ontario Medical Audit and Review Process." *Ontario Medical Review*, the Honourable Peter Cory, http://www.petercory.org.

Ouston, R. 1998. "Controversial Doctor Faces Possible Loss of Privileges." *Vancouver Sun*, 24 November, A3.

Oziewicz, E. 1996. "Doctor Vanishes in Midst of Overbilling Case." *Globe and Mail*, 21 August, A1 and A6.

Phillips, A. 2002. "MD Gets Ban for Life in $592K Fraud Case: College Hands Alex Scott Harshest Punishment Ever for Bilking Health System." *Kingston Whig-Standard*, 3 April, 1.

Robinson, M.B. 2001. "Wither Criminal Justice? An Argument for a Reformed Discipline." *Critical Criminology* 10, 2: 97-106.

Rosoff, S.M., H.N. Pontell, and R.H. Tillman. 2004. *Profit without Honor: White-Collar Crime and the Looting of America*, 3rd ed. Upper Saddle River, NJ: Pearson Education.
Saul, J.R. 1999. "Health Care at the End of the Twentieth Century: Confusing Symptoms for Systems." In *Do We Care: Reviewing Canada's Commitment to Health*, ed. M.A. Somerville, 1-20. Montreal and Kingston: McGill-Queen's University Press.
Shinkle, P. 2005. "Doctor Who Exposed Fraud at Gambro Will Get $56 Million." *Knight-Ridder Tribune*, 26 March, n.p.
Sibbald, B. 2000. "MDs Get Jail Terms, Fines as New Police Squad Targets Health Fraud." *Canadian Medical Association Journal* 163, 5: 591.
Simon, J. 2007. *Governing through Crime: How the War on Crime Transformed American Democracy and Created a Culture of Fear*. Oxford: Oxford University Press.
Smart, C. 1989. *Feminism and the Power of Law*. London: Routledge.
Snider, L. 1998. "Towards Safer Societies." *British Journal of Criminology* 38, 1: 1-39.
–. 2000. "The Sociology of Corporate Crime: An Obituary (or: Whose Knowledge Claims Have Legs?)." *Theoretical Criminology* 4, 2: 169-206.
–. 2001. "Abusing Corporate Power: The Death of a Concept." In *[A]busing Power: The Canadian Experience*, ed. S.C. Boyd, D.E. Chunn, and R. Menzies, 112-29. Halifax: Fernwood Publishing.
–. 2003. "Researching Corporate Crime." In *Unmasking the Crimes of the Powerful: Scrutinizing States and Corporations*, ed. S. Tombs and D. Whyte, 49-68. New York: Peter Lang.
Social Assistance Review Committee. 1988. *Transitions*, a report. Toronto: Queen's Printer.
Sparrow, M.K. 2000. *License to Steal: How Fraud Bleeds America's Health Care System*. Boulder, CO: Westview Press.
Statistics Canada. 2001. *Occupation 2001 National Occupational Classification, Canada, Total Labour Force*. Catalogue no. 97F0012XCB01017. Ottawa: Statistics Canada.
Sutherland, E.H. 1940. "White-Collar Criminality." *American Sociological Review* 5, 1: 1-12.
–. 1983. *White Collar Crime: The Uncut Version*. New Haven and London: Yale University Press.
Sykes, G., and D. Matza. 1957. "Techniques of Neutralization." *American Sociological Review* 22, 6: 664-70.
Tombs, S., and D. Whyte. 2003. *Unmasking the Crimes of the Powerful: Scrutinizing States and Corporations*. New York: Peter Lang Publishing.
Tremayne-Lloyd, T. 2007. "Commentary: Proposed Law Offers Doctors Relief from Heavy-Handed Medical Audit System." *Lawyers Weekly* 26, 48, http://www.lawyersweekly.ca/.
Upton, S. 1991. "MD Jailed for Bilking Health Plan." *Ottawa Citizen*, 1 September, A6.
Wilson, P.R., D. Chappell, and R. Lincoln. 1986. "Policing Physician Abuse in BC: An Analysis of Current Policies." *Canadian Public Policy* 12: 236-44.
Young, A.M. 2003. *Justice Defiled: Perverts, Potheads, Serial Killers, and Lawyers*. Toronto: Key Porter Books.

List of Cases
Carstoniu v. The General Manager, Ontario Health Insurance Plan, 13 August 2004, Case 03-HIA-0050 (Health Services Review and Appeal Board).
College of Physicians and Surgeons of Ontario v. Artinian, [1992] O.C.P.S.D. No. 11.
College of Physicians and Surgeons of Ontario v. Bogart, [2001] O.C.P.S.D. No. 9.
College of Physicians and Surgeons of Ontario v. Moore, [2002] O.C.P.S.D. No. 5.
College of Physicians and Surgeons of Ontario v. O'Connell, [1994] O.C.P.S.D. No. 5.
College of Physicians and Surgeons of Ontario v. Paikin, [2003] O.C.P.S.D. No. 36.
College of Physicians and Surgeons of Ontario v. Scott, [2002] O.C.P.S.D. No. 4.
College of Physicians and Surgeons of Ontario v. Tolentino, [2002] O.C.P.S.D. No. 2.
College of Physicians and Surgeons of Ontario v. Verma, [2001] O.C.P.S.D. No. 27.
College of Physicians and Surgeons of Ontario v. Wai-Ping, [2004] O.C.P.S.D. No. 33.
MacDiarmid v. College of Physicians and Surgeons, [2003] O.J. No. 277.
Moore v. College of Physicians and Surgeons of Ontario, [2003] O.J. No. 5200 (Sup. Ct. J.).
Order PO-1881-1 (Institution: Ministry of Health and Long-Term Care), [2001] O.I.P.C. No. 55.

R. v. Bogart, [2002] S.C.C.A. No. 398.

R. v. Bogart (2002), 167 C.C.C. (3d) 390.

R. v. Bogart, [2001] O.J. No. 2323.

R. v. Chen, 5 and 20 November 2001, Provincial Court of British Columbia, Vancouver, British Columbia, No. 115882-1 (unreported).

R. v. Devlin, 9 and 15 May 2001, Provincial Court of British Columbia, Port Coquitlam, British Columbia, No. 61170-01 (unreported).

R. v. Ing, [2001] B.C.J. No. 2855 (Prov. Ct.).

R. v. Lee, 27 January 1992, Provincial Court of British Columbia, Rossland, British Columbia, No. 11480 (unreported).

R. v. MacDiarmid, [2001] O.J. No. 243 (C.A.).

R. v. Paikin, 16 January 2001, Ontario Court of Justice, Toronto (Metro North) (unreported).

R. v. Scott, 8 May 2000, Ontario Court of Justice, Kingston, Ontario (unreported).

R. v. Stokic, [1999] B.C.J. No. 1312.

R. v. Théroux, [1993] 2 S.C.R. 5.

Verma v. College of Physicians and Surgeons of British Columbia, [1994] B.C.J. No. 2701.

R. v. Verma, 9 May 1994, Provincial Court of British Columbia, Vancouver, British Columbia, No. 64501C (unreported).

R. v. Verma, 6 May 1994, Provincial Court of British Columbia, Vancouver, British Columbia, No. 64501C (unreported).

R. v. Zlatic, [1993] 2 S.C.R. 29.

Yip v. Audit Committee, Medical Services Commission, 26 January 1993, Provincial Court of British Columbia, Vancouver Registry, No. A924879 (unreported).

3
Pimatsowin Weyasowewina: Our Lives, Others' Laws
Lisa Chartrand and Cora Weber-Pillwax

A non-status Aboriginal man ventures out onto unoccupied lands in northern Alberta in order to secure food for his family. Successful in the hunt, he returns with a bull moose that he and his wife distribute among thirty-five immediate and extended family members. Subsequently, the man is charged by Fish and Wildlife officials under the provincial legislation for hunting without a licence. The man loses his vehicle, his guns, and the meat that has already been preserved for the families' use.

This is a composite description of traditional Aboriginal harvesting incidents that occur on a regular basis throughout northern Alberta.[1] Under provincial laws, the unlicensed killing of big game animals, even for sustenance purposes, is a "criminal activity" that is punishable by fines and/or incarceration. The negative outcomes of these events are exacerbated by the fact that many individuals, families, and communities of Aboriginal people in this country live under conditions of severe poverty. Despite a logic that seems to support a "poverty leads to crime" argument in these situations, and even within the context of high poverty levels in Aboriginal communities, this argument is not an accurate explanation for the fact that many Aboriginal persons continue to be "criminalized" for engaging in traditional hunting and gathering activities within their own traditional territories.

Across the northern parts of the western provinces where boreal forest conditions prevail, various Aboriginal peoples continue their traditional practices of harvesting and gathering. These activities are the expressions of distinct ontologies and epistemologies just as deeply and certainly as they are the sources and means of distinct Aboriginal peoples' collective and individual physical and social existence and survival. In many of these boreal regions, the people continue to practise their traditional ways of life, and extended families will rely, in some cases almost exclusively, on the capacity of key individuals in the family network to hunt, fish, and trap as the primary means of subsistence. This reliance of families and communities on the

resources that accrue from hunting, fishing, and gathering is integrally connected to social practices that encompass the trading, sharing, and, sometimes, selling of particular resources. The vitality of this connection signifies
an assurance that individuals with highly developed skills that are used to
serve the people's needs are greatly respected and honoured because they
ensure the people's survival. Aboriginal peoples who continue to reside in
their original territories, as individuals and as groups, also continue to practise
their traditional forms of harvesting and gathering, thus holding to their
values and customs despite provincial and federal laws that criminalize both
them and their practices.

Since the personal experiences of Aboriginal people, like those shared in
this case study, almost always depict law enforcement techniques as expressions of unequal power and authority, and are often connected with threats
and abuses of such power and authority, interactions between law enforcement officials and Aboriginal people are presented as tenuous at best and
often hostile and openly antagonistic. The nature of this relationship can
and does have a negative and lasting impact on the quality of life of the
Aboriginal people involved. Where power and authority reside with the one
who holds the breadbasket, or, in this case, the moose licence, the one who
needs the licence offends authority at grave risk of going hungry. When the
people fear that their traditional ways of personal and communal living are
being threatened or are endangered, they live in constant mental, physical,
emotional, and spiritual distress. Aboriginal peoples as individuals and as
collectives are forced to live within this state of constant stress as a result
of the existing provincial and federal laws and policies that inhibit, prevent,
and, in many cases, criminalize their traditional harvesting and gathering
practices.

The cumulative effect of these situations in the long term is the construct-
ive criminalization of Aboriginal cultures and peoples. Although the long-
term personal, cultural, and social impact of this criminalization has never
been fully and impartially investigated, the personal narratives shared during this work describe a clearly negative impact. Neither the *Criminal Code*
prohibitions nor criminal law processing is necessary to render persons
"criminal" either in terms of how they experience their interactions with
others or in how others perceive them and their conduct.[2] This project
demonstrates that one major impact of criminalizing Aboriginal traditional
subsistence practices is the criminalization and consequent imprisonment
of the mindsets, psyches, and bodies of generations of Aboriginal people.
This imprisonment of the beings of Aboriginal peoples has happened over
decades and generations of externally defined and imposed systems of licensing and criminalization of their traditional harvesting activities. Such
criminalization and imprisonment deny the providers of Aboriginal peoples

access to significant traditional sources of their own spiritual and physical nourishment and sustenance, thereby mutilating and smothering the life of the peoples they were meant to protect.

While the historical and legal records of Canada reveal clearly that the spiritual practices of the Aboriginal peoples were prohibited and criminalized through government legislation, the connections between these legal actions and policies of the state and the physical, intellectual, and psychological development, well-being, and/or survival of Aboriginal peoples have yet to be fully analyzed. Similarly, the fact that traditional harvesting and gathering practices continue to be deeply intertwined with the spirituality of Aboriginal peoples is rarely considered a significant factor in the development and enforcement of law and policy. Thus, the state's ongoing criminalization of hunting and gathering activities can be understood merely as an extension in time and a contemporary expression of the state's earlier criminalization of Aboriginal spiritual practices. The laws that govern and ban hunting and fishing are, in critical ways, the same as those that banned Indigenous America's earlier spiritual practices such as the sun dances, the ghost dances, and the potlatches. These criminalization practices may be understood as different expressions through time of an unchanging state positioning in relation to Aboriginal peoples. The practice in Canada of criminalizing, through law, the subsistence activities upon which depends the spiritual and physical survival of Aboriginal peoples has to be recognized for what it was and is – a deep and complex level of violence against human consciousness and life. In addition to taking away the right to live physically, the laws against traditional harvesting practices have resulted in the repression, denial, and destruction of peoples' rights to express and live out their own spiritualities.

As will be described later in the methodology section, the most significant component of this research project was the involvement and active participation of Aboriginal people who have been directly impacted by the laws and policies relating to traditional harvesting practices. The refrain that rang throughout the community sessions described how young people grew up learning to lie and to distrust the laws and their enforcers. They watched the people of their parents' generation lie to law enforcement officials, hiding the meat and fish that were food for the family. Although not one of the research participants believed that such actions were "criminal," neither did any one of them deny the potential negative impact of such experiences on their individual personal development.

One of the first things I learned was how to hide a deer so the Fish and Wildlife wouldn't find it. I remember watching the blood dripping down on the snow as my uncle stood and talked casually to the Fish and Wildlife officer who had

stopped us on the bush road. Lying didn't seem wrong then. But what else did
that experience teach me? What were the long-term impacts of those experiences?
Will I ever know?[3]

Background

Generally, when individual or group behaviour is "criminalized" through
the laws of a society, a significant percentage of the members of that society
are comfortable in the belief that their lawmakers have engaged in a considered and careful analysis of the social context of this particular behaviour,
prior to its formal and legal denunciation through the law. The confidence
of mainstream Canadian society is based on the belief and broad understanding that the ethos of a democratic society guarantees all of its members the
right to full participation in the processes of their own government, including law making.

Most Aboriginal people have been, and continue to be, excluded from
these processes of law-making in Canada. The reasons for this lack of involvement are many and complex, often related to legal, political, linguistic,
and accessibility issues. The democratic approach, then, cannot and does
not work in this context. In fact, the ongoing creation of laws, policies, and
formal agreements that threaten Aboriginal peoples' survival continues
without their full and informed participation as peoples. They remain objects
of the legislation and are neither equal members of Canadian democracy
nor cultural beings within their own acknowledged and respected distinct
societies.

This research was prompted by a belief, rooted in Aboriginal community
knowledge and experience, that the necessity and significance of traditional
Aboriginal harvesting practices to the well-being and survival of Aboriginal
peoples are not understood by most members of contemporary Canadian
society. An unfortunate but logical consequence of an ill-informed public
is that the values, beliefs, customs, and cultural significance of traditional
harvesting practices for Aboriginal peoples have not been reflected in the
laws and policies that impact directly upon and, in effect, criminalize these
practices.

There is no substantiated evidence to suggest that loss of resources for
non-Aboriginal Canadians will occur if Aboriginal people are "permitted"
to engage in their traditional harvesting practices without criminalization
and punishment. However, community discussions during this project
pointed to the ways in which this argument continues to feed and keep alive
existing societal tensions around "rights" in relation to Aboriginal peoples,
tensions that exist primarily because most members of the non-Aboriginal
public remain uninformed about the historical context and legal bases
of Aboriginal rights. As long as this ignorance persists, a variety of social

tensions between Aboriginal people and non-Aboriginal people will continue, often concluding with racialization as the core point of differentiation.[4]

The history of Canada is based on the economic benefits of colonialism that accrued first to Europe and then to Canada. With economics as the guide for state laws and policies, Aboriginal peoples' traditional ways of life and laws, including those relating to hunting and gathering, were eroded slowly but inexorably. European laws and policies, driven by economic pressures, both impeded and re-defined the sustainability of Aboriginal lives through the wholesale slaughter of the buffalo herds and the establishment of a large-scale export fur trade. These early colonial laws were the beginnings of the criminalization of Aboriginal peoples and their ways, establishing bounded "Indian" reserve lands where tribal peoples lived as wards of the government, often breaking the "law" if they tried to travel, or otherwise live, as they had done traditionally for tens of thousands of years.

Our research reveals, in a similar fashion noted by Durkheim (1938) over seventy years ago, that the participation of the Aboriginal peoples themselves in the fulfillment of the European laws was significant and necessary for the legitimization of such laws. Without the fulfillment, albeit enforced, of the Aboriginal person's functions/roles as the "criminal" and the "punished," the larger society might have challenged the notion that such laws were necessary for its well-being. Without these laws and the forms of colonialism that they allowed, Aboriginal peoples would have continued to live their lives according to the ways of their own traditional societies. Their children would have learned in traditional ways, and their cultures and communities would have remained strong, supporting the men, women, and children that comprised them. The lands and resources would have been shared with the newcomers under different systems of respect if the peoples had come to the meeting table under different conditions and in different relations to each other. The question remains: Is there a way to measure or describe the impact that accrued to Aboriginal societies, families, and individuals after years of legally sanctioned abuse through the criminalization of Aboriginal traditional harvesting practices? This research is one small attempt to make that impact known to the larger Canadian society and to Aboriginal people who have felt isolated under the various labels and practices of legalized criminality.

This chapter offers a more comprehensive knowledge base and, therefore, a deeper understanding of the harvesting practices of Aboriginal individuals, families, and communities in northern Alberta. The work is carried out with the underlying premise that Aboriginal populations across the northern parts of each of the Prairie provinces share a history of similar experiences in relation to their traditional harvesting and gathering practices in their home territories. The people who participated in this research shared their personal and familial histories in ways that demonstrated their own ancestral connections with traditional harvesting and gathering territories. The rivers, lakes, creeks, hills, muskegs, meadows, and ranges were all described as being inseparable from the lives of the persons themselves. The passion of relationships and spiritual connections with the land, its natural forms, and the life these supported was the elemental force behind the narratives. Harvesting and gathering were not activities to be carried out with motions and prowess for the purposes of physical survival. They were, and are, the expression of the fullness of human being and spirit.

In this work, Aboriginal community members spoke openly and shared their stories to inform lawmakers and other Canadians about their views and experiences in the area of traditional harvesting and gathering activities. Their intent was to contribute to public and official understanding of the overall circumstances surrounding Aboriginal peoples' harvesting of wildlife, fish, and plants as means of subsistence and survival. The hope is that an enhanced understanding will positively affect future definitions and legal responses to traditional Aboriginal practices and that formal consideration of hunting, trapping, and gathering behaviours will be viewed from a perspective outside the realm of criminal behaviour and sanctions.

While criminal law and enforcement are often used as default means of securing social control, they comprise only one available strategy. Alternative methods include co-management arrangements, mediation, formal or informal agreement, self-regulation and codes of conduct, and education and awareness. Each of these formal responses to traditional Aboriginal behaviours has distinct personal, social, and legal consequences. Given the broad range of options available for state management and social control of Aboriginal behaviours with respect to traditional harvesting practices, this chapter speaks to several questions:

- What were the legal, social, and cultural factors that influenced the decision to criminalize or not criminalize specific behaviours for specific Aboriginal peoples?
- Was/is it necessary that these particular behaviours be criminalized?
- What are some of the personal and social consequences of the criminalization of these behaviours?

To ensure the validity and integrity of the research, the people most directly impacted by the criminalization of their traditional activities were invited to participate by sharing their experiences as Aboriginal people who continue to live in ways that rely on traditional forms of harvesting and gathering. These individuals were asked to speak also to the issues that arise where such activities have been historically considered illegal and where engaging in these activities left them open to criminal charges and severe penalties under state laws. The context and content of their responses are crucial to several generations of Aboriginal peoples from the past, the present, and the future. It also cannot be denied that the answers implicate all Canadians.

Pimatsowin means life, within itself, and with its own laws. The term encompasses the relationships that Indigenous peoples have with the land and all forms of life. These laws of life are embedded in, and given expression through, the ways that relationships are lived out between and among people and land and all created life forms, sustaining each other and surviving together. *Weyasowewina* refers to externally imposed laws, distinguishing these from beliefs and laws that come from within and from the forces of creation (*Pimatsowin*). Together, *Pimatsowin Weyasowewina* speaks to the impacts that these externally imposed laws have on the way of life of a people. It is our intent that *Pimatsowin Weyasowewina* will consider the harvesting and usage of wildlife and other natural resources by Aboriginal peoples for subsistence and related cultural purposes as well as the legal categorization of criminality that has tended to accompany these practices and activities. Traditional Aboriginal harvesting practices are often portrayed through public education and popular media either as primitive and outdated or as exotic and frivolous. In either case, their significance in contemporary society is often not known or understood, whether that society is Aboriginal or not.

Many Aboriginal persons, families, and communities rely on hunting, fishing, and/or trapping as an important means of subsistence. In addition, people hunt, fish, and gather for reasons that relate to their own and their children's psychological and spiritual well-being and to the long-term vitality of the cultural groups to which they belong. This well-being is guaranteed through the intergenerational transmission of values, customs, and traditions that evolved from, are embedded within, or are acquired through these traditional practices. Without the practices, there is limited, distorted, or no transmission of Aboriginal knowledge systems and ways of being.

In most instances, Aboriginal peoples in both rural and urban settings continue to maintain their values and connections to traditional harvesting practices. Research on migration patterns and movements of urban Aboriginal peoples indicates that Aboriginal people will usually maintain connections with their home territories for purposes of cultural identity (Graham and Peters 2002). In our work, several of our participants moved between urban and rural settings regularly. For most participants, cultural identity was connected to hunting and gathering practices in their home territory and to the related "illegal" transportation of the natural products of such harvesting into the urban setting for sustenance purposes and in support of family.

Despite the intention of state rules and laws to prohibit or prevent traditional harvesting practices, Aboriginal people continue to hunt, fish, and gather for physical, as well as other cultural, survival reasons. The following quote is a good example of the participants' general response to the federal rules and laws that criminalize both them and their practices directly and indirectly:

You know they have a job to do, but I think they could do it in such a way that they don't make you feel like such a criminal. When we got charged, they came in at seven o'clock in the morning. It was still dark in October. Why couldn't they have come at a decent hour when we were up? There must have been seven Fish and Wildlife vehicles out there. We had trespassing signs on our property – we had them there for a reason – because we couldn't drive over the water lines. They ignored everything. They barged in and went straight to my bedroom. I don't have a habit of keeping fish in my bedroom. That's what I mean about the way they do things. They could have done the same thing in a different way.

When we went to court, we had no lawyer. We were refused Legal Aid, and we couldn't afford our own lawyer. The way that was set up with the undercover cop – he still has my net – he came and borrowed from me so he could fish in the river – he befriended the family and the community – he just lived there, and he's the one who supplied the transportation, he supplied the ammunition, he supplied the guns and the young people with dope, and we tried to get them to admit that this is entrapment. They said, "He's not the one who is being charged, it is you guys." There was not a whole lot we could do – even a lawyer can't do anything.

I didn't fish, and I didn't sell fish. I accepted money for someone else who had arranged to give the undercover cop some fish. The way the undercover cop talked, we were outlaws, we were thieves.

Like he said in court, the people he stayed with didn't have to go fish to make a living because they had a coloured TV. Now what does that have to do with food in your cupboard?

When we went to court, I was fined two thousand dollars. They also said, "Even though you are a Treaty Indian, you have to report when you pick up your licence for certain lakes, you have to report twenty-four hours before you set the net, where you set the net, what lake you set it in, and you have to report in twenty-four hours after you lift the net exactly how many fish you caught.

Like most of the contributions from the community gatherings and interviews, these narratives express clearly the view that laws, lawmakers, and law enforcement officials commonly display a lack of understanding and appropriate respect for Aboriginal ways of life and traditional harvesting practices. Along with many other narratives, these excerpts also underscore the difficulty in developing an understanding or respect if there is no knowledge base on which to build such understanding.

To exacerbate this difficulty, Aboriginal people and communities have generally lacked opportunities to interact with officials and policy-makers in ways that can best fulfill governments' obligations to protect the resources that have sustained Aboriginal peoples for centuries. State systems of conservation and protection are relatively recent (both temporally and experientially) in comparison to the many ancient Aboriginal forms of sustainability and resource protection that are usually not considered in Canadian law and policy development processes. To continue using a foundation of criminal law and enforcement to manage those natural resources that are the life source of Aboriginal societies is to purposefully structure the demise of these ancient cultures:

> *Fish and Wildlife laws are assimilation policies. The aim is to have Aboriginal peoples live as the "other" Canadians. Canadian laws so we can't practise our traditions. Whose values do the laws reflect?*

Description and Methodology
The research process unfolded as a rich community experience of knowledge creation. To honour the voices of the Aboriginal community participants, and to better reflect an Aboriginal perspective, the chapter does not present information in a sequential and linear pattern. Rather, its contents must be considered in its totality. This type of reading will most accurately depict the responses that evolved as the events and activities took place. An important traditional Cree teaching will help to situate the reader in relation to the text. The teaching points out that, in a dialogue, the listener has as much responsibility as the speaker. The speaker is responsible for what she or he says but not for what is heard. The listener is totally responsible for what she or he hears and for any actions that ensue from that hearing (Stan Wilson, personal communication, 2001). In a similar manner, the reader "dialogues" with the text and forms his or her own understanding.

The text does not *merely* record a response to the questions stated earlier. The text does respond, however, like a mist and covers the ground in a manner that blurs the edges, causing any boundaries in the response to disappear. In this manner, the text offers readers an opportunity for a deeper understanding of how Aboriginal harvesters contextualize, describe, and interpret the issues that surround their traditional harvesting and gathering practices. To maintain consistency in this approach, there is also no separate analysis section to explain or interpret the "findings." The reader is expected to make personal interpretations and to act on his or her own findings.

The research plan for this case study was composed of several components. First, literature-based research was conducted through available and accessible written records of traditional harvesting practices of Aboriginal peoples in northern Alberta. A part of this research was completed by graduate students working under the guidance of the principal researchers at the

University of Alberta. Second, a significant component of the research project involved semi-structured and formal interactions and gatherings within selected communities. The dialogues and community workshop sessions enabled the collection of personal narratives from Aboriginal community members. These narratives effectively present Aboriginal perspectives about historical and contemporary harvesting practices as well as the attitudes and beliefs of Aboriginal peoples towards these practices. As such, this record forms a body of new knowledge related to the research topic.

The community-based research component involved participation by approximately 100 First Nations, Métis, and non-status Aboriginal persons.[5] This diverse representation provided an excellent opportunity for academic professionals, law- and policy-makers, and Aboriginal community members to discuss a broad range of issues affecting traditional Aboriginal harvesting practices. The Aboriginal participants in this research project self-identified themselves as Aboriginal, Cree, Chipewyan, First Nation, and Métis. Community representatives participated from each of the following five geographical areas in northern Alberta: Calling Lake/Wabasca/Sandy Lake; Grouard/Gift Lake/East Prairie; Lac La Biche/Conklin/Fort McMurray/Kikino; Fort Vermilion; and Paddle Prairie.

The research communities were selected by the principal investigators on the basis of personal relationships and knowledge of traditional Aboriginal harvesting practices in these particular regions. Personal contact and engagement within these communities over many years had established a trust that is essential for open and safe dialogue between researchers and community members on this topic. Most of the participants from these communities were Métis and would potentially benefit greatly from the research process in that they represented the population in Canada that had been most highly criminalized for practising traditional hunting and gathering. As such, they could speak with the greatest depth of personal knowledge to the issue of the criminalization of Aboriginal harvesting. The research design thus relied on the important legal distinction of identity that effectively defines and discriminates between the harvesting practices of persons who are categorized as First Nations or Indian and those persons who are categorized as Métis or non-status Indian.[6] With respect to the data-gathering process, one-on-one interviews were conducted intermittently with group sessions and formal workshops involving participants and the research team.

Planning the community fora involved careful consideration of traditional forms of Aboriginal protocols governing respect and group dialogues while simultaneously addressing the requirements for standard research ethics and the technical aspects of recording data and facilitating group processes in settings that did not necessarily appeal to traditional Aboriginal people. Careful and culturally sensitive planning with community members led to many valuable opportunities to discuss Aboriginal harvesting practices in welcoming and safe community environments. These environments permitted the community research groups to identify, describe, and interpret the complexities of the legal characterization of Aboriginal harvesting practices, including the appropriateness of defining and treating some Aboriginal harvesting behaviours as criminal actions.

The community-based participation approach to the case study facilitated open discussion in the communities about intervention strategies that have been explored in the various regions in order to deal with traditional harvesting practices outside the context of the law. This process, in turn, enabled the research team to compare the appropriateness and effectiveness of intervention strategies known to community participants with those identified by the research team through Western research methods, including legal research and literature reviews. The principle that research will benefit the community in which it is conducted is a critical element of Indigenous research methodology as well as a strongly recommended ethical practice in contemporary social science research (Weber-Pillwax 1999). Adherence to this principle was assured through the active participation and guidance provided by respected community members from each of the five regions in northern Alberta. Their presence on the research team was also a visible statement of trust in the research objectives and methodology.

The significant connection and direct relationship between cultural identity and harvesting practices, as described by participants in this research, have not been investigated or explored to any significant depth. However, in the world of formal research and critical scholarship, and among Aboriginal scholars and community members, there is a general agreement that the elucidation of issues embedded in the relationship between cultural identity and traditional harvesting practices is best made by Aboriginal knowledge holders and scholars who have lived the experience of this connection. Given that the numbers of Aboriginal scholars remain small, the articulation of the specific, subtle, and complex nature of this connection is rare. This work then takes on additional significance with the recognition that the community members, including the Aboriginal researchers, are in fact the living expressions of this relationship or connection and that their words are spoken from this position. They embody the new knowledge that is being created through the research process in which they are engaged.

At the final workshop involving the whole research group, including the research team, community members, and "new" community participants, the final draft report was presented, and more narratives were shared in response. The report itself seemed to serve as an inspiration and an invitation to community members to express their views and to share more of their stories. The final workshop brought forth more powerful stories of how the criminalization of traditional harvesting practices is simultaneously a historical and a contemporary phenomenon. While the people recognized and expressed their concerns regarding the long-term impact of such criminalization on themselves and their children, they left no doubt that they would not – could not – give up their rights to practise their ways of living. These practices were explained as the sources of their beliefs and their values – the practices represented key elements of expression for the people's cultures and, as such, were critical aspects of their identities as individuals and as collectives.

The participants did not describe identity as being separate from traditional harvesting activities. Further, during all phases and events of the project, every participant articulated clearly a belief that no one had the right to prevent another person from engaging in traditional harvesting practices in order to provide food and sustenance for their family. These traditional harvesting activities were not ever understood or described as criminal, although there was a stated awareness that, officially, such actions were often considered "criminal" acts by the authorities. Stories involving prison and harassment were common. A shared vocabulary was evident in the workshop sessions that further demonstrated the breadth of commonality of such experiences, including the nature of the relationship between the authorities of wildlife, birds, fisheries, and plants and the Aboriginal peoples who relied on these resources. Many participants observed and commented critically on the criminality that is inherent but unnoticed in the laws and acts that prevent persons from living out their traditional ways of providing for their families' needs.

Traditional Harvesting Practices as Crime

Traditional Aboriginal Harvesting Practices

"Aboriginal harvesting practices" is a general term commonly used to refer to the traditional hunting, fishing, trapping, and gathering practices of Aboriginal people and communities. The research team identified these four activities as the core traditional practices of the Aboriginal communities involved in this study. In northern Alberta, these subsistence activities are well documented, with hunting, fishing, and gathering of plants and other naturally occurring resources from the land cited as the main traditional occupations (Daniel 1970, 18). Each of these practices implied unique considerations and issues relevant to the project.

Hunting as a Traditional Practice

Hunting has for millennia been one of the principal harvesting activities of Aboriginal peoples and communities in northern Alberta. Moose, deer, bear, and, to a lesser extent, caribou are the primary big game animals used by local Aboriginal populations for subsistence purposes. Waterfowl, depending on species, seasons, community locations, and circumstances, also continue to be an important staple for subsistence as well as a recognized delicacy and healing source.

Even one moose a year, a deer, a bunch of ducks – this was all a part of our living. My sister did the tanning of the hides. All parts of the moose were used.

I did do some trading of moose meat for potatoes with other Aboriginal communities. It was a crime – I had to eat, my kids had to eat.

The importance of hunting and the continuing opportunities to hunt and to transmit traditional knowledge about hunting practices extend beyond meeting subsistence needs. Our participants recounted how the ability of one generation of harvesting practitioners to pass these traditions on to the next generations facilitates and ensures the cultural survival of Aboriginal groups:

Hunting is something that we value, and we always want to maintain. Hunting means a lot to us as our life depends on animals around us, the wildlife. We want to make sure that it is protected in the future. Hunting is something that makes us Indian and it is something that we feel strongly about ... We don't want to lose our traditional way of living. (Al-Pac Environmental Assessment Board 1990, quoting Chief Walter Janvier)

Hunting, fishing, and trapping are more than physical subsistence activities. They are an educational and spiritual process. We all have a responsibility to our children to teach them this whole process. If we don't have the land, we can't do that.

Trapping as a Traditional Practice

Commercial trapping of fur-bearing animals continues to be a traditional harvesting activity for many Aboriginal people and communities. During the 1970s, Métis and Treaty Indians in the Wabasca-Desmarais area were still actively trapping and maintaining registered trap lines, despite negligible economic returns (Piepenberg et al. 1974, 99 and 102). Reports from the Department of Indian Affairs regarding northern Alberta Indian bands in the late 1970s similarly indicate small numbers of individuals participating in trapping activities on a regular basis (Canada 1981). These references suggest that the continuation of trapping as a traditional harvesting activity is not necessarily for subsistence reasons alone.

Community members and participants confirmed that trapping is being sustained as a traditional cultural activity and that family trap lines continue to be handed down from one generation to the next.[7] Strong, Hall, and Associates (1980) support the community statements and in their impact assessment work point out that trapping continues to be described as one of the few ways in which Aboriginal people can live out their relationships with the land (*ibid.*, 69). Research participants described their complex issues, relationships, and histories with trap lines in their families and communities:

> *We used to pick berries there, too, and cut hay, wild grass in the summer. We had a trapper shack along the lake where we stayed in the winter, trapping, and where we cut and hauled wood on weekends. I was young.*

> *Selling furs is an issue. Aboriginal people need permits and licences to sell fur if they have no registered trap line, yet Hutterites and farmers sell fur as "protecting their home."*

> *That trap line had been ours from the beginnings of time, my great-grandfather and all them. If they didn't trap the furs themselves, they bought it from others. All the brothers, even my mother trapped there. Brothers on both sides. There were five cabins there, some had barns too.*

> *We lost them all. This mooniyaw [white man] came one year, and my dad let him hunt and stay with us. The next year he was there already, had signs up, it was his now. He applied with his ten dollars, and the government gave it to him. Not only us, a lot of Métis lost their trap lines here. One uncle fought it and got his trap line back. That line is still in his family, his son has it. But that's the way: the white man came, and the old man (grandfather) was easygoing – he couldn't read anyway, so he just let it (the land) go. They said, "You just go home, we paid the registration – this is our place." So we went home. I was about thirteen or fourteen at that time. What are you going to fight with if you have no money?*

Fishing as a Traditional Practice

> *When Fish and Wildlife first came out, they would open fishing in spawning season. You could catch so many fish and store them. Then they would close the season. If you had more fish than what you were supposed to have, they burnt them. You were allowed so many fish according to the size of your family. If you got caught with more fish than you were allowed to have, you were pinched. You would go to court and pay a fine. Lots of people who could not pay fines ended up in jail.*

> *Throw the fish back in the lake is only destroying them. I don't know who makes those laws.*

> *When I come along to fish, I was scared all day long because they made a criminal out of you. If they sell you a licence, they look all over your boat, your nets little bit tighter, not enough ice, get tickets for this, for that. If your buoys not painted right, give you a ticket for that. Harassment – they could jump into your boat just like you were nothing, open the vents. I felt violated – used to be scared when I saw the Fish and Wildlife coming with their boat. My brother used to say, "a person has to be scared of that big window," referring to the windshield of their boat.*

Commercial and sport fishing developments have had serious implications for traditional Aboriginal fishing practices in northern Alberta. They have contributed widely to the decimation of fish populations in northern Alberta lakes, making subsistence fishing difficult (and even impossible) or illegal in some areas. Traditional harvesters believe that it is the regulation of the fishery itself that by interfering with the natural order, is having a detrimental impact on the vitality and survival of the fish populations. In other cases, they have pointed out that the fish populations are intact and strong but Aboriginal peoples are being prevented from harvesting by provincial regulations that favour sport or commercial fishing.

Some discussion at the community sessions indicated popular beliefs that there are species of fish that are on the brink of destruction from pollutants. Investigation and validation or proof of these claims, according to Western scientific standards, are restrained by a lack of financial and/or legal resources, and, consequently, for unknown reasons communities of Aboriginal people are left in a situation where a once stable and reliable food source has deteriorated, or is deteriorating, into a precarious resource.

In the late 1970s, for example, Lesser Slave Lake was "fished out," preventing the local Indian bands from relying on this resource either commercially or for subsistence purposes (Canada 1981).[8] Around the same time, Utikuma Lake was also fished out and was restocked in order to support a commercial fish industry run by the local First Nation (*ibid.*). Madeline Bird and Agnes Sutherland (1991, 69) recall the dramatic decline in fish populations in Lake Athabasca: "There was lots of good fish in Fort Chipewyan. The fish was so good and plentiful in Lake Athabasca. Even the dogs were treated with trout. Big tubs of trout for them until the commercial fishermen came and they soon emptied the lake of good fish." Today, despite the degradation of the northern Alberta fishery, fish remains a staple in the diet of most Aboriginal peoples who grew up and continue to live in communities alongside northern lakes and rivers.

Gathering as a Traditional Practice

There were seasonal activities, and we knew what those were. There were berries every year in those years: we would start by picking gooseberries, then wild strawberries, then raspberries, saskatoons, blueberries, cranberries. These were good all winter.

Knowing these seasons, and where the berries were, when they were available, how much to pick. These were our conservation systems.

In this chapter, gathering refers to the seasonal picking of berries, roots, eggs, plants, and herbs. While government-designed and government-monitored forms of health care and education have profoundly affected the use of plants and other naturally occurring resources, most Aboriginal peoples continue to gather and use plants in traditional ways to support personal health. Medicine people, referring to those who have acquired, hold, and use the traditional knowledge related to physical, emotional, psychological, and/or spiritual health and wellness of the individual, are the primary teachers and practitioners of the gathering and usage of plants for health purposes.

The training for such responsibility and knowledge takes a lifetime for the learner and entails a long apprenticeship to learn the "correct" and respectful ways to gather and use the plants. Herein lies the significance of gathering practices as sources of teaching and learning for the transmission of cultural values and ways of knowing and being. With nothing to gather, and a diminishing number of persons who know how and what to gather, this form of knowledge is being lost to the people, along with its associated values and ways of being. The implications of this potential loss are beyond the understanding of most people.

The gathering of herbs or plants, shrubs, or parts of trees and plants is not limited to those items that support food or medicinal purposes. Some gathering activities are related to spiritual practices and the needs of the people. In such cases, threats to the environment involve more than endangering specific plants and herbs. They also threaten the survival of the people themselves by striking at the deepest level of spiritual being and undermining those practices that sustain the strength of individual and collective psyches. Where such gathering activities are prevented or prohibited because particular ecological systems have been destroyed, the Aboriginal people themselves face the threat of the extinction of whole systems of Indigenous thought and meaning that are tied directly to the vitality of these specific plants and plant life.

In most contemporary settings, however, this knowledge and these practices continue to be protected by the practitioners and the people themselves as being sacred. Ironically, precious plant resources and their interrelated Indigenous knowledge are at a critical risk of loss partly because of the esoteric nature of the various components of the system itself. Often those persons with the highest degree of knowledge about medicines are the farthest removed, physically as well as cognitively, from mainstream society. Protection of medicinal and other plant resources and appropriate support for those persons who hold the significant and related traditional knowledge require an informed and sophisticated advocacy. However, most Aboriginal people remain reluctant to discuss this topic openly, especially with those whom they perceive as representing the greatest threat. Placed in a historical context, the notion of a "sophisticated" advocacy that will support traditional knowledge and medicine people is a difficult one to promote among Aboriginal peoples.

Factors Affecting Traditional Harvesting Practices

The earlier description of traditional harvesting practices makes it apparent that a variety of traditional practices continues into the present day, that these have an economic, cultural, and spiritual value to Aboriginal communities, and that they are grounded in an elaborate body of knowledge that must be transmitted from one generation to another. It would seem that constitutional entrenchment of Aboriginal and treaty rights would ensure Aboriginal peoples an increased access to their traditional lands and therefore a continuation of their traditional practices. There are, however, many factors that work against the continuation of these practices or that make it extremely difficult for Aboriginal communities to maintain them. Among the constraints discussed briefly in this chapter are (1) natural resource development on traditional harvesting lands; (2) economic development and employment initiatives; (3) provincial land tenure; (4) federal and provincial laws affecting traditional harvesting practices; (5) abuse of discretion by law enforcement officials; (6) Indian land claims; and, finally, (7) environmental pollution affecting harvested food.

Natural Resource Development

Indigenous peoples throughout the world have experienced profound changes in their land use and occupancy as a result of resource development and exploration occurring on their traditional lands. In northern Alberta, oil and gas exploration and development and industrial-scale forestry have impacted the economy and traditional land use of Aboriginal communities to the greatest extent. These industries were noted to be increasingly disruptive and destructive to trapping practices, wildlife habitat, and wildlife populations, thereby negatively impacting harvesters' ability to maintain their traditional practices (Espiritu 1997, 51-57; Ross 2003, 1-2; Northern Alberta Development Council 1984). As the following excerpts reveal, many contributors to our study made similar observations:

> *Twenty-two years of mining operations has destroyed our trapping area. Now the claim is being made that the land, the water, the medicine plants will be restored to their natural original states. I see fish floating down the river. You cannot put the land back to what it was.*

> *Now they are experimenting with air injection into oil wells and lighting fires down in the wells. This is very scary to even think about what could happen. The threat to wildlife and humans has to be there. I have no information – I don't know how this works, but it can't be too safe or good for the environment.*

> *Trap lines have been destroyed by oil and gas industry. Talking compensation doesn't usually solve anything. Even here they will use tactics to avoid addressing*

the long-term impact of their presence on the trap lines. There is always more than damage to snares or traps, but they don't want to recognize that. The trails that are destroyed, for example, have been in use for many decades and generations of trappers and animals' movements. To change these through industrial actions is permanently disruptive to the trapping potential for unpredictable lengths of time into the future.

When traditional harvesters are refused access, or their access is restricted due to third-party interests, their continuing or insistent presence is often characterized as illegal. Although provincial regulations and policies require consultation with all interested parties, Crown-granted leases and licences are often issued on the understanding that consultation will take place at some future date. It has become standard industry practice for companies to advertise their intent to develop the lands in question in local regional newspapers. Sometimes the company will also hold an "open house," where corporate business plans are made available to the attendees. The environmental and socio-economic impact of these developments is often presented in the form of highly scientific and formal environmental impact assessment reports, which are not readily available to the traditional land user. Moreover, consultants who have no real connection to the land in question, but who may have attended the area for the sole purpose of drafting the assessment, often complete these reports. In most instances, there will have been little or no involvement by Aboriginal traditional land users, particularly those who oppose such development, in the compilation of the assessment.

It is a safe assumption that most Aboriginal traditional land users do not accept a local newspaper's notice of hearing to be adequate consultation regarding land development. Neither do most users accept an environmental impact assessment report filed at a distant corporate head office as consultation. Notwithstanding their rejection of these industry practices, when Aboriginal peoples challenge the industry or the Crown on the issue of land development and the lack of consultation, the company's conduct is often recognized by the Crown as having met the accepted standards for consultation purposes. According to those individuals that we interviewed, this response from the Crown leaves members of the Aboriginal communities feeling powerless and ignored:

Consultations ought to be an ongoing part of the plans to deal with trappers. In most cases of development, plans have been in place long before the trapper is notified. There is no excuse for not meeting with the trappers. Even then the notice to the trapper about scheduled and already approved and government-licensed activity is usually late.

If you ask questions about proposed developments to Aboriginal traditional territories, you get sent a huge box of books and papers to read. I am not trained in what I have to read, so I cannot respond. This is frustration and helplessness.

Once a lease or licence has been issued, the presence of third parties on that particular piece of land can be legally characterized as trespass. Accordingly, land users who continue to hunt on their traditional hunting territory, which is now legally and formally designated as a forest management agreement area, or as an oil sands development project, can be (and often are) considered trespassers.[9]

We are muzzled against industry – have to keep quiet and follow the rules. How do we get around this is the question. This will get worse. Who keeps the big industries "in line"?

Alternatively, many Aboriginal groups have attempted to use the legal system to protect their interest in traditional lands.[10] Such a claim must typically be raised in the context of a breach of treaty and Aboriginal rights relating to the land in question or, at the very least, of a claim based on lack of consultation. Alternatively, or additionally, the claimant group may allege a breach of the Crown's fiduciary obligation. These types of claims typically entail lengthy, complicated, and expensive legal proceedings. When prompted by land development disputes, governments will often put in place legislative and administrative schemes that require compliance with statutorily mandated hearing processes. The role of the court will be to determine, through judicial review, whether these administrative procedures have taken place. Only if the court determines, after the judicial review, that it does in fact have the jurisdiction to hear the complaint will it begin to resolve the substantive matters.

In a resource-rich province such as Alberta, where resource development is the economic foundation of the society, Aboriginal interests have little, if any, priority in the resolution of these matters. Even if they are aware of, and have the means to support, bringing a matter before the courts or an administrative tribunal for determination, Aboriginal people are often left with a sense of frustration and distrust in the system.

I have seen that it is the same people who are working together with industry and government. In one case, we had our lawyer, and industry and government each had their lawyers present. During the break, the government lawyers and the industry lawyers were socializing, laughing, and touching, obviously together. Our lawyer was excluded. Even with such poor examples of professionalism, it was obvious that the government regulators were simply a part of the whole "development" system. How could they regulate to address environmental and 'Aboriginal concerns?

If you challenge the AEUB [Alberta Energy and Utilities Board], you get branded. Government and industry talk, and you get black-balled.

Aboriginal people and communities throughout Alberta have generally accepted that natural resource development is an inevitable occurrence. Often this development will occur directly in their traditional use areas and in the face of their active political and sometimes legal opposition. Recognizing this fact, Aboriginal communities will often take strong political positions with these third parties, who may have a duty to consult with the local Aboriginal populations. Their demands may include compensation for damages to traditional harvesting areas. However, more often, these demands will serve to guide negotiations for increased levels of employment and training and more and improved opportunities for the economic advancement of the Aboriginal people.

Aboriginal Economic Development and Employment Initiatives
Since the latter portion of the twentieth century, some Aboriginal people and communities have benefited from the employment opportunities created by the development of their traditional lands.[11] Spin-off opportunities have also been created by industry developments in neighbouring areas (Canada 1981; Northern Alberta Development Council 1991). These mainstream means of earning a livelihood held out much promise to local Aboriginal communities in northern Alberta, especially in the early 1970s and 1980s. However, it soon became evident that there would be detrimental impacts on traditional practices and minimal long-term benefits to Aboriginal people from the increasingly intense oil activities in their regions.

The structure and time commitments required of those employed within a wage labour economy affect their ability to spend time on the land practising traditional activities. Nonetheless, most individuals continue to engage in such pursuits and to teach the next generation; the time restrictions fail to diminish the value that is attributed to the traditional activities and the meaning of these to the life of the individual and the family. Often there are conflicts of interest that arise in relation to land use in areas of economic development and those of traditional harvesting. Such lands that are tied to economic development, for example, would be considered occupied for the purposes of provincial laws. Hunting thereon would, for the purpose of provincial legislation, be considered illegal activity. Indirectly, then, Aboriginal employment and economic development initiatives, while "legal" and indeed sought by many Aboriginal communities, contribute to the criminality of traditional harvesting practices.

Government forced adaptation with criminalization of who we are. We need jobs, but we want to continue our practices and to teach our kids. As leaders, we're under great pressure to get jobs for our communities. What are we supposed to do?

Federal and Provincial Law

Look at statistics to see who is actually killing off the moose? In 1985, with Bill C-31, many Indian people came back with rights to hunt, but since then moose numbers have increased. Calculate that there were 30,000 Aboriginal men in Alberta: 10,000 of these are Indians, and of these 2,000 can legally hunt. Yet 10,400 licences were sold in Alberta in 1985.

Provincial legislation and regulations that have a direct effect on Aboriginal people's harvesting practices have become the subject matter of numerous cases heard by the Supreme Court of Canada since the constitutional entrenchment of Aboriginal and treaty rights in section 35 of the *Constitution Act, 1982*.[12] It is apparent, when one considers many of these cases, that implementation of the commitment reflected in this constitutional provision continues to require prompting by Aboriginal people's actions. More importantly, these actions tend to occur in the context of alleged criminal conduct by Aboriginal persons. Thus, notwithstanding the legal standard of "innocent until proven guilty," Aboriginal persons seeking recognition of their Aboriginal practices, which are integral to the continued existence of themselves and their communities, enter into this arena as criminals. From the data-gathering process and workshops, we were able to discern two common legal situations affecting traditional Aboriginal harvesting practices in northern Alberta – hunting without a valid provincial licence and being in possession of wildlife without a valid licence to possess it.[13]

Who has the right to determine what my rights are? Laws are like cobwebs dropping on us, and we can't move.

Hunting without a Valid Licence

The procedure and requirements for acquiring a subsistence-hunting licence from the province are very stringent. As an example, the following sections of the *Alberta Wildlife Regulations* illustrate the predicament that occurs in the context of Aboriginal hunting practices. Sections 39(1) and 40(1) of Alberta Regulation 143/97 state:

39(1) A person is eligible to obtain or hold a subsistence hunting licence if and only if

(a) he is an individual who resides outside the boundaries of a city,
town or village and in the subsistence hunting area described in
subsection (2), and

(b) the Minister is satisfied that he is in dire need of sustenance for
any of his family members, including his adult interdependent
partner.

40(1) A subsistence hunting licence authorizes its holder, if any of his family
members, including his adult interdependent partner, is in dire need
of sustenance, to hunt one animal (and one only) from among the
following kinds of animals, namely, moose, mule deer and white-tailed
deer during the period, and in the area, specified in the licence.[14]

As noted earlier, Aboriginal people are moving to urban centres at unprecedented rates. In many instances, this migration is for employment, education, and/or health commitments. Our research indicates that, notwithstanding this fact, traditional practices are usually maintained, implying significant and regular connections with the home community. Often it is the primary provider who relocates to the urban centre, but, even from this location, this individual remains the primary provider in terms of traditional hunting practices. However, section 39 of the regulations would prevent this person from obtaining a subsistence-hunting licence. Notwithstanding the continuing connection to his or her home community and traditional territory, the applicant would be considered a resident of the urban centre and therefore ineligible.

Section 40 restricts the licence holder to harvesting one animal for subsistence purposes. This restriction flies in the face of the needs of many Aboriginal families and communities and their cultural practices where it is common practice for specific individuals to be the community hunters and providers. These individuals will hunt and kill numerous animals to meet their own subsistence needs as well as those of their extended families, community elders, and others who may otherwise not be able to hunt. The restriction of one animal per licence implies that these traditional hunters and providers are committing a criminal act by meeting these familial and societal needs and expectations.

There was usually one person who hunted for the family. One uncle, the oldest one, did most of the hunting. All the brothers supplied him with shells and the gun. He could walk and run better than the others. I recall one winter he killed and we ate nineteen deer, a bear, and three moose, and we butchered a steer. There were big families to feed. Everything was shared. That was the way it was. In those days, Fish and Wildlife didn't bother you. You could skin (game) outside and not be scared.

In our extended family, I hunt and share meat with about thirty-five people.

One thing I don't like, I am a Bill C-31 now, and I used to be Métis. Now I can't even give this old man some fish or moose meat or I will get charged. How do the old people survive? That's how we survived. Young people went and hunted and fed the old people. That's how we survived. Now I am told I can't give you a chunk of moose meat.

Transportation and Possession of Wildlife

Provincial legislation rigorously regulates the manner in which wildlife is to be transported from the harvesting location.[15] In many instances, the facts of these situations would have supported a legitimate defence based on section 35 of the *Constitution Act*. However, for circumstantial reasons, most notably the financial burden of carrying a constitutional legal defence through the court system, and the emotional stress of facing stringent criminal penalties, many Aboriginal accused elect to resolve these cases by way of a guilty plea or through plea bargaining to a lesser charge. The overall consequence, then, is the criminalization of these traditional harvesting practices and the accompanying social debilitation of Aboriginal persons pursuing their own ways of life or *Pimatsowin*.

We were told, "You're a Treaty. If you need help to get your moose out of the bush, you have to pay these people (Métis) in cash." But that has always been our way of life, you know, to share our meat.

My grandfather was sick. He can't hunt, so I give him moose meat and fish because that is the only way, and that's how the old people survive. I set a net, and I drive around and give them fish. I still do that.

They tell me that the Treaty people, they are not supposed to give away anything – not even a fish. There was a case where a Treaty man was selling fish door to door. In this community, a Métis man with a large family bought one of the fish. But it is illegal to buy fish from the Treaties ("Indians"). The man was charged with a big fine. He bought this fish to feed his family probably because he could get it at a reasonable price, but he was slapped with a fifteen-hundred-dollar fine.

Provincial Land Tenure and Relocation Programs

Introduced in the 1970s and 1980s, Alberta's land tenure systems and family relocation programs were promoted as opportunities for northern Aboriginal families. Housing programs went along with the land tenure system, and family home locations were disrupted as housing programs re-designed Aboriginal community spaces into models of "white" suburban spaces. Land taxes and mortgage payments were introduced to people who had never heard of such concepts – these payments were tied to the land, and many people were threatened and/or lost their homes and their land in this process. The relocation program offered families the opportunity to be relocated from their traditional territories and into nearby towns where they were promised training and employment opportunities for better futures. Very few of these promises were ever brought to fruition. In fact, many families, once removed from their traditional lands and stripped of the opportunity to practise their traditional harvesting activities and live out their values in relation to the land, succumbed to the prisons of enforced housing and social organization in ghettos within the "white" town. Many people disappeared into this darkness and emptiness without a sound, others disappeared into alcohol, and still others clung to the hope that they would eventually be able to return to their original home territories.

It is not within the scope of this study to elaborate and trace the development of land tenure and relocation programs in northern Alberta. However, these topics are included because they demonstrate the struggles that Aboriginal peoples in northern Alberta have had in maintaining their connections to the land and carrying on their traditional harvesting practices. Resource development has been inextricably connected to the land tenure systems and other social programs affecting Aboriginal communities in the northern areas, and the laws and policies under which these systems operate do not usually reflect the perspectives of Aboriginal peoples who continue to rely on traditional harvesting practices for their own well-being and survival. The focus on oil and gas development in northern Alberta as an investment for Alberta's economic future was one that carried devastating impacts for many tiny, isolated Aboriginal communities. In too many cases, whole families gave up their lives as their rights and opportunities to practise their traditional ways were taken away from them through provincial legislation, policies, and regulations.

Harvesting and cultural practices are not separable, and within these traditions are embedded the cultural values and beliefs of the people. The threats and impact of the law through state-sanctioned resource development are integrally related to the destruction of the relationship between the Aboriginal people and the land. Without this relationship, the people will not survive. Is this then not an issue that moves beyond land control, ownership, and development and into the arena of human rights and crimes against humanity? If the right of a people to live is taken away from them for financial benefits to another, does this not constitute a crime against humanity in some definition, in some generation, in some location, and in some future?

Abuse of Discretion by Law Enforcement Representatives
With respect to law and policy enforcement, participants discussed numerous and varied experiences of alleged abuse by conservation officers. They

described investigations as interrogatory in nature, often resulting in verbally and sometimes physically abusive exchanges between the two parties. It is obvious that most of these investigative inquiries did not result in criminal or civil findings of guilt against the harvester when one considers the low number of provincial and superior court decisions involving these practices. It is arguable, then, that such abusive conduct by Crown representatives is unwarranted and may itself be criminal conduct.

When Fish and Wildlife first came out, they would open fishing in spawning season. You could catch so many fish and store them. Then they would close the season. If you had more fish than what you were supposed to have, they burnt them. You were allowed so many fish according to the size of your family. If you got caught with more fish than you were allowed to have, you were pinched. You would go to court and pay a fine. Lots of people who could not pay fines ended up in jail. I was convicted of setting a net in too shallow water.

I was sixteen when I was charged for killing a moose with no licence. I had a criminal record from then on. I got other charges since then. One was for tagging a moose on the antler instead of the hock. The officer stood there and watched me put the tag on the moose and then charged me.

In many communities, hunting and fishing are primary subsistence activities. Where regulations and legislation are enacted and enforced in relation to these practices, the effect is a restriction on traditional practices that have sustained cultures and indeed peoples' survival for millennia. These restrictions have caused a fundamental shift in the lifestyle of these people, including dietary adjustments and the diminishment and loss of cultural practices. Moreover, these laws and policies are preventing whole populations of Aboriginal peoples from living out their values and ways of life. The personal narratives collected during this work describe the negative impact that interactions with law enforcement officials have had on Aboriginal people, clearly and repeatedly, from every region:

We were told, "You're a Treaty. If you need help to get your moose out of the bush, you have to pay these people (Métis) in cash. But that has always been our way of life, you know, to share our meat."

My grandfather was sick. He can't hunt, so I give him moose meat and fish because that is the only way, and that's how the old people survive. I set a net, and I drive around and give them fish. I still do that. I was taught that by the elders. I spent a lot of time with my grandfather.

Much of the community discussion pointed to the negative impact that laws relating to wildlife and fish have on human physical well-being. One young woman shared the story of how her mother's health had deteriorated quickly and devastatingly when she could no longer include wild meat and fish in her diet because her sons, who provided her with food, could no longer legally hunt or fish. They had been refused licences and permits to hunt and fish after their father, a man with Indian status, had passed away. Another woman told of how her doctor had prescribed her a diet of wild meat and fish intended to prevent her from developing heart problems. To fulfill the diet, she required a fishing licence or permit. When she went to apply for a licence from Fish and Wildlife with a letter from her doctor, the officer filled out her licence and was prepared to hand it to her. Before doing so, he asked her who was going to set the net for her. She named her husband, whereupon the officer ripped up the licence, saying, "I know those people from Mariah River, they are all Métis and poaching all the time." He refused her the licence. Thereafter, the woman's heart condition worsened, and she eventually required major heart surgery. She attributes her declining health, in part, to her inability to sustain herself with traditional foods.

Abusive interrogations by enforcement officials often leave harvesters and their families with a general sense of apprehension of authority figures. As a result of these interactions, people begin to feel that simply by walking on their traditional lands they are guilty of some illegal act – in essence, that they are criminals. The following quotes were given earlier but bear repeating here:

> You know they have a job to do, but I think they could do it in such a way that they don't make you feel like such a criminal. When we got charged, they came in at seven o'clock in the morning. It was still dark in October. Why couldn't they have come at a decent hour when we were up? There must have been seven Fish and Wildlife vehicles out there. We had trespassing signs on our property – we had them there for a reason – because we couldn't drive over the water lines. They ignored everything. They barged in and went straight to my bedroom. I don't have a habit of keeping fish in my bedroom. That's what I mean about the way they do things. They could have done the same thing in a different way.

> I didn't fish, and I didn't sell fish. I accepted money for someone else who had arranged to give the undercover cop some fish. The way the undercover cop talked, we were outlaws, we were thieves.

In many instances, it is the intergenerational impact of such abuse of authority that is of great concern. In one community, the abuse became evident when an officer's son taunted a harvester's son at school: "My dad's going to come to your house and arrest your dad." The harvester dad, a Métis man from northern Manitoba, had shot and killed an elk to feed his family for the winter. The animal had been shot and killed on unoccupied Crown land. One week after the school taunting, at exactly the same time of day as the school bus arrived to pick up the Métis children, Fish and Wildlife officers and representatives of the local RCMP arrived at the family residence to charge the man for killing the animal. They roared into the yard in front of the school bus and marched into the house uninvited. They seized all of the meat that had been wrapped and stored in the family freezer. The impact of this incident was intensified by the involvement of the sons. The school taunting discloses the officer's breach of professional conduct and confidentiality in relation to an ongoing investigation. The arrival of the investigating team at the family residence at the same time as the school bus, while perhaps coincidental, effectively confirms to the son and to his school peers that the father is guilty of criminal conduct and is, therefore, a criminal.

The impact of this incident must have been devastating and immeasurable on both the man as the provider for his family and on the family as a cohesive unit engaged in and dependent upon traditional hunting practices. Notwithstanding this negative personal and familial impact, the conduct of the officers in this situation would be considered legal and defensible in terms of existing law and policy enforcement practices. However, from another, more human and respectful, perspective, the evident criminality in this situation lies in the conduct of the enforcement officers. From the perspective of a children's counsellor, the psychological damage to the children in this case constitutes a form of child abuse, likely with negative impacts on learning capability and self-esteem, trust, and general school and societal achievement. The professional and ethical conduct of the enforcement officials or authority figures could be open to challenge. However, notwithstanding the gravity of the situation, none of these perspectives would likely enter into the legal considerations of this case, should it ever be tried.

Ironically, the Manitoba government has made reference to the need for respect of Métis rights to hunt for subsistence purposes. At an annual general assembly of the Manitoba Métis Federation (MMF) in September 2004, Premier Gary Doer pledged that his government would follow the Supreme Court of Canada's decision in *R. v. Powley* (2003) and respect the Métis right to hunt.[16] Notwithstanding this pledge, Métis people in Manitoba continue to be charged for practising their traditions:

"I was chair of the MMF annual general assembly. I was within ten feet of the premier when he promised to respect Métis rights and follow the *Powley* decision," said Goodon, chairperson of one of the local Métis organizations. Goodon was subsequently charged with illegal possession of a migratory bird for not holding a valid provincial hunting license. His gun and the carcass were seized by the Department of Conservation and he was charged under the Migratory Birds Act for being in possession of the bird. "After hearing his message to the Métis people, I didn't think I would have to skulk in the bush like a criminal. Métis hunters have the right to feed their families in our traditional ways. The minister has no right to play games with the lives of our people" (Dolha 2004).

During this study, specific reference was made by community participants to situations in a number of northern Alberta communities where individuals would be charged with illegal possession and/or selling of meat and fish derived from traditional hunting practices. In these instances, undercover officers would approach the harvester, requesting meat or fish for sale. Incidents were also described where enforcement officials reportedly offered substances such as drugs and alcohol to Aboriginal harvesters in their investigations of illegal harvesting activities.[17]

Even taking the kids out snaring in the creeks and rivers in the spring time, the Fish and Wildlife will be there watching and waiting, stopping the children and questioning them about what they are doing at the river. Everyone knows, and everyone is watching and waiting too to see where the officials go and what they do. Why do I have to teach my kids to hide what they enjoy and what they know we do as Native people? What am I teaching them?

Now, as Métis, we have to teach our kids how to hunt legally; we are not poaching. We need to re-program our kids. But because of the law and how it is enforced, we can't take our children out to teach them. They don't know enough. They don't have the foundations to learn.

It is a humiliating experience to have to hunt at night to feed your family.

Indian Land Claims Settlements
When a claim is settled between Canada and a First Nation, the traditional territory of that group is identified and becomes a central component to the final agreement. Often the traditional territory will form part of a co-management area between Canada and the First Nation. Where there are overlapping traditional lands between different Aboriginal groups who may not be parties to the agreement, this can cause problems relating to the continuation of traditional practices of the non-party Aboriginal group. In terms of the law, the legal use of lands for traditional harvesting by the signatory First Nation will imply illegal use of other non-signatory Aboriginal peoples.

As an example, lands near the Cold Lake Air Weapons Range in northern Alberta were subject to a claims settlement made by the Cold Lake First Nation against Canada.[18] Finalized in 2002, this agreement compensated

members of the Cold Lake First Nation for loss of access to traditional territory as a result of the air weapons bombing range. The agreement included
$25.5 million in cash compensation, additional reserve land, and access
agreements to the Primrose Lake Air Weapons Range, which straddles the
Alberta/Saskatchewan border. The Cold Lake agreement enables Cold Lake
band members' access to lands within the air weapons range, which is a part
of the band's traditional territory. Although the Cold Lake–Canada agreement was a positive one for this particular First Nation, there are numerous
other Aboriginal persons and communities that have used this same geographical area as their traditional territory. However, the Cold Lake agreement
is not binding on Canada vis-à-vis non-band members (Cold Lake First Nation) since they are not party to the land claim agreement. Consequently,
non-band member harvesters are detrimentally affected by the land claim
agreement in that they are legally refused continuing access to these lands.
Non-band members also do not benefit from the $25.5 million in cash
compensation or from additional reserve land. Consequently, Aboriginal
people who arguably might also have a legal claim to this land as a part of
their traditional territory find themselves in a situation where their presence
on these lands will be considered illegal, particularly given that the land is
used as a military air weapons test range.

> *The bombing range scared our people away from their traditional territories. The
> Métis families scattered across the province, leaving their homes, trap lines, etc.
> They were threatened with bombs if they remained in the area. The planes would
> fly low to terrorize them.*

Environmental Pollution
In various areas throughout Canada, health research focuses on warning
and educating Aboriginal peoples on how to live without their relationships
to the land and its resources that have sustained them for millennia. A
primary focus of health research, for example, is the education of northern
populations of Indigenous peoples, through health pamphlets and other
written information, on the dangers of eating too much traditional food
that is polluted. Such health information emphasizes the dangers of eating
fish and meat gathered from traditional harvesting activities because of
widespread pollutants and poisoning amongst these food sources and com-
municates increasing dangers to women of childbearing ages if they continue to rely on traditional food sources for their sustenance. However,
notwithstanding the promotion of such scientific "knowledge," people in
the north continue to eat fish, for example, as a staple food. They do this
in spite of the fact that their fish are showing extremely high levels of
mercury poisoning.

The underlying message from the pamphlets seems to be asking the northern Aboriginal peoples to set aside their relationships with the animals, the land, and the water since these are poisoned and will die. The people are being educated and advised not only to eat in a different way but to "be" in a different way; they are being asked to live in a way that excludes other forms of life from within the shared environment of the earth. This way of seeing the earth and other life is foreign to Aboriginal peoples; if the fish are dying, will we not also die?

In this project, the stories that were relayed by community members in northern Alberta spoke to their thinking about traditional harvesting and gathering activities in relation to the larger environment.

Elders teach us that, in the old days, the animals ate all kinds of plants. When we eat the animals, we receive the sources of the minerals, vitamins, etc. that the animal has eaten. In this way, our health is maintained. However, today the animals are suffering and cannot find healthy food for themselves. They are diseased and sick because of the contaminants in the environment.

Farming "wild" animals and fish farms are leading to sickness amongst the animals.

Our doctors are recommending moose meat instead of beef, but the environment is impacting on the quality of wild meat today.

The taste of wild game has changed drastically, and I don't eat deer meat anymore. It just doesn't taste that good, it tastes different. The deer are eating different food too. There is nothing really solid in meat these days. The deer go out and eat in the fields, and they are just as bad as cattle. They are not eating natural foods either.

Intervention Strategies

This community-based research has demonstrated how, under the guise of regulation and management, state laws and policies have effectively criminalized the traditional ways of living and being of Aboriginal peoples. However, there are alternative methods and strategies possible to reasonably and respectfully regulate Aboriginal harvesting practices outside of the context of the civil and criminal law. These include (1) bilateral harvesting agreements; (2) co-management agreements; (3) domestic legal mechanisms; and (4) international legal mechanisms.

Bilateral Harvesting Agreements

After the Supreme Court of Canada's decision in *R. v. Powley* (2003), the argument that governments have a fiduciary duty to recognize the rights of Métis people to hunt for subsistence motivated some provincial governments to take steps to implement the principles espoused in this case.[19] In Alberta, the right of Métis communities to exercise traditional harvesting practices was reflected in agreements between the provincial government and two Métis organizations: the Métis Settlements General Council representing Métis residing on, and members of, one of the eight Métis Settlement communities throughout the province and the Métis Nation of Alberta representing Métis individuals not associated with the Settlements. These harvesting agreements enabled Métis persons to harvest fish and wildlife for sustenance purposes on all unoccupied Crown land in Alberta. The agreements recognized traditional practices of food sharing and the mobility of families between traditional areas and urban centres. Although provincial justice departments maintained prosecutorial discretion with regard to the laying of charges in certain instances, the agreements nonetheless provided an alternative to prosecution under provincial regulation and the criminal law.[20]

Co-Management Agreements

The co-management of wildlife on Aboriginal traditional lands is another mechanism that has been used as an intervening strategy against increased criminalization of traditional harvesting practices. Wildlife co-management boards are often created pursuant to land claims settlements, with the intention that Aboriginal peoples will directly participate in wildlife management and conservation in specific areas. There is no apparent reason why this strategy could not be applied to regions where there is no ongoing claim, such as within existing state-run wildlife management areas. Restructuring existing systems to increase Aboriginal representation and involvement would have a positive effect at multiple levels of government–Aboriginal people relationships. In this context, co-management offers an alternative to criminal and civil law for resolving disputes related to Aboriginal harvesting practices.

Domestic Legal Mechanisms

As reflected in the common law, recognition of Aboriginal rights is based on the fact that Aboriginal peoples historically existed in Canada as distinct Aboriginal societies prior to European contact and the assertion of sovereignty. The practices, customs, and traditions that these societies historically exercised, and still continue to exercise, will be afforded constitutional protection in accordance with section 35 of the *Constitution Act, 1982*. While section 35 recognizes and affirms existing Aboriginal and treaty rights, Aboriginal peoples must prove the continued existence, nature, and scope of their traditional practices if they are to receive constitutional protection. The test for proving the existence of unextinguished Aboriginal rights is set out in the decision by the Supreme Court of Canada in *R. v. Van der Peet*

(1996, para. 46), where the court stated that "in order to be an Aboriginal right an activity must be an element of a practice, custom or tradition integral to the distinctive culture of the Aboriginal group claiming the right."[21]

Once a right has been established according to the *Van der Peet* criteria, extinguishment can only occur if a "clear and plain intent" by Parliament is demonstrated.[22] Notwithstanding this restriction, Aboriginal rights are not absolute and may be justifiably infringed upon. For example, conservation and resource management have been upheld by the courts as valid legislative objectives for infringing upon Aboriginal rights.[23] The hierarchy of interests noted by the Supreme Court of Canada in *R. v. Sparrow* (1990) clearly gives priority to traditional Aboriginal harvesters to fish for food purposes as a constitutional entitlement, second only to conservation measures that may be undertaken by federal legislation. Subsequent Supreme Court of Canada decisions have strictly characterized the fiduciary obligation of the Crown to consult with affected Aboriginal peoples where claims to Aboriginal title and rights have been stated but not yet determined by the courts. With respect to the extent of infringement, the court in *Van der Peet* (1996, para. 1111) reinforced its earlier decision in *Guerin v. The Queen* (1984), that infringement of Aboriginal rights must be minimal and in accordance with the Crown's fiduciary relationship with the Aboriginal group in question. In *Haida Nation v. British Columbia (Minister of Forests)* (2004) and *Taku River Tlingit First Nation v. British Columbia (Project Assessment Director)* (2004), the Supreme Court of Canada concluded that the Crown has a legal duty to consult and that these consultations must take place in good faith and, in certain instances, extend to an obligation to accommodate the needs and interests of the claimant group.[24]

The combined effect of the Supreme Court of Canada decisions in *Sparrow*, *Haida Nation*, and *Taku River Tlingit* is that Aboriginal people whose traditional practices or Aboriginal rights are infringed by government regulations, laws, or policies have legal grounds to have their interests protected and, in certain instances, accommodated. Laws can, however, be constructed in such a manner that they do not infringe upon Aboriginal peoples' constitutional rights to harvest. In this manner, domestic law in Canada is capable of respectfully regulating Aboriginal harvesting practices outside of the context of the civil and criminal law.

International Legal Mechanisms
Indigenous peoples have consistently maintained that, if they are to survive as distinct societies, intact with their unique cultures, identities, and institutions, their ability to use the land, to practise their traditions – indeed, to protect the land – must be assured. The United Nations rapporteur on Indigenous land rights aptly noted this inherent connection:

A profound relationship exists between Indigenous peoples and their lands, territories and resources; (ii) this relationship has various social, cultural, spiritual, economic and political dimensions and responsibilities; (iii) the collective dimension of this relationship is significant; and (iv) the inter-generational aspect of such a relationship is also crucial to indigenous peoples' identity, survival and cultural viability. (Stavenhagen 2002)

No single issue affects the survival of Indigenous peoples as much as state appropriation of land and its resources. To remove or fundamentally alter Indigenous peoples' access to the land and its resources, which, for many, goes to the core of their existence as distinct peoples, is to strip away their identity, their religious beliefs and practices, and their means of survival.

In cases of human rights claims where domestic processes have proven ineffective in addressing conditions that are contrary to the concept of self-determination – as that concept is accepted and defined in international law – the matter will become one of international concern and therefore no longer essentially within the domestic jurisdiction. In such instances, state sovereignty may be made to yield to an appropriate level of international scrutiny.

International Covenant on Civil and Political Rights (ICCPR)

It was within this context that the Human Rights Committee considered the submission of the Lubicon Cree of northern Alberta. Chief Bernard Ominayak first communicated the claim of the Lubicon Cree to the Human Rights Committee in 1984. Ominayak claimed that Canada had violated the band's right of self-determination under the ICCPR.[25] Specifically, Ominayak cited Article 1 on the violation of the right to self-determination, the right to dispose of natural wealth and resources, and the right to have a traditional means of subsistence protected (*Bernard Ominayak and the Lubicon Lake Band v. Canada* 1984, para. 2.1). The Human Rights Committee received statements from both the federal government and Ominayak over a period of six years before rendering its concluding comments in 1990. Much of the extensive record in this matter related to two main points of contention:

(1) whether or not the Lubicon Cree were "a people" as that term pertains to the right of self-determination; and (2) whether or not the Lubicon Cree had exhausted all domestic remedies available to it, thereby enabling sub-mission of a communication to the Committee. With respect to the right of self-determination, Canada maintained that the Lubicon Cree were not a people within the meaning of article 1 of the Covenant. Canada further maintained that Chief Ominayak did not have standing to bring a com-munication before the Committee under the Optional Protocol, which

stipulated that communications were only to be brought by individuals or groups of individuals claiming a breach of their individual rights. In this instance, Chief Ominayak had submitted the Lubicon communication as representing the collective interests of the Band as a people. Canada maintained that the complainant lacked standing before the Committee. *(Ibid.)*

With respect to the exhaustion of domestic remedies, Canada maintained that the Lubicon Cree could be, and indeed were, party to actions in domestic courts seeking substantive recognition of their Aboriginal and treaty rights and that such a determination would resolve the issues at bar. To the extent that they would offer any meaningful redress of the claims concerning the destruction of its means of livelihood, Ominayak (on behalf of the band) maintained that in fact all domestic remedies available had been exhausted. Ominayak maintained that any domestic processes available had proven ineffective in ensuring the continued ability of the Lubicon Cree to maintain itself and its survival as a people:

> The recognition of aboriginal rights or even treaty rights by a final determination of the courts will not undo the irreparable damage to the society of the Lubicon Lake Band. [It will] not bring back the animals, will not restore the environment, will not restore the Band's traditional economy, will not replace the destruction of their traditional way of life and will not repair the damages to the spiritual and cultural ties to the land. The consequence is that all domestic remedies have indeed been exhausted with respect to the protection of the Band's economy as well as its unique, valuable and deeply cherished way of life. *(Ibid.*, para. 11.2)

In its final decision, the Committee stated that whether or not the Lubicon Cree constituted "a people" for the purpose of the ICCPR was not an issue to be considered under the Optional Protocol *(ibid.*, para. 32.1).[26] However, the committee did note that Article 27 of the ICCPR would enable a group of individuals similarly affected by breaches of individual rights to submit a communication alleging a breach of their rights. The committee went further in applying Article 27 to the claim of the Lubicon Cree, stating that the provision could be interpreted as including the right of a group of persons to engage in economic and social activities, which are part of the culture of that community. It is arguable, then, that land and the resources, subsistence, and participation rights of Indigenous persons are protected by Article 27 of the ICCPR. Although these rights are defined as individual rights in international law, they may be exercised by individuals living in community with other members of the group, thereby providing some measure of protection of the collective rights of Indigenous peoples to continue their traditional harvesting practices.

Inter-American Commission on Human Rights (IACHR)
The Organization of American States (OAS) is a regional international organization encompassing thirty-four member states, including Canada and the United States. The human rights component of the OAS is the IACHR. The primary mandate of the IACHR is to promote respect for, and defence of, human rights in the hemisphere.[27] This mandate is fulfilled through a number of functions, including advisory services to the member states, preparation of reports and studies pertaining to human rights issues, and various other mechanisms, including on-site visits and the oversight of member state conduct with respect to progressive measures taken to uphold human rights. Most notably for the purpose of this chapter, the commission may also receive complaints, conduct hearings, and render decisions regarding complaints of human rights violations by OAS member states.

The commission has had the opportunity to hear matters pertaining specifically to claims by Indigenous peoples of violations of their collective human rights. The case of *Mary and Carrie Dann v. United States* (2002) effectively illustrates how Indigenous peoples' grievances in relation to land use and occupation can be addressed in the context of human rights violations. Mary and Carrie Dann were members of the Western Shoshone peoples, who have historically and continuously used and occupied a vast area of land in the state of Nevada for traditional purposes.[28] In 1951, the Danns' property was appropriated by the United States and subsequently developed for mining purposes. Notwithstanding that a "land claim" had allegedly been settled on behalf of the Western Shoshone, the Danns claimed, pursuant to a number of articles set out in the proposed American Declaration on the Rights of Indigenous Peoples, that the expropriation of their lands constituted a violation of their human rights.[29] In particular, the Danns claimed that the state had deprived them of the use and continued occupancy of their traditional lands in the absence of full informed consent and that this was a violation of their individual and collective interests as Indigenous peoples.

Consideration of the Danns' claim in the context of the human rights system and the rights of Indigenous peoples is promising. Based on its factual and legal analysis of the Danns' situation, the commission concluded that there had indeed been a violation of the Danns' rights and that in order to rectify this violation an effective remedy would include respect for their right to property through legislative amendments. More generally, the commission also directed the state to conduct a review of laws, procedures, and practices to ensure that the property rights of Indigenous persons were determined in accordance with the declaration. Despite this positive decision, the Danns have continued to experience violation of their rights to their lands because there are currently no mechanisms to enforce the findings or judgments of the commission. Clearly, petitioners of such mechanisms remain subject to the discretion of the state (see Weber and Weber-Pillwax 2005).[30]

Conclusion

Aboriginal peoples shall be recognized as a permanent voice in fish and wildlife and natural resources management everywhere. The strict interdependence of Aboriginal peoples and the land with all its resources is a relationship that needs to be formally built into the process of land and resource management. The survival of the Aboriginal peoples is not assured without an assurance that the land itself and all wildlife, fish, and natural resources will survive. The gravity of this relationship is not outside the knowledge of Aboriginal community members.

Societal norms are a projection of the behaviours expected of members of a given society. "Crime" exists within that society where there are at least two sets of normative ideologies that conflict with one another and where one social group has the power to enforce its ideology over other groups. The law (criminal or otherwise) is the standard means by which these societal norms and morals are regulated and enforced. The research discussed in this chapter provided an opportunity to consider and record social norms as they relate to traditional harvesting activities in particular Aboriginal communities. The work demonstrated the dichotomy of values and perspectives that often exist between mainstream society and Aboriginal peoples and communities regarding the legal characterization of traditional harvesting practices.

The formation of Aboriginal peoples' social structures and mores, including those governing spiritual practices and traditions and those guiding relationships with other peoples and other forms of life, have evolved as part of the people's relationships with the land and its resources. Most Aboriginal communities remain centred on ceremonies, teachings, and practices associated at a deep level with traditional hunting, fishing, and gathering. Traditional practices, in addition to fulfilling subsistence needs, play a significant role in the preservation of Aboriginal culture, values, and belief systems. Aboriginal community members as a whole have judged the criminalization of these traditional harvesting practices as an act of criminality in itself. Hence, the research itself had to encompass much more than the issue of legally defined criminal behaviours as the stated subject matter.

Hunting, fishing, and trapping are activities that encompass more than food objectives. They involve teaching and cultural preservation. Everyone has the responsibility to teach the children. There is a ceremony that accompanies this responsibility:

It's our responsibility to show them and to take them out on the land to practise these traditions, our responsibility to teach the humanness of traditional education and practices. If we have no land, or if there are so many regulations governing our use of the land, how are we supposed to do that?

Community members were clear that, if they are to survive as distinct societies with unique cultural identities and institutions, opportunities to practise their traditions on the land, including traditional harvesting practices, must be assured – not criminalized. This work points clearly to an integral connection between all of the aspects of the traditional harvesting and gathering practices of Aboriginal peoples' life-ways, including ancient and embedded epistemologies and ontologies. The research further substantiates international declarations endorsed by various nations of the world that land, and the ability to live off the land, is the basis of Indigenous being and knowledge. The effective criminalization of traditional harvesting practices through alteration or control of access to the land and its resources strips away Aboriginal identities, traditional beliefs and practices, and, ultimately, the means of individual and collective Aboriginal survival.

Pimatsowin Weyasowewina demonstrates that reconciliation of the law and recognition and affirmation of traditional harvesting practices as integral aspects of Aboriginal culture are only at a beginning stage. If reconciliation is to occur between the various Aboriginal peoples within Canada and with Canada itself, more dialogue is needed on the development of alternative approaches to the enforcement of *Weyasowewina*. These alternatives must recognize the legitimacy of the laws and principles that govern *Pimatsowin,* ensuring strong relationships between Indigenous peoples and the land from which their subsistence is drawn. Simultaneously, the alternatives must recognize and incorporate the knowledge that these relationships are enacted through the traditional harvesting and gathering practices of the people.

Aboriginal harvesting practices emerge from, and are integrally interconnected with, traditional knowledge, values, beliefs, and practices. Without these practices, Aboriginal people cannot relate meaningfully to their past, nor do they have the means by which to pass on their traditional knowledge to the next generation. Existing and ongoing Aboriginal harvesting practices point to the need for formally recognized Aboriginal harvesting rights. The knowledge, beliefs, identities, and histories of the people are carried within the practices that have continued through the generations. The Aboriginal people contributing to this study have described a repository of this ancient knowledge and have pointed out a direct means of accessing it – through the traditional harvesting and gathering practices and ceremonies, as they are lived out in relation to the land. The land as totality is the basis of the cosmologies, epistemologies, and ontologies of Aboriginal peoples in their societies and cultures. The rights to engage in the activities that express that traditional relationship to the land must be legally recognized and protected as a foundation to the continuing survival of Aboriginal peoples in Canada.

Appendix A: List of Community Participants

Joe Adam	Melvin Goulet	George Quintal
Robin Auger	Lauralyn Houle	Margaret Ross
Lawrence Berland	Cecile Howse	Isadore Shott
Doreen Boucher	Mable Howse	M. Smith
Joe Bourque	Kevin Howse	Robert Smith
Greg Calliou	Marty Howse	Herman Sutherland
George Cardinal	Ronald Johnston	Adam la Tourneau
Gerald Cardinal	Betty Ladouceur	Skipper Villeneuve
Jeff Chalifoux	Cindy Ladouceur	Ivan Villeneuve
M. Chalifoux	Hillaire Ladouceur	Paul Weber
Karen Collins	Jerry LaRose	Arly Roe
Gloria Desjarlais	Patrick Mercredi	Rick Martin
Kenny Gairdner	Carolyn Merkle	Billy Martin
L. Gairdner	Fred Pruden	

Appendix B: Recommendations from Interviews and Workshops

The following are direct quotes provided by research project participants. The recommendations were generated through both one-on-one interviews with participants and through group workshops held throughout the duration of the project. The recommendations have been grouped according to topic.

Impact of Law and Policy on Aboriginal Identity and Traditional Lifestyle

If we are going to retain our languages and our traditional cultural practices, accessibility to the land is imperative. If we are to keep/retain our Aboriginal identity as Aboriginal people, and not just as Canadians, we must have access to our traditional lands. Is not only about the practice itself, but is about retention of cultural values, identity as Aboriginal.

We need to educate/make our children aware that you don't need to choose to be Aboriginal or white, to live only a modern lifestyle or a traditional Aboriginal lifestyle. You can have both, and it's okay to have both. They're not being taught this. They're being taught that it's criminal to be Aboriginal, to practise our traditions. That's criminal.

Sure, it's our responsibility at home to teach our kids about the law as well as what our traditional beliefs are. But poverty takes away our rights, our belief systems. The government controls what we can and can't have, especially when we're poor.

Government has historically had economic control over us. This is the contemporary problem too. They control our economy and, in doing so, take our traditional ways of earning a livelihood away.

The mainstream law-making process is distinct from Aboriginal means of law making and social control. Laws affecting Aboriginal lifestyle need to be communicated in ways that our people understand. This will lead to less criminalization of traditional practices.

Any interpretation of laws, policies, regulation needs the development of a vocabulary for shared meanings amongst the Aboriginal peoples as well as the policy and lawmakers. We need to come to the process with understanding of terms, including understanding the legal implications of using words like "historical" and "traditional."

When people are charged and go to court on charges for practising their traditions, the court needs to take all factors of that person's life into consideration. This doesn't happen automatically, and our people don't talk for themselves in court.

Need to have Métis hunting rights in particular recognized so that Métis can exercise their rights without fear of persecution and prosecution.

All laws and policies and regulations affecting the lives of Aboriginal peoples need to be communicated in ways that the people can understand. Processes can be written down, but Aboriginal systems tend to be oral traditionally.

Aboriginal people need to be involved in the making of laws and policies that affect their traditional ways of knowing and being.

In the administration of justice and law, when Aboriginal persons go to court on conservation issues, all spiritual and economic aspects in connection to the law must be taken into consideration.

In cases dealing with hunting and trapping infringements, there is a need for an advocacy position or a place to go for resolution besides the courts.

Why is pressure always being put on Aboriginal people to protect animals?

Who are the Fish and Wildlife, RCMP, conservation officers? Why aren't our people better represented in these positions?

Impact of Resource Development on Traditional Harvesting Practices

We are muzzled against industry – who watchdogs big industry?

We should be making a policy for future generations – conservation harvesting, negotiating with oil companies who are entering into our traditional areas.

Aboriginal peoples shall be recognized as a permanent voice in fish and wildlife and natural resources management everywhere. The strict interdependence of Aboriginal peoples and the land with all its resources is a relationship that needs to be formally built into the process of land and resource management. The survival of the Aboriginal peoples is not assured without an assurance that the land itself and all wildlife, fish, and natural resources will survive. The gravity of this relationship is not outside the knowledge of Aboriginal community members.

Consultations with respect to law making and infringement of Aboriginal practices: all Métis and Aboriginal peoples should be included in consultation processes by government. Right now, they only consult with First Nations and Indians.

Regulation of traditional practices by white society – is not practice-based, is theory.

Any forum intended to discuss Aboriginal traditional land use – policy and regulations – needs the full and equal participation of Aboriginal people.

Need to have more meetings with elders and traditional teachers.

Is it more important to have the white man's education than Aboriginal education? I am starting to see it is not.

Co-Management and Intervention Strategies

We should encourage and promote agreements between the Métis and First Nations. In order to protect our traditional practices. We have the same practices. These are human rights, to live and take care of our families.

Aboriginal peoples together should have a master plan. This is important to do and to focus on.

There should be promotion of partnerships between Aboriginal peoples and the federal and provincial governments on issues relating to conservation and regulation. Co-management regimes can be entered into between and within regions, involving Aboriginal, experienced, and knowledgeable representation.

We should have our own policing of harvesting practices.

The harvesting agreements that the Métis are entering into with the provinces – these agreements should be reflected in legislative changes. They have not, so government can still charge and harass us as they please, can't they?

There needs to be more direct involvement by knowledgeable Aboriginal people in policy making and law making. This does not necessarily mean our political leaders.

There needs to be more attention and validity given to our traditional ecological knowledge. There is merit in giving equal consideration to our scientific knowledge in policy making.

Whatever takes place in our own environment, people have to be an active part of the process of development of activities, policies, etc. If you don't want to consult with me, you are making a criminal out of me.

An elder made this recommendation before he passed on: that Native people take responsibility and control for the conservation of all lands north of baseline twenty-four degrees.

We need to be involved in co-management of conservation and development in our own traditional territories.

In our communities, we know who hunts, and we know the practices of our own people and our own community members. We regulated our own hunting capacity and practices.

Notes

1 See, for instance, the following cases accessible through the Alberta Courts judgment database, http://www.albertacourts.ab.ca: *R. v. Quinney* (2003); *R. v. Ferguson* (2001); *R. v. Breaker* (2000); *R. v. Lamouche* (2000); *R. v. Rodgers* (1998); and *R. v. Jacko* (1998).

2 *Criminal Code*, R.S.C. 1985, c. C-46.

3 All quotes from those who participated in this research project appear in italics (all participants are listed at the end of the chapter (Appendix A). Quotes from other sources are non-italicized.

4 The situation in Alberta is a case in point. The Métis Nation of Alberta, on behalf of its membership, had negotiated a formal agreement with the Alberta government following the decision of the Supreme Court of Canada in *R. v. Powley* (2003). This formal agreement provided the means by which Alberta Métis could hunt and fish according to subsistence guidelines and traditional practices within traditional Métis harvesting territories. This agreement had been interpreted in some northern towns and by some non-Aboriginal persons as rights based on preferential differentiation along racial lines. They "saw" that Métis hunters no longer required licences to hunt and fish and had no seasonal and seemingly no territorial restrictions. To the Métis hunter, the agreement had meant simply that traditional harvesting activities would not be "criminalized" and that she or he would not be charged for killing a moose or setting a net to feed the family. What remained unaddressed was the very high probability that neither party had been informed about the historical and legal foundation that underlay this situation and the formal agreement. In 2007, the newly elected Conservative government terminated the agreement within a

month of coming into power and legislated its own version of criteria for Métis Aboriginal "rights" to practise traditional hunting, fishing, and gathering.

5   A list of individual community participants who gave consent to their names appearing in this report is included at the end of this chapter in Appendix A.

6   The most common list of Aboriginal identifiers at present includes "First Nations," "Indian," "Bill C-31," "non-status," "Métis," and "Inuit." Only those persons who are legally identified as "Indians" under the *Indian Act, R.S.* 1995, c. I-5, including but not limited to members of an Indian band that is signatory to a formal treaty with Canada (or Britain), are permitted to harvest and gather in traditional ways, but always within the parameters of location and practice established by a treaty or the *Indian Act*. In this work, several participants self-identified as Indian, as their social identity, but would be categorized as Métis under Canadian legislation.

7   Information gathered from community consultations in Lac La Biche, Alberta. Community members from the Conklin area confirm this practice.

8   This descriptor, "fished out," refers to the depletion of the species that had customarily been relied on as a food source.

9   There are currently twenty management agreements in effect in Alberta. This map effectively illustrates how all of the province's natural forest area has been licensed to the pulp industry.

10 Here "legal system" refers to both administrative law mechanisms – for example, environmental control authorities such as the Alberta Energy and Utilities Board – as well as standard civil litigation through the courts.

11 Although not the subject of this report, these positions tend to be seasonal, temporary, and not at the managerial level. Accordingly, the sustainability or long-term benefit of such employment opportunities is tempered.

12 *Constitution Act, 1982,* being Schedule B to the *Canada Act 1982* (U.K.), 1982, c. 11. The majority of cases heard by the Supreme Court of Canada since 1982 involving Aboriginal defendants have involved claims based on unextinguished Aboriginal and/or treaty rights pursuant to section 35 of the *Constitution Act, 1982.* These include *R. v. Sparrow* (1990); *R. v. Van der Peet* (1996); *R. v. Badger* (1996); *R. v. Gladstone* (1996); *R. v. Powley* (2003); and *R. v. Blais* (2003).

13 It should be noted that there may be other laws that negatively impact Aboriginal peoples' exercise of traditional practices. Further, laws and enforcement in other jurisdictions were beyond the scope of this project.

14 *Alberta Wildlife Regulations,* Alta. Reg. 143/97.

15 To illustrate this fact, see section 138 of the *Alberta Wildlife Regulations, supra* note 14, which mandates possession of a licence and a bill of lading if the transporter is not the licensee. Where certain species of wildlife are involved, a wildlife manifest may be required, and the specifics of this requirement are detailed in the Wildlife Regulations.

16 This was the first Supreme Court of Canada decision to recognize that Métis have existing Aboriginal rights to hunt for subsistence purposes.

17 This information was shared at the final Edmonton roundtable by workshop participants who requested that their identities not be disclosed.

18 See *The Encyclopedia of Saskatchewan,* "Cold Lake (Primrose Lake) Air Weapons Range, 4 Wing," http://esask.uregina.ca/entry/cold_lake_primrose_lake_air_weapons_range_4_wing. html for a description of the Cold Lake/Primrose Lake Air Weapons Range claim.

19 It should be noted that the Court in *Powley* did not provide any concrete definition of Métis. Consequently, if litigation is the context, the courts would need to determine on a case-by-case basis whether certain communities constitute Métis communities and, *then,* whether or not the practices constitute rights to be accorded constitutional protection. This discussion is beyond the scope of this report but is covered extensively in Weber (2005).

20 For example, see http://www.afga.org/documents.html?fileID=80 to view the Interim Métis Harvesting Agreement made between the Métis Nation of Alberta and the Alberta government. In other jurisdictions, interim agreements have similarly been negotiated and entered into, http://www.metisnation.ca/press/07-june12.html. Note, however, that the enforceability

of these and other similar agreements is questionable. None refers to the arrangements being based on the recognition of Aboriginal rights. It follows, then, that in the absence of substantive changes to legislation to reflect the terms of the agreements, provincial discretion will prevail. This concern was noted by participants at the roundtable discussions (see Appendix B at the end of this chapter). It should further be noted that the interim Métis harvesting agreements were terminated by the Alberta government in July 2007.

21 With respect to the claims of Métis people for protection of their traditional practices (which are often the same as First Nations or Inuit people), the test set out in the 2003 Supreme Court of Canada decision in *R. v. Powley* (2003) applies.

22 The Supreme Court of Canada first contemplated the meaning of section 35 in the landmark decision *R. v. Sparrow* (1990). Speaking for the Court, Chief Justice Dickson (as he then was) held that the Crown must prove a "clear and plain intention" to extinguish an Aboriginal right and that Aboriginal rights were not to be interpreted as frozen in time.

23 "The nature of government regulations cannot be determinative of the content and scope of an existing aboriginal right. Government policy can however, regulate the exercise of that right, but such regulation must be in keeping with s. 35(1)" (*R. v. Sparrow* 1990, para. 44 [per Dickson CJ and La Forest J]).

24 Originating in the province of British Columbia, the Haida Nation and Taku River Tlingit First Nations sought injunctory relief against the province of British Columbia to stop logging activities on their traditional territory. In November 2004, the Supreme Court of Canada rendered their decisions in these two cases. *Haida Nation v. British Columbia (Minister of Forests)* (2004) and *Taku River Tlingit First Nation v. British Columbia (Project Assessment Director)* (2004).

25 International Covenant on Civil and Political Rights, 23 March 1976, G.A. Res. 2200A (XXI), 21, U.N. GAOR Supp. (No. 16), 52, UN Doc. A/6316 (1966), 999 U.N.T.S. 171.

26 Optional Protocol to the International Covenant on Civil and Political Rights, http://www2.ohchr.org/english/law/ccpr.htm.

27 In addition, the Organization of American States is currently drafting an American Declaration on the Rights of Indigenous Peoples, to which member states will be subject on adoption and ratification.

28 Mary Dann is now deceased, having passed away as a result of an accident in the spring of 2005.

29 Proposed American Declaration on the Rights of Indigenous People, approved by the IACHR at its 1333rd sess., 26 February 1997, Doc. OEA.Ser.L/V/II.95, doc. 7 rev. (1997). The declaration has not been finalized and is still in the negotiation phase.

30 In the case of the Danns, the United States has reportedly refused to implement the findings of the commission and, instead, has proceeded to develop the traditional lands. To make matters worse, the state has taken steps against the Danns and other Shoshone for trespass and has seized and sold livestock without compensating the Danns.

References

Al-Pac Environmental Impact Assessment Review Board. 1990. *The Proposed Alberta-Pacific Pulp Mill: Report of the EIA Review Board.* Edmonton: Alberta Environment.

Bird, M., and A. Sutherland. 1991. *Living Kindness: The Dream of My Life: The Memoirs of Métis Elder, Madeline Bird.* Yellowknife: Outcrop.

Canada. 1981. *Socio-Economic Profiles for Northern Alberta Indian Bands for 1977.* Ottawa: Department of Indian Affairs and Northern Development.

Daniel, R.C. 1970. *Indian Rights and Hinterland Resources: The Case of Northern Alberta,* master's thesis, University of Alberta, Edmonton [unpublished].

Dolha, L. 2004. "Métis Fighting over Implementation of Right to Harvest." *First Nations Drum,* http://www.firstnationsdrum.com/Winter%202004/CulMetis.htm.

Durkheim, E. 1938. *The Rules of Sociological Method,* 8th ed., ed. George E.G. Catlin, trans. Sarah A. Solovay and John H. Mueller. Chicago: University of Chicago Press.

Espiritu, A.A. 1997. "'Aboriginal Nations': Natives in Northwest Siberia and Northern Alberta." In *Contested Arctic: Indigenous Peoples, Industrial States, and the Circumpolar Environment,* ed. E. Alden Smith and J. McCarter, 51-57. Seattle and London: University of Washington Press.

Graham, K., and E. Peters. 2002. *Aboriginal Communities and Urban Sustainability*. CPRN Discussion Paper No. F/27. Ottawa: Canadian Policy Research Networks.

Northern Alberta Development Council. 1984. *Research Report: Trapping in Northern Alberta*. Peace River: Northern Alberta Development Council.

–. 1991. *Profiles of Regions and Communities in Northern Alberta*. Peace River: Northern Alberta Development Council.

Piepenburg, R.L., et al. 1974. *Wabasca-Desmarais Land Tenure Research Project: Report of Community Survey*. Wabasca-Desmarais: Resident Workers of Wabasca-Desmarais.

Ross, M.M. 2003. *Aboriginal Peoples and Resource Development in Northern Alberta*. Calgary: Canadian Institute of Resources Law, University of Calgary.

Stavenhagen, R. 2002. *Report of the Special Rapporteur on the Situation of Human Rights and Fundamental Freedoms of Indigenous Peoples, Mr. Rodolfo Stavenhagen, Submitted Pursuant to Commission Resolution 2001/57*. UN Doc. E/CN.4/2002/97, United Nations Human Rights Council.

Strong, Hall and Associates. 1980. *Wabasca and Pelican Projects: Community Impact Assessment*. Calgary: Gulf Canada Resources.

Weber, L. 2005. *Metis Aboriginal Rights in a Post-Powley Era*, LL.M. thesis, University of Manitoba, Winnipeg [unpublished].

Weber, L., and C. Weber-Pillwax. 2005. *Pimatsowin Weyasowewina: Aboriginal Harvesting Practices Considered*. Ottawa: Law Commission of Canada.

Weber-Pillwax, C. 1999. "Indigenous Research Methodology." *Journal of Educational Thought* 33, 1: 31-45.

List of Cases

Bernard Ominayak and the Lubicon Lake Band v. Canada. 1984. Communication No. 167/1984, Doc. CCPR/C/38/D/167/1984, United Nations Human Rights Committee.

Mary and Carrie Dann v. United States. 2002. Case No. 11.140, Report 75/02, Annual Report of the Inter-American Commission on Human Rights.

Guerin v. The Queen, [1984] 2 S.C.R. 335.

Haida Nation v. British Columbia (Minister of Forests), [2004] 3 S.C.R. 511.

R. v. Badger, [1996] 1 S.C.R. 771.

R. v. Blais, [2003] 2 S.C.R. 236.

R. v. Breaker, [2000] A.B.P.C. 179.

R. v. Ferguson, [2001] A.B.P.C. 215.

R. v. Gladstone, [1996] 2 S.C.R. 723.

R. v. Jacko, [1998] A.B.P.C. 10.

R. v. Lamouche, [2000] A.B.Q.B. 461.

R. v. Powley, [2003] 2 S.C.R. 207.

R. v. Quinney, [2003] A.B.P.C. 47.

R. v. Rodgers, [1998] A.B.P.C. 127.

R. v. Sparrow, [1990] 1 S.C.R. 1075.

R. v. Van der Peet, [1996] 2 S.C.R. 507.

Taku River Tlingit First Nation v. British Columbia (Project Assessment Director), [2004] 3 S.C.R. 550.

4

Incivilities: The Representations and Reactions of French Public Housing Residents in Montreal City

Frédéric Lemieux and Nadège Sauvêtre

In recent years, incivility has been the object of particular attention from public actors in Quebec. For example, a security review conducted over the course of 2003 by the Montreal Municipal Police Service (MMPS) revealed that incivilities remain a central concern within the community, whose members expressed a strong sense of insecurity in the face of such incivilities. To attend to this concern, the MMPS implemented local responses in 2004, which later translated into the strategic distribution of a police presence in "hot" neighbourhoods and the development of partnerships with local community organizations. The review also identified twenty-six new call codes, with incivilities broken down into two categories: (1) physical disorder (signs of incivility), and (2) social disorder (acts of incivility). In the first category, we find "incivilities" that involve the degradation of the environment (for example, graffiti, rubbish, vandalism, and so on). The second category comprises social behaviours that are regarded as inappropriate and are frowned upon by the community (for example, verbal aggression, disorderly parking, noisy neighbours, presence of prostitutes and solicitation, and so on). The codification of such behaviours by the Montreal police department is clearly setting the first stage for the criminalization of incivilities. The choice of intervention against perceived incivilities favoured by public authorities needs to be called into question because incivility is a matter of security that falls more under the social order than under the legal domain. Thus, we ought to ask the question: Are these the sort of acts that require criminalization and penal regulation?

In fact, a considerable number of studies have shown that uncivil behaviours are a determining factor in the deterioration of interpersonal ties between social actors and, by extension, in the aggregation of disorder within difficult urban zones. Further, several North American studies have shown that communities that are marked by weak social cohesion, instability in interpersonal networks, and an absence of collective mobilization are also distinguished by higher levels of disorder. Yet empirical studies of the ecology of crime in disadvantaged neighbourhoods have often failed to cast attention on the specific structures, such as social housing, that make up these urban zones. Social housing is characterized by different modes of management that generate variable degrees of collective mobilization and social control. Thus, by taking an interest in the governance modes at work in the most impoverished communities, and the underlying social processes, public authorities would be better equipped to understand the mechanisms for regulating deviant behaviours, even within difficult neighbourhoods.

As noted, research on the issue of incivilities and disorder in disadvantaged neighbourhoods tends to underestimate the relevance of the institutional context in which the social actors exist. They often fail to acknowledge that disadvantaged urban zones are composed of "microstructures" in which different modes of governance affect the living conditions of individuals, interpersonal relationships, and the capacity for collective mobilization. In Montreal, disadvantaged neighbourhoods are characterized by the presence of several types of social housing. For the purposes of this research, we call particular attention to two managerial or governance frameworks that, depending on the case, generate variable degrees of responsibilization and collective mobilization. The first involves low-income housing in which a public type of governance has been adopted – that is, a model in which the state takes charge of residents by defining their housing conditions. The second involves housing co-operatives, which operate essentially on the basis of a process of democratic participation in which residents have a right to examine and affect how their housing is managed. In effect, co-operatives are managed by their members and are equipped with a board of directors, offering residents the possibility of participating in devising strategies for maintaining or improving their living conditions.

Furthermore, some empirical studies have shown that structural factors, such as the concentration of disadvantages, can weaken the capacity of communities to deploy collective intervention strategies. By contrast, those communities that have been able to maintain a high level of social cohesion are better equipped to counterbalance the criminogenic effects that are linked to structural factors. Thus, we postulate that the operating rules inherent in the mode of management in social housing shape the perceptions of individuals with regard to what is or is not acceptable to a particular membership group, affect the degree of tolerance of the residents when confronted with uncivil behaviour, and exert an influence on the process of regulating incivilities. In addition, we know that the notion of incivility remains ambiguous due to the influence exerted by factors that act on individual perceptions. The definition of incivility emanates from subjective representations that refer to the mores and moral considerations of the actors who are subjected to, or in the vicinity of, incivility. Thus, knowing that the residents of social housing hold varied socio-economic and socio-demographic characteristics, it is plausible that these attributes shape the subjective representation of incivility and modulate the intensity of the disapproval from residents in response to uncivil behaviour.

In this chapter, we will draw the reader's attention to the points of view held by francophone residents of social housing in Montreal who are confronted by incivilities on a daily basis. The perspective of these social actors is vested with a crucial importance at a crossroads where public powers and communities will need to find lasting solutions to this social phenomenon. Our research is especially interested in the representations and intervention strategies used by the residents themselves to deal with incivilities. On the one hand, it is plausible that the different personal characteristics of the residents of social housing can contribute to their subjective perception of incivility and their varied intensity of disapproval, as well as their intervention strategies, in dealing with uncivil behaviour. On the other hand, it is also possible that the modes of governance in social housing can exert an influence on the representations and reactions of individuals.[1] As mentioned previously, we find two main types of management in the city of Montreal, one that is geared towards state/public responsibility for the residents' housing conditions (low-income housing) and one that is geared towards residents' collective responsibility for housing conditions (co-operatives). We argue that the operational rules inherent in the governance of housing complexes modulate what is or is not accepted by the community, set a tolerance limit with regard to incivilities, and influence the process of regulating uncivil behaviour.

Incivilities

Preliminary Distinctions

Philip Milburn (2000, 338) suggests that the inability of researchers to clearly delineate the concept of incivility has to do with the fact that often these varied behaviours "are only experienced as uncivil by those who are the witnesses or victims" [translation]. According to Albert D. Biderman et al. (1967), disorder or incivilities are easily perceptible signs that result in unruly and disruptive behaviours taking place in the community. Studies by Christiane Bonnemain (2000, 60) suggest that incivilities involve interpersonal conflicts (within the family, the neighbourhood), impairment of the enjoyment of premises (due to noise, obstructions), social misconduct (impoliteness, swearing), and misdemeanours (vandalism, destruction of property). Wesley Skogan (1990) categorizes the manifestations of incivility by type into social incivilities and physical incivilities. It is important to note that this categorization proposed by Skogan appears to have been central to the Montreal police department code call reform regarding incivilities. The social form of incivility designates experiences that can be directly perceived by the social actors involved, such as impoliteness, loitering, and noise making. The physical form, by contrast, designates signs that suggest an unhealthy, deteriorating environment, such as litter, graffiti, and vandalism. In general, research shows that physical incivilities correspond to recurring, lasting behaviour, while social incivilities tend to be expressed as a series of episodic events.

Sebastian Roché (1996) groups uncivil behaviour into four categories: degradation (for example, graffiti, fires); neglect (for example, litter, filth); spontaneous tension (for example, aggressive or threatening behaviour); and recurring conflicts (for example, obstructions, noise). Finally, Robert Sampson and Stephen Raudenbush (2001) measure the concept of disorder using the following elements: the presence of litter, graffiti, abandoned vehicles, needles, syringes; the occurrence of loitering; the consumption of alcohol in public; and the presence of groups of youths showing signs of affiliation with a street gang. Overall, uncivil behaviour refers to a wide variety of events and situations that disrupt the everyday social order and contribute to an increased fear of crime.

Studies by Roché (2000) show that behaviour that is considered to be uncivil is judged less severely than actual infractions of law. Using data from a number of surveys of respondents from different urban environments, the author finds that physical harm and theft are less tolerated than degradations, grime, and a lack of tidiness. However, these results do not shed any light on the specific dimensions of behaviour that affect respondents' perceptions of the seriousness of the incivilities. Drawing from research that deals with the perceived gravity of criminal acts, we can postulate that the severity of the social actor's judgment of uncivil behaviours would be modulated by a set of dimensions, including (1) the nature of the incivility; (2) the aggravating or attenuating circumstances; (3) the personal characteristics of the respondents; and (4) the standards in effect within their particular social group (Sellin and Wolfgang 1964; Ackman, Normandeau, and Turner 1967; Normandeau 1970; Wolfgang et al. 1985; Hamilton and Sanders 1988; Cusson 1998; Hough and Roberts 1999). Thus, an analysis of the perceived gravity of various types of disorder enables us to better understand the process by which uncivil behaviours are qualified and which modes of intervention are favoured by the social actors involved.

Controlling Incivilities: Public Intervention and Community Response
Even though many incivilities may appear to be relatively harmless forms of behaviour, they are nevertheless strongly associated with a fear of crime and a feeling of insecurity (Roché 1996). The presence of disorder in the urban environment contributes to an increasing mistrust among members of the community and generates a state of heightened vigilance, which is activated by the fear of being victimized. Thus, incivilities represent a break

with the order of everyday life, which weakens the social ties between citizens and erodes their trust in public institutions (Roché 1994). In effect, a decline in order in disadvantaged urban zones, manifested as a proliferation of in-civilities, is thought to trigger the flight of social actors and to create favour-able conditions for the development of predatory delinquency. On this point, the "broken windows" theory, proposed by James Q. Wilson and George Kelling (1982), suggests that, if in a given neighbourhood broken windows are not replaced and the authorities do not seek to punish those responsible for such degradation, then acts of incivility will multiply rapidly. In such a context, the authors posit that inaction on the part of social actors and public authorities sends the implicit message that the rules of proper conduct can be ignored without transgressors incurring any negative consequences. This assertion is also supported by the works of Marcus Felson (1998), whose results indicate that deterioration in living conditions and the proliferation of deviant behaviours of lesser importance contribute to the decay of a neighbourhood and an increase in serious crime.

Over the course of the 1980s and 1990s, the "broken windows" theory became, in a way, the dominant "doctrine" in the strategies that were imple-mented by the authorities in both North America and Europe to hold neighbourhood deterioration in check and block the conditions precedent for an increase in criminality. As a result, the theory became central to a considerable number of repressive and preventive police initiatives in these jurisdictions. This doctrine is reflected in the zero-tolerance model, the system of community policing, the problem resolution approach, and local security contracts (a French model of collective security). Building upon a dualistic logic, the quasi-totality of the strategies being deployed by public actors has taken as their target the most disadvantaged communities within the major urban agglomerations. First, there was a preference for more formal control by increasing police presence while, at the same time, advocating intransigence towards those who disrupt public order. However, the broken window approach posed numerous limits. Reducing actual levels of disorder will not remedy psychological discomfort since this discomfort stems from more insidious sources (for example, racial issues, stereotypes, structural factors, and so on). Simply removing graffiti may lead to nothing in terms of stabilizing the neighbourhood (Sampson and Raudenbush 2004). Faced with the limited success of such an approach, political decision makers also turned to preventive projects, the main objective of which was to rehabilitate the most disadvantaged individuals, notably by making it easier for them to access training and conflict resolution programs as well as workshops on parenting skills development (Earls and Carlson 1996).

Preventive strategies to reduce disorder represent a laudable effort on the part of authorities. Nonetheless, by placing the focus on individualized programs, public actors have locked themselves into a process whereby social problems are fragmented and the influence of the structural factors and the social processes that are central to the urban ecology are neglected. For example, a number of studies have shown that there is a link between poverty, social inequality, and urban violence (Curry and Spergel 1988; Smith and Jarjoura 1988). With regard to residential mobility, we see the presence of a positive correlation between residential instability and serious crimes (Block 1979; Sampson 1985, 1986; Taylor and Covington 1988). In the matter of ethnic heterogeneity, there is a strong connection between the racial composition of neighbourhoods and violent crime. However, this relationship disappears when socio-economic and family structure factors are kept constant (Messner and Tardiff 1986). Indeed, the proportion of single-parent households and the level of poverty seem to capture the effects of racial composition on the rate of violent crime (Smith and Jarjoura 1988).

Even though all of these empirical studies deal with the ties between structural factors and urban violence, it must be remembered that the results indicate the criminogenic effects of social disorganization. The theory of social disorganization refers to the incapacity of certain communities to carry out common objectives, such as maintaining or improving living conditions and regulating deviant behaviour (Messner and Rosenfeld 1994; Sampson and Groves 1989). The inverse reasoning is equally true since this theoretical approach makes it possible to understand neighbourhoods or suburbs as complex systems of family ties and networks of friends and acquaintances, which together generate a process of ongoing socialization that ensures that social control is maintained among the members of the community (Bursik 1988). Thus, the theory of social disorganization suggests that the stronger the density and interconnectedness of interpersonal networks in a community are the better the community will be able to ward off deviant behaviour and the victimization of its members (Sampson 2002).

This theoretical approach is particularly interested in the study of incivilities because, as Roché points out, the proliferation of incivilities in a neighbourhood increases not only the feeling of insecurity but also the rates of crime once the informal mechanisms of social control start to deteriorate. Yet an analysis of the structural factors alone is not enough to explain the variation in disorder from one neighbourhood to the next. In effect, while the concentration of disadvantages can cause an increase in the level of disorder, other forces can counterbalance or neutralize the criminogenic effects of structural factors. This latter premise supposes that the desire to live in a secure social environment can encourage, among the members of a community, the deployment of common strategies that are intended to guarantee order in their living environment (Sampson and Raudenbush 2001). On the neighbourhood scale, the willingness of residents to intervene beyond public strategies of formal control depends essentially on the capacity for mobilization and the trust between members of a given community.

Taken together, mutual trust and the willingness to act for the well-being of everyone concerned constitute what Sampson, Raudenbush, and Earls (1998) call collective effectiveness. An empirical validation of this concept on levels of criminality shows that the more the residents of a neighbourhood uphold close ties and the more they mobilize to reach common objectives, the lower the rates of violent crime (homicides), even when the concentration of social disadvantages – residential instability, racial composition, and the socio-economic and socio-demographic characteristics of the residents – is kept constant (Sampson, Raudenbush, and Earls 1998; Morenoff, Sampson, and Raudenbush 2001; Sampson and Raudenbush 2001).

Incivilities and the Governance of Social Housing
Empirical studies of disadvantaged neighbourhoods contain a considerable number of methodological limits (Sampson 2002, 236). In effect, we can see that they presuppose that such factors as distrust and the incapacity of residents to mobilize, sparse and dysfunctional interpersonal networks, the weakening of social control in public spaces, an absence of institutional and organizational bases, and weak participation by residents in volunteer associations increase the risk of public disorder and interpersonal violence. In addition, we see that research conducted on incivilities, disorder, and delinquency has primarily examined the prevailing situation in disadvantaged neighbourhoods, without really paying attention to the "microstructures" involved, notably social housing.

During the 1970s, one strategy that Western public authorities used in the fight against poverty was the development of a vast network of social housing. These state interventions were intended to enable access to minimum housing conditions for the most impoverished communities. Today the residents of social housing are increasingly poor, multi-ethnic, single-parent households, and socially isolated without resources. This geographic concentration of disadvantages inevitably poses the problem of an aggregation of disorder and degradation in the living conditions of the communities that live in these residential spaces. Moreover, the French model of *"cités"* has shown us all too well the problems of disorder that are tied to exclusion and the concentration of poverty (Boyer 2000; Roché 2000; Merlin 1999).

Studies by William Brill (1975) identify the cause of disorder in social housing as weak social structure, the absence of support groups, a lack of trust, and all of those factors that inhibit the capacity of a community to protect itself and for its members to help one another. Such circumstances may lead to varying degrees of deterioration of the social fabric, depending on the characteristics of the interventions made by public authorities. The authorities of the city of Montreal avoided building "ghettos," relying rather on a model of blocks dispersed within neighbourhoods. And yet the problem remains fundamentally the same – demobilization, deresponsibilization, and a lack of social cohesion and social control. Studies by Victor Rouse and Herb Rubenstein (1978) indicate that the problem of deviance that afflicts social housing is associated with a lack of both social cohesion and informal social control. These authors also report that these weaknesses at the level of social mechanisms contribute to the vulnerability of residents in the face of crime. They also reveal the influence that social cohesion and the level of informal social control (collective effectiveness) have on the levels of criminality in low-income housing.

According to Jeffrey Fagan et al. (1998), the manifestations of disorder and incivilities in social housing are the consequences of a system that is deficient in managing living conditions. Moreover, studies by Susan Saegert, Gary Winkel, and Charles Swartz (2002) show that the implementation of social programs that promote the development of the informal social capital of residents has tended to lower the levels of criminality in public housing in New York City. In effect, the authors conclude that the wealth of informal social capital (measured in terms of resident participation in tenants' committees, the pro-social standards of tenants, and formal organizations within social housing) is directly tied to a reduction in different types of crime. The results of this study indicate that disorder is not endemic to communities that reside in low-income housing and that a deeper knowledge of the mechanisms of governance in these communities is needed (for example, organizational structure and administrative rules) in order to locate the dysfunctional elements (Weisel 1998). In addition, the works of Walter Dekeseredy et al. (2004) show that public authorities need to spend more money in the public housing sector and avoid financing the construction of oversized housing in poor urban areas. They also highlight the importance of building a partnership between public and private sectors to develop housing subsidy and refurbishment programs, improve public transportation, and create job opportunities for youths.

Methodology

For this study, we chose to use field surveys in the form of structured interviews (questionnaires) with 364 francophone residents in social housing, of whom 217 were from low-income housing and 147 were from co-operatives.[2] We also limited our study to five neighbourhoods in the city of Montreal: Centre Sud; Hochelaga-Maisonneuve; Mercier; Plateau Mont-Royal; and Ville Marie.[3] An analysis of the personal characteristics of the respondents indicates that there are few differences between the two populations studied in terms of socio-demographic characteristics examined: age, sex, ethnic group, and marital status. By contrast, it seems that the levels of schooling and income are strongly associated with the living environment. Put another way, the residents of low-income housing are more socio-economically disadvantaged than the members of co-operatives.

Note that this difference between the two groups can be explained primarily through the criteria inherent in the selection of tenants. That is, in order to be admitted to low-income housing (LIH), applicant income must not exceed the poverty line (below approximately $25,000, depending on the family size). Yet co-operatives, unlike LIH, are based upon socio-economic diversity among their members. Persons who wish to live in a co-operative and become members must formally agree to respect the operating rules set down in Article 4 of the *Cooperatives Act*.[4] This agreement holds great importance because it grants members a substantial reduction in their housing fees, conditional upon their involvement in managing the co-operative. Even though housing co-operatives use selection criteria that are geared towards a mix of income levels, we nonetheless consider them to be a form of social housing because most co-operativess receive "public" financial aid, which enables them to offer their members rents that are typically below rents in the private market. For the purposes of this study, we chose co-operatives that reserve 25 percent of their rental space for a low-income clientele, which ensures congruence in the comparison of the two living environments.

Manifestations and Representations of Incivility among Residents of Social Housing

With regard to representations, our results indicate that a high number of respondents found it difficult to define the notion of incivility in their own words. The analyses herein reveal that a considerable proportion of these respondents reside in low-income housing. By comparison, the members of co-operatives found it easier to express their concept of incivility. Nonetheless, the operationalization of this concept enabled us to note that respondents are able to describe incivility, albeit in different terms and based on various manifestations. Thus, when we asked respondents about the meaning they attributed to the concept of incivility, our results indicate that 58 percent associate incivility with "a lack of proper manners," while 27 percent associate it with "a failure to respect the established rules in their housing complex," another 5 percent associate it with "an infraction against the law," and the remaining 10 percent do not know what this concept refers to.

It is interesting to note that social actors, in contrast to the institutional actors surveyed in Bonnemain's study (2000), are less likely to associate incivility with behaviour that is legally punishable. The difficulty of defining a concept as abstract as incivility is hardly surprising in and of itself. Indeed, it was to be expected that the conceptual representation of this notion would not be accessible to all respondents. On this point, when controlling for the type of management, we found that it was primarily individuals who self-identify as visible minorities, those with a declared income below the poverty line, and the heads of single-parent households who have the greatest difficulty in explaining the concept of incivility. We would do well to remember that incivility is first a semantic artefact developed in political discourse and taken up by the legal system in order to qualify a complex social phenomenon.

Using a list of twenty-one incidents, respondents were asked to identify behaviours that they consider uncivil. This list included legally punishable behaviours (for example, assault and theft), behaviours tied to physical disorder (for example, graffiti and rubbish), and behaviours tied to incivilities of a social nature (for example, insults and noise). Although it may be difficult to organize the results into a clearly defined typology, they nonetheless indicate that the incidents that received a large consensus are, generally speaking, associated with physical disorder (for example, degradation of the environment) and a lack of hygiene.[5] After these behaviours come those that result in an alteration of social ties and interpersonal trust. More specifically, these are behaviours that are likely to generate tension and interpersonal conflicts.[6] Finally, those situations that trigger a strong divergence of opinion from respondents are those associated with marginal behaviour.[7] Consequently, a majority of respondents do not perceive the actions of squeegee kids or itinerants to be uncivil behaviour.

Generally speaking, our results indicate that residents in LIH and co-operatives agree upon which acts are or are not considered incivilities. Nonetheless, it appears that, compared to residents in LIH, the members of co-operatives are less categorical about describing behaviours associated with marginality as uncivil. We also see the same tendency when it comes to legally punishable behaviours. In effect, a greater number of residents in LIH than co-operative members consider physical assault and theft to be incivilities. These statistically significant differences suggest that the members of co-operatives take a more nuanced approach towards qualifying acts that are legally punishable and those that have to do with marginality than residents of LIH. Yet the differences between the representations of residents in LIH and those of co-operative members can also be explained by the socio-economic status of respondents. Indeed, our results show that only the levels of schooling and income distinguish respondent responses in terms of marginal behaviours and criminal acts, and these relationships are statistically significant. More precisely, the results indicate that those respondents who have a low level of schooling and a declared income below the poverty line are more inclined to consider marginal behaviours (for instance, the presence of squeegee kids), and to regard criminal acts (for instance, stealing goods), as incivilities.

With regard to the manifestations of uncivil behaviour, we asked each subject to indicate the number of times he or she was a witness to, or a victim of, each of the twenty-one situations on the list over the course of the six months preceding the survey.[8] Using the information collected, we drew up a scale of exposure by adding the frequency of victimization and

Table 4.1

Frequency of incivilities according to personal characteristics of respondents, as a function of personal characteristics and the type of management (variance analysis, n = 329)

Factor	Mean	F	Sig
Model		33.92	0.01
Ethnic group			
Caucasian	12.64	0.69	0.40
Visible minority	9.47		
Education			
Post-secondary diploma completed	10.66	0.04	0.83
High school diploma or less	11.44		
Family income			
$19,999 or less	11.64	0.09	0.75
$20,000 or more	10.46		
Type of management			
LIH	15.25	4.89	0.02
Co-operatives	6.38		

the number of times where the respondents affirmed that they had been witness to incidents that they considered incivilities. Our results show that the respondents' weekly exposure to each of the twenty-one behaviours on the list is relatively low. Nonetheless, we do see that respondents are on average exposed more often – twice or more per week – to behaviours of a *physical* nature that are connected with an "unhealthy" environment. A smaller proportion of respondents were exposed to disorders of a *social* nature (one to two times per week). These results are consistent with those from Skogan (1990), which underscored the persistent and lasting character of physical incivilities and the episodic nature of interpersonal tensions. More-over, we observed that, in general, exposure was not associated with the representations of the respondents. That is, our analyses indicate that the average frequency of exposure does not determine perceptions as to the civil or uncivil nature of incidents on the list. This observation is particularly interesting because it suggests that the fact of qualifying behaviour as uncivil is not so much founded on the *frequency* of irritating situations as it is on a normative judgment.

In addition, the results indicate that the type of management in social housing is a determining factor in the propensity to be exposed to incivilities. Residents in LIH report that they are more often exposed to incivilities than residents in co-operatives. We also see that respondents with limited educa-tion, who identify as Caucasian, or who declare low family income report more exposure to incivilities than the residents of co-operatives. In order to separate the effects that are attributable to personal characteristics and the type of management, we undertook a multivariate analysis (UNIANOVA).[9] The results presented in Table 4.1 show that, when personal characteristics are kept constant, the living environment remains the only factor that is significantly associated with the individual being a witness and/or victim of uncivil behaviour ($r^2 = .14$). This result is particularly interesting because it shows that the low frequency of occurrence of incivilities in co-operatives cannot be attributed to an effect induced by the urban ecology as a result of our sampling method.

Perceptions of Incivility among Residents in Social Housing
By reference to the list of twenty-one incidents, we asked respondents to report on the emotions that they experienced in response to behaviours they had previously identified as incivilities. Specifically, respondents were asked about their perceptions (their feelings) upon being confronted with each of the twenty-one incident types. These responses were then categorized as follows: (1) indifference; (2) insecurity; (3) anger; or (4) discomfort. Based on the responses from the participants, we prepared a scale for each feeling experienced, taking into account only those incidents that were perceived by residents as incivilities. These measurement scales enabled us to analyze the discriminating effects of personal characteristics and management type.

In general, we can state that uncivil behaviours *do* disturb the residents of social housing. In fact, our results indicate that only a small proportion of respondents express a feeling of indifference in the face of incidents that they qualify as uncivil. In more than half of the proposed situations (twelve times out of twenty-one), incivilities triggered anger in the respondents, particularly when it was a matter of an unhealthy environment, theft, vandalism, and incivilities of a social nature. Moreover, it is interesting to note that the majority of incidents featured on the reference list generate little insecurity among respondents. Nonetheless, we see that behaviour that seems to be innocuous, such as "the presence of loiterers" and "the presence of squeegee kids," elicits more insecurity than an "assault against a person." On this point, we note that over the course of several interviews many respondents in LIH associated loiterers with the presence of "seedy" characters or vagabonds having a bad reputation. This result suggests that insecurity in the face of "marginal" behaviours may originate in the fear of being victimized.

Variance analyses show that women and respondents who are ethnic minorities are less indifferent to uncivil behaviours. By contrast, the respondents of Caucasian origin feel greater anger in the face of incivilities than do respondents from ethnic minorities. In addition, we see that respondents who declare a household income above $20,000 are those who experience the most embarrassment when confronted with uncivil behaviour. Moreover, we see that women and respondents who declare a low income feel more insecurity due to incivilities. Finally, it appears that the type of housing management is linked to three of the four emotions in the study, namely discomfort, insecurity, and indifference. The mean analysis indicates that more members of co-operatives experience a feeling of embarrassment in the face of uncivil behaviour. By contrast, more residents of LIII experience feelings of insecurity and/or indifference in the face of incivilities.

The results for the feelings triggered by the occurrence of uncivil behaviours led us to examine the perceived seriousness of disorder. An analysis of the perception of the seriousness of disorder is essential if we wish to know what principal dimensions are associated with the severity of judgment from respondents when faced with uncivil behaviours and if we wish to better understand how the dynamic that underlies the process of social reaction is articulated. In order to measure this concept, we took inspiration from surveys on the perception of the relativity of crime seriousness (Sellin and Wolfgang 1964; Wolfgang et al. 1985). The measure of relative seriousness was distributed across four grids presented separately to respondents in order to avoid memorized responses. For each scenario proposed to respondents, we varied the frequency, social proximity, and geographic proximity of disorders. Yet, in contrast to studies of the perception of crimes, we opted for a measure of seriousness that compared each uncivil act to the others rather than to a reference statement (module).[10]

First of all, we see that the scores for seriousness vary according to the nature of the uncivil behaviours involved (physical or social), according to frequency (more or less frequent), and according to their proximity (closer to or farther away from the respondents). The results indicate that the mean scores are higher for social incivilities than for physical incivilities. In effect, it appears that uncivil behaviours that alter social ties and interpersonal trust are perceived as more serious than incivilities that degrade the environment. This initial finding is consistent with studies conducted on the seriousness of crimes and showing that offences against the person were perceived as more serious than crimes against property. In addition, we see that respondents tend, on average, to accord higher scores for seriousness to criminal acts than to offences or to behaviours that are not legally punishable.[11] Thus, the weighted mean for these scenarios also respects a ranking according to which the more an uncivil behaviour is inscribed within the penal domain the more severely it is judged. On the one hand, these results are interesting because they qualify the classic studies on the severity of crimes by introducing acts that are outside the penal sphere. On the other hand, and contrary to studies by Roché (2000), our analyses show that the mean scores for severity attributed to incivilities are relatively high compared to legally punishable behaviours. These results indicate that, despite their innocuous nature, uncivil acts are of considerable concern to respondents.

Moreover, although the differences may be modest, our analyses show that respondents have a tendency to accord a higher severity score to behaviours of a recurring nature compared to isolated acts, and this is independent of the proximity of the incivility. In addition, independent of the frequency, we find that respondents accord a higher severity score to uncivil behaviours that occur within their housing complex (proximity). These results serve to confirm the hypothesis that perceived severity varies as a function of the nature of the act (physical or social), its frequency, and its geographic or social proximity.

From Table 4.2, it is possible to specify the ranking held by each of the uncivil behaviours presented to the respondents. The table was structured to present the mean scores attributed by respondents to each of the scenarios in the four grids.[12] First of all, with regard to the sample, we note from these rankings that the highest mean seriousness scores are attributed to assault (8.39), theft of goods (8.10), and vandalism (7.56), while the lowest mean seriousness scores are assigned to the presence of flyers (4.65) and to obstructions (5.81). Finally, we see that the mean seriousness scores granted to scenarios located in the centre of the continuum of seriousness show an increasing standardized weight, even while the difference in scores remains low, varying from 6.24 (noise) to 6.72 (loitering). These differences between the mean seriousness scores can be explained by intra-group and inter-group variance (Francis, Soothill, and Dittrich 2001). Indeed, our scale is composed of two broad categories of behaviours (1) behaviours that arise from a real intention to do harm;[13] and (2) behaviours that do *not* arise from a real intention to do harm.[14] In other words, the ranking of mean seriousness scores follows a logic that is comparable to the one seen in studies on the severity of crimes – that is, behaviours that receive an elevated score are those that emanate from a real intention to do harm. In addition, the standard deviations show that respondents have less difficulty agreeing on the perceived seriousness of acts such as assault, theft, and vandalism than for other types of behaviours.

Next we focused in particular on the differences that exist between management types and the perceived seriousness of uncivil behaviours. First, a longitudinal interpretation of Table 4.2 shows that a consensus exists on behaviours located at each extreme of the seriousness continuum. That is, whatever the living environment, respondents consider "throwing flyers on the floor" and "obstructing passageways with packages" as relatively harmless acts compared to "vandalizing the mailboxes," "stealing property," and "physical assault." Nonetheless, we see that the ranking of behaviours at the centre of the continuum differs with the living environment. Notwithstanding the behaviours on which there was consensus, an examination of the

Table 4.2

Mean scores of incivilities seriousness (scale 0-9)

Total sample	Flyers	Obstructions	Noise	Insults	Spitting	Loitering	Vandalism	Theft	Assault
(n = 364)	(4.65)	(5.81)	(6.24)	(6.32)	(6.59)	(6.72)	(7.56)	(8.10)	(8.39)
SD	2.54	2.21	2.14	2.19	2.20	2.19	1.75	1.34	1.33

Type of management	Flyers	Obstructions	Insults	Noise	Spitting	Loitering	Vandalism	Theft	Assault
LIH (n = 217)	(4.69)	(5.71)	(5.87)	(5.92)	(6.42)	(6.72)	(7.35)	(7.97)	(8.21)
SD	2.66	2.36	2.39	2.44	2.20	2.19	1.96	1.48	1.52

Co-operatives	Flyers	Obstructions	Noise	Insults	Spitting	Loitering	Vandalism	Theft	Assault
(n = 147)	(4.61)	(5.95)	(6.67)	(6.69)	(6.84)	(6.96)	(7.88)	(8.31)	(8.72)
SD	2.35	1.99	1.58	2.07	1.88	1.70	1.29	1.06	0.82

Notes:
SD: Standard deviation.
Scale: Least serious (0); most serious (9).

rankings indicates that the members of co-operatives consider the fact of insulting a person as more serious (first in centre) than any other behaviour located in the centre of the continuum, while, for residents in LIH, the most serious behaviour was the presence of loitering in and around their housing complex.

A priori, it seems difficult to explain the logic that underlies the ranking of behaviours located at the centre of the continuum. Nonetheless, the ranking held by insults and loitering may stem from values that are inherent to the living environments being studied. Thus, notwithstanding the behaviours for which there was a consensus, the members of co-operatives more severely judge uncivil behaviours that result in an alteration in social ties and interpersonal trust. In this case, it is clear that insults represent an attack on good neighbourly relationships and "threaten" social cohesion in some way, at least more than the fact of spitting, loitering, or creating a noise disturbance. By contrast, if we consider the fact that, on average, residents in LIH experience more insecurity when faced with uncivil behaviours than the members of co-operatives, the ranking held by loitering along the continuum of seriousness could be explained by the feeling it generates among residents in LIH. Moreover, recall that respondents often associated loitering with prowlers or vagrants with a bad reputation. Finally, we see that there exist between the two living environments statistically significant differences for assault, theft, vandalism, insults, and noise making. For these five behaviours, we see that the members of co-operatives assign higher mean seriousness scores than do residents in LIH.

Further, we see that none of the socio-demographic characteristics is associated with the judgment of respondents. By contrast, we do see that a statistically significant relationship exists between income and education level. On average, respondents declaring income above $20,000 and those who completed post-secondary studies assign higher seriousness scores. Overall, except for these two factors, the discriminating effect of personal characteristics is rather disparate, which makes any form of interpretation risky. In addition, although income and education levels are the most convincing personal characteristics in the assignment of seriousness scores, we cannot underestimate the fact that they reflect the living environment.

The Reactions of Residents When Faced with Uncivil Behaviour

We questioned respondents regarding the strategies they adopted when they were witness to, and/or victims of, uncivil behaviour. Each time a respondent affirmed having been exposed to one of the twenty-one behaviours on the list, he or she was asked to describe his or her reaction, as follows (1) do nothing; (2) react personally; (3) ask an acquaintance for help; (4) inform the superintendent; (5) complain to the municipal inspector; (6) complain to the managers of the housing complex; or (7) complain to the police. Our results indicate that the primary strategy used by respondents is to remain impassive when faced with uncivil behaviour (65.36 percent). By contrast, we find that those respondents that do react after having been witness to, or victim of, uncivil behaviour opt for *informal* intervention strategies. Indeed, when we aggregate the percentages associated with personal reactions, with the intervention of an acquaintance, and with informing the superintendent (26.62 percent), we see that respondents are less inclined to engage in a formal process (for example, contacting police, managers, city inspector) to report incivilities (8.02 percent). However, when we break reactions down by living environment, we find a number of interesting differences. First, we see that the choice of doing nothing after exposure to uncivil behaviour is slightly higher in co-operatives than in LIH (68.44 percent versus 63.57 percent). In addition, the members of co-operatives are less likely, when they react, to opt for formal intervention strategies (3.74 percent) compared to residents in LIH (10.49 percent).

The list submitted to respondents reveals a certain number of behaviours for which the perceived seriousness might influence the reactions of respondents when they witness or are victims of such acts. A variance analysis indicates that the fact of reacting or doing nothing is not associated with the perceived seriousness of uncivil behaviours. By contrast, it appears that the greater the perceived seriousness of an assault or insult (behaviours associated with interpersonal tensions) the more respondents opt for formal intervention strategies ($T = 1.99$; $p \leq .05$ and $T = 2.36$; $p \leq .05$). Nonetheless, the low number of statistically significant relationships does not allow us to conclude that the perceived seriousness of uncivil behaviours is associated with the reaction of respondents.

Moreover, the frequency of occurrence of incivilities is correlated to respondent reaction.[15] Thus, we see that the more often a person is a witness to, or a victim of, uncivil behaviour the more likely he or she is to react ($r = .43$; $p \leq .01$), and the more he or she tends to opt for intervention strategies that are formal in nature ($r = .30$; $p \leq .01$). In addition, the tests of means indicate the existence of statistically significant differences in respondent reactions depending on their living environment. On the one hand, residents in LIH react more to uncivil behaviours than the members of co-operatives ($T = 3.79$; $p \leq .01$). On the other hand, the members of co-operatives tend to favour informal intervention strategies, while residents in LIH tend to turn to formal strategies ($T = 4.67$; $p \leq .01$). Finally, we see that none of the socio-demographic or socio-economic factors significantly discriminates respondent reactions or intervention strategies.

Nevertheless, these results can only be considered partial because they do not enable us to dissociate the respective effects exerted by the living environment and the frequency of occurrence of incivilities on the reaction

Table 4.3

Reaction and intervention strategies of respondents, according to frequency of incivilities and type of management (covariate analysis)

Factors	Reaction scale ($n = 363$)		Intervention strategy scale ($n = 315$)	
	Mean	F-Test	Mean	F-Test
Model	–	847.76[b]	–	285.04[b]
Exposure	–	60.94[b]	–	16.46[b]
Type of management				
LIH	12.34	0.29	4.50	5.28[a]
Co-operative	12.12		3.72	

Notes:
[a] $p \leq .05$
[b] $p = .00$

of respondents. In order to compensate for this limit, we conducted covariance analyses (ANCOVA).[16] The results presented in Table 4.3 indicate that the living environment does not discriminate for the fact of reacting or remaining impassive, provided the frequency of uncivil behaviour remains constant. Although the model presents a relatively modest explained variance ($r^2 = .19$), it appears that the frequency of occurrence of incivilities (covariate variable) represents the best "predictor" of respondent reactions. By contrast, we see entirely different results when we conduct a second modelling regarding intervention strategies. Although the variance explained by our covariance model is relatively weak ($r^2 = .11$), the living environment remains statistically significant ($F = 5.28$; $p \leq .05$) in determining the intervention strategies used by respondents. When the frequency of incivilities is kept constant, the members of co-operatives favour informal intervention strategies (3.72) in contrast to residents in LIH, who turn to more formal modes of intervention (4.50).

Collective Effectiveness and the Control of Incivilities in Social Housing

Without minimizing the discriminating effects generated by the personal characteristics of respondents on the representations of incivilities, it appears that the type of management constitutes one of the most convincing factors in explicating the differences in the perception of the seriousness of uncivil behaviours and the intervention strategies taken by respondents. An interesting avenue to explore can be found in the level of social cohesion and the degree of informal social control present in the two communities studied. To better understand how these social processes are manifested, we drew up two scales measuring the degree of social cohesion and the level of informal social control in the living environment of respondents. The development of these scales was largely inspired by the work of Sampson, Raudenbush, and Earls (1998). The first scale measures respondents' feeling of belonging to their community (cohesion), notably the ties of trust and solidarity that they have developed within their neighbourhood. Meanwhile, the second scale measures the level of informal social control, according to the respondents' perception. More specifically, this scale involves examining the degree of efficacy demonstrated by residents of social housing in managing collective problems (for example, deviant behaviour, local problem, and so on).

According to the literature, informal social control is primarily determined by the degree of social cohesion among members of a given community. Variance analyses indicate that residents in LIH have a lower level of social cohesion than the members of co-operatives ($T = -6.84; p \leq .01$). In addition, we see that informal social control is also associated with the living environment – that is, residents in LIH report a lower mean level of informal social control than the members of co-operatives ($T = -8.28 ; p \leq .01$). These results help clarify the mechanisms that lead the members of co-operatives to judge incivilities more severely than the residents of LIH, who are less exposed to uncivil behaviours and who favour intervention strategies that are informal in nature. In addition, our analyses serve to qualify numerous empirical studies that suggest that disadvantaged neighbourhoods are primarily characterized by a weak capacity for mobilization and an inability to regulate deviant behaviours. Our results suggest that modes of governance of "microstructures," such as social housing, can generate variable degrees of cohesion and social control in the most resourceless communities.

Conclusion

Taken as a whole, the results presented in this chapter indicate that respondents with accumulated socio-economic disadvantages have greater difficulty in conceiving the notion of incivility, are more often exposed to disorder, are more tolerant of uncivil behaviour, and prefer formal modes of intervention. These observations are also associated with the types of governance in social housing. Nonetheless, multivariate analyses show that the *type of management* remains the most convincing element for explaining the frequency with which uncivil behaviours occur in social housing, the perceived seriousness of the incivilities, and the preferred intervention strategies of the residents. Moreover, we see that the level of cohesion and informal social control is higher in co-operatives than in public housing (LIH).

In light of the literature, our results suggest that those communities (even the most resourceless) that are equipped with mechanisms that foster collective participation in decision-making processes and in the implementation of strategies intended to improve living conditions (collective effectiveness) are more capable of preserving themselves against incivilities (controlling for education, income, and ethnicity). In order to support this hypothesis, additional analyses will need to explore the variations that may exist within the two groups studied. Indeed, we know that certain LIH complexes have particularly active tenants' committees, while certain management committees in co-operatives are characterized by internal tension and a lack of motivation. Yet, by examining the factors that modulate the vitality of pro-social mechanisms encouraging the *empowerment* of the most disadvantaged communities – independent of the type of management – we would be able to better understand the dysfunctional elements that contribute to the slackening of interpersonal ties, the demobilization of communities, and the weakening of informal social control.

Downstream from the problem of incivilities, political discourse makes disorder out to be a matter of security that increases the feeling of insecurity within a population. Yet, returning upstream, we see that incivility arises above all from a weakening of mores and the deterioration of interpersonal ties between social actors. Such observations inevitably push us to reconsider action plans put in place by public actors. In particular, we need to question the real capacity of the legal apparatus to resolve problems of incivility and to participate in the regeneration of the social structure. Less spectacular than large-scale interventions, improvements in a life setting can exert an influence on the quality of social relations on which the fundamental principles of community living are founded. Public actors would do well to focus on interventions that stimulate the vitality of pro-social mechanisms in difficult neighbourhoods rather than on implementing strategies that run a strong risk of even further *codifying* and *judicializing* social relationships.

Notes

1 Governance is distinguished from the traditional notion of "government," which, in the French language, is an organized, rational, and coherent form of power. In contrast, governance suggests increased participation by civil society in reaching and implementing decisions. For our purposes, this concept refers to the means by which members of a community organize themselves to participate in decision-making processes in order to increase control over their living conditions.

2 In order to improve the representativeness of the samples, we used a simple random sampling approach, which allowed for comparable socio-demographic characteristics in both sub-groups.

3 Two considerations justified this choice. First, a significant proportion of public housing was concentrated in these neighbourhoods. Second, geographic delimitation allowed us to control for structural factors (for example, poverty and residential mobility), which characterize these heavily disadvantaged urban areas.

4 *Cooperatives Act* (*Loi sur les coopératives*), L.R.Q., C-67.2.

5 More precisely, these results include acts of vandalism such as drawing graffiti (93.6 percent), destroying mail boxes (93.3 percent), setting fires in park garbage cans (93 percent), damaging public services (91.5 percent), and other unhygienic acts such as not picking up dog

feces (98.5 percent), urinating in public places (90 percent), and spitting in lobbies (96.7 percent).

6 These results include insults (90 percent), stealing goods (87.2 percent), parking vehicles in another tenant's reserved spot (87.8 percent), having loud neighbours (85.7 percent), physically assaulting another person (83.6 percent), not paying for bus tickets (79.9 percent), not respecting smoking bans (76.9 percent), spitting on the street (76.6 percent), and obstructing entrance hallways (73.9 percent).

7 These results include public intoxication (52.3 percent), loitering (44.7 percent), the presence of "squeegee kids" (41.9 percent), and the presence of the homeless (33.4 percent).

8 This time frame addresses two goals. The first was methodological and ensured that respondents would not "telescope" perceptions of the occurrence of incidents. The second goal was more pragmatic and involved selecting a time frame that was long enough to capture rare incidents such as robbery or assault.

9 The choice of UNIANOVA allows for regression and variance analyses for a continuous dependent variable and one or several independent dichotomous or categorical variables.

10 This approach allowed us to obtain perceptions of the relative severity for all nine scenarios using our scale. Accordingly, respondents had to score between zero (least serious) and nine (most serious) for each scenario in relation to their scores for the other scenarios. We chose this rating method over that of Wolfgang et al. (1985), the original scale is coming from Sellin and Wolfgang (1964) in order to avoid biasing respondents' judgment with reference statements and to allow the free expression of perception of severity in relation to behaviours with variable attributes. We would like to thank Julien Piednoir for his judicious advice in developing this measuring tool.

11 The "criminal acts" category consists of theft and assault. The "offences" category includes vandalism and making excessive noise, and the "non-punishable" category consists of discarding flyers, obstructing movement, spitting, insulting people, and loitering.

12 More specifically, calculating the means for severity scores recognizes the internal consistency of aggregate scores. Indeed, between-scenario analyses yielded high correlation coefficients, ranging from .45 to .80 ($p \leq .01$).

13 The first category is composed of the following acts: assault, theft, and vandalism.

14 The second category is composed of the following behaviours: loitering, spitting, noise pollution, insulting, obstructing passageways, and littering the ground with brochures.

15 To measure respondent reactions, we designed two scales. The first measures reactions, where respondents were victims or witnesses, to each behaviour in a list of twenty-one incidents. It allows for the measurement of responses in relation to a scale that ranges from one (not reacting) to an upper limit of twenty-five (reacting). We applied similar logic to the second scale for the nature of responses on a scale that ranges from one (informal) to an upper limit of eleven (formal).

16 The ANCOVA procedure allows for regression analysis and analysis of variance for continuous dependent variables in relation to one or more independent variables, while controlling for a covariant.

References

Ackman J., A. Normandeau, and P. Turner. 1967. "The Measurement of Delinquency in Canada." *Journal of Criminal, Criminology, and Police Science* 58: 330-37.

Biderman, A.D., L.A. Johnson, J. McIntyre, and A.W. Weir. 1967. *Report on a Pilot Study in the District of Columbia on Victimisation and Attitudes toward Law Enforcement.* Washington, DC: US Government Printing Office.

Block, R. 1979. "Community, Environment, and Violent Crime." *Criminology* 17: 46-57.

Bonnemain, C. 2000. "Les incivilités: Usage d'une nouvelle catégorie." In *Prévention et sécurité: Vers un nouvel ordre social,* ed. F. Bailleau and C. Gorgeon, 55-66. Paris: Les Éditions de la DIV.

Boyer, J.C. 2000. *Les banlieues en France.* Paris: Armand Colin.

Brill, W. 1975. *Victimization, Fear of Crime, and Altered Behaviour: A Profile of Four Housing Projects in Boston.* Washington, DC: US Department of Housing and Urban Development.

Bursik, R. 1988. "Social Disorganization, and Theories of Crime and Delinquency: Problems and Prospects." *Criminology* 26: 519-52.

Curry, G.D., and I. Spergel. 1988. "Gang Homicide, Delinquency, and Community." *Criminology* 26: 381-406.

Cusson, M. 1998. *Criminologie actuelle*. Paris: Presses Universitaires de France.

Dekeseredy, W.S., S. Alvi, M.D. Schwartz, and E.A. Tomaszewski. 2004. *Under Siege: Poverty and Crime in a Public Housing Community*. Lanham, MD: Lexington Books.

Earls, F., and C. Carlson. 1996. "Promoting Human Capability as an Alternative to Early Crime Prevention." In *Integrating Crime Prevention Strategies: Propensity and Opportunity*, ed. R.V. Clarck, J. McCord, and P.O. Wikström, 141-68. Stockholm: National Council for Crime Prevention.

Fagan, J., T. Dumanovsky, J.P. Thompson, and G. Davies. March 1998. "Crime in Public Housing: Clarifying Research Issues." *National Institute of Justice Journal* 235: 2-9. Washington, DC: US Department of Justice, Office of Justice Programs.

Felson, M. 1998. *Crime and Everyday Life*. London: Pine Forge Press.

Francis, B., K. Soothill, and R. Dittrich. 2001. "A New Approach for Ranking 'Serious' Offences." *British Journal of Criminology* 41: 726-37.

Hamilton, V.L., and J. Sanders. 1988. "Punishment and the Individual in the United States and Japan." *Law and Society Review* 22, 2: 301-28.

Hough, M., and J. Roberts. 1999. "Sentencing Trends in Britain: Public Knowledge and Public Opinion." *Punishment and Society* 1, 1: 11-26.

Merlin, P. 1999. *Les banlieues, Que sais-je?* Paris: Presses Universitaires de France.

Messner, S.F., and R. Rosenfeld. 1994. *Crime and the American Dream*. Belmont, CA: Wadsworth.

Messner, S.F., and K. Tardiff. 1986. "Economic Inequality and Levels of Homicide: An Analysis of Urban Neighbourhoods." *Criminology* 24: 297-318.

Milburn, P. 2000. "Violence et incivilités: De la rhétorique experte à la réalité ordinaire des illégalismes." *Déviance et société* 24, 4: 331-50.

Morenoff, J.D., R.J. Sampson, and S.W. Raudenbush. 2001. "Neighbourhood Inequality, Collective Efficacy, and the Spatial Dynamics of Urban Violence." *Criminology* 39, 3: 517-60.

Normandeau, A. 1970. "Études comparatives d'un indice pondéré de la criminalité dans 8 pays." *Revue internationale de police criminelle* 235: 15-18.

Roché, S. 1994. "Les incivilités, défis à l'ordre social." *Projet* 238, été: 37-46.

–. 1996. "Les incivilités vues du côté des institutions: Perceptions, traitement, et enjeux." *Les cahiers de la sécurité intérieure* 23, 1: 86-99.

–. 2000. "La théorie de la vitre cassée en France: Incivilités et désordres en public." *Revue française de science politique* 50, 3: 387-412.

Rouse, W.V., and H. Rubenstein. 1978. *Crime in Public Housing: A Review of Major Issues and Selected Crime Reduction Strategies*. Washington, DC: Department of Housing and Urban Development, Office of Policy Development and Research.

Saegert, S., G. Winkel, and C. Swartz. 2002. "Social Capital and Crime in New York City's Low-Income Housing." *Housing Policy Debate* 13, 1: 189-226.

Sampson, R.J. 1985. "Neighbourhood and Crime: The Structural Determination of Personal Victimization." *Journal of Research in Crime and Delinquency* 22: 7-40.

–. 1986. "Neighbourhood Family Structure and the Risk of Personal Victimization." In *The Social Ecology of Crime*, ed. J. Byrne and R. Sampson, 25-46. New York: Springer-Verlag.

–. 2002. "The Community." In *Crime: Public Policies for Crime Control*, ed. J.Q. Wilson and J. Petersilia, 225-52. Oakland, CA: ICS Press.

–. 2004. "Seeing Disorder: Neighborhood Stigma and the Social Construction of 'Broken Windows.'" *Social Psychology Quarterly* 67, 4: 319-42.

Sampson, R.J., and W.B. Groves. 1989. "Community Structure and Crime: Testing Social Disorganization Theory." *American Journal of Sociology* 94: 774-802.

Sampson, R.J., and S.W. Raudenbush. 2001. *Disorder in Urban Neighbourhoods: Does It Lead to Crime?* Washington, DC: US Department of Justice, National Institute of Justice.

Sampson, R.J., S.W. Raudenbush, and F. Earls. 1998. *Neighbourhood Collective Efficacy: Does It Help Reduce Violence?* Washington, DC: US Department of Justice, National Institute of Justice.

Sellin, T., and M.E. Wolfgang. 1964. *The Measurement of Delinquency.* New York: John Wiley and Sons.

Skogan, W.G. 1990. *Disorder and Crime: Crime and the Spiral of Decay in American Neighbourhoods.* Toronto: Macmillan.

Smith, D.R., and G.R. Jarjoura. 1988. "Social Structure and Criminal Victimization." *Journal of Research in Crime and Delinquency* 25: 27-52.

Taylor R., and J. Covington. 1988. "Neighbourhood Changes in Ecology and Violence." *Criminology* 26: 553-90.

Weisel, D.L. 1998. "Crime and Public Housing." Police Executive Research Forum, National Institute of Justice, Rockville, MD.

Wilson, J.Q., and G.L. Kelling. 1982. "Broken Windows." *Atlantic Monthly* March: 29-38.

Wolfgang, M.E., R.M. Figlio, P.E. Tracy, and S.I. Singer. 1985. *The National Survey of Crime Severity.* Washington, DC: US Government Printing Office.

5
The Legalization of Gambling in Canada
Colin S. Campbell, Timothy F. Hartnagel, and Garry J. Smith

The focus of this chapter is on gambling in its particularly modern form as it has emerged in Canada since 1970.[1] Although gambling has ancient roots and traditions in a variety of cultures, the overview and analysis of this chapter consider those forms of gambling that have emerged as a result of a complex pattern of related developments: global expansion of the gambling industry; technological innovations with respect to electronic games; the popularity of gambling as a mass leisure activity; and, finally, its utilization as a state fiscal tool (Reith 1999, 89-90). In Canada, the distinctive feature of legal gambling is that it has become a public policy instrument used by provincial governments and is marketed as a form of mainstream entertainment for consumers by state-run corporations in partnership with private sector interests for the purpose of revenue generation (Cosgrave and Klassen 2009, 3). The purpose of this chapter therefore is to review the transformation of the social control of gambling in Canada and to examine some of its consequences.

In Canada, while criminal prohibitions against gambling formally remain firmly in place, there has been a widespread contraction of the scope of the criminal law against it. This transformation is exhibited in the extent to which provincial governments can (and often do) grant exemptions to the general prohibitions on gambling contained in the *Criminal Code*.[2] Provincial exemptions have culminated in the emergence of a multi-billion-dollar legal gambling industry. This chapter identifies not only the nature and extent of legal gambling within Canada but also the contentious legal, behavioural, and public policy issues that have accompanied the move from strict prohibition to provincial licensing regimes. The chapter presents a distinctive case study in the use of the criminal law. More specifically, the chapter presents a case study in how sub-national governments have acquired the discretion to exempt gambling from strict criminal prohibition for the purpose of generating state and private sector income. It is apparent that the use of criminal law in Canada with respect to gambling consolidates a provincial monopoly rather than mitigating social harm. As a case study, the chapter therefore underscores that what is and is not defined as "crime" is indeed the outcome of political choices.

The chapter subsequently briefly contrasts Canada's experiences in regard to gambling with those of Australia, Great Britain, and the United States. The chapter concludes with a consideration of four theoretical perspectives that provide insight into the sources and effects of the transformation in the social control of gambling in Canada. Due consideration is given to the role of neo-liberal state policies in fostering gambling's commercialization and expansion as a mass leisure activity and its utilization as a state fiscal tool.

The Evolution of the Criminal Code's Gambling Provisions

Until several decades ago, most forms of gambling in Canada were illegal, while permissible gambling (for example, on track betting at horse races) was narrowly restricted. This situation was transformed with *Criminal Code* amendments in 1969 and 1985, which spurred a proliferation of legal gambling formats that were licensed, operated, and regulated by provincial governments over the past thirty years. Many gambling activities and behaviours have been transformed from the status of being criminal and prohibited to a status of legal and licensed. Given the current provisions of the *Criminal Code*, it is our view that modern criminal law in Canada has not been deployed for the purpose of controlling or preventing either the operation of, or participation in, gambling activities. Rather, existing provisions have facilitated a widespread expansion of a variety of gambling activities, provided they are conducted and managed under provincial jurisdiction.

As provincial governments have moved to legalize and exploit gambling's economic potential, regulatory systems have been constructed to investigate, monitor, inspect, license, audit, and control gambling in the interest of sustaining gambling's integrity as a government revenue source. However, "gambling" remains an elusive term in Canada because, depending on the format and circumstances surrounding it, a variety of legal statuses are possible. Legalization has thus tended to blur public perceptions about the status of gambling, with some forms of legal gambling such as electronic gambling machines (EGMs) being singled out for continuing social censure.[3] Furthermore, crime and gambling remain linked in numerous ways, and new forms of "deviance" associated with gambling (for example, "excessive" or "problem" gambling) have emerged (Campbell and Smith 2003; Smith and Wynne 1999, 2004).

For the majority of participants, gambling may be a harmless amusement; however, because of the potential for chicanery, exploitation, and overindulgence, "the law has historically taken a stern view toward gambling" (Bowal and Carrasco 1997, 29). Despite its drawbacks, modern commercial gambling appears to be well entrenched within Canadian culture and within provincial fiscal policies. History has taught us that the complete suppression of an activity such as gambling is virtually unachievable (Dixon 1991). Given this reality, modern legislators have tried generally to strike a balance between regulation and prohibition. Inevitably, efforts to control gambling result in policies stipulating where, when, and under what conditions the activity is permissible. Consequently, gambling can be legal or illegal depending on the context, the circumstances, and the operators of the game. For example, the *Criminal Code* of Canada contains provisions that dictate when gambling is an indictable offence and outlines the range of sanctioned gambling formats that provincial governments can license or operate if they so choose.

When the Canadian *Criminal Code* was first enacted in 1892, under a section titled "Offences against Religion, Morals and Public Convenience," a series of gambling offences that had been created by acts of Parliament in 1886 and 1888 was simply incorporated therein. From 1892 to 1969, there was a series of ad hoc and seemingly minor amendments to the sections of the code on gambling. Taken together, these early amendments facilitated a very gradual expansion of legal gambling in Canada. While there was some public lobbying, beginning in the 1930s, in favour of reform and a gradual shift in public opinion towards more liberal attitudes, these *Criminal Code* amendments were typically made in the absence of any significant public debate (Campbell and Smith 1998; Morton 2003). Indeed, the last public review of the gambling sections of the *Criminal Code* took place in 1954-55 when a special joint committee of the House of Commons and Senate examined the issues of lotteries (Campbell and Smith 1998; Canada 1956). The work of the special joint committee on lotteries had its genesis in 1949 when the government of Canada established a royal commission with a mandate to systematically review and update the provisions of the *Criminal Code* for the first time since its codification in 1892. The royal commission reported in 1954 but chose not to address the gaming provisions of the code due to their controversial nature. Subsequently, the task of reviewing the lottery provisions fell to the 1954 special joint committee (Campbell 1994, 228; Osborne 1989, 48-49).

When the joint committee tendered its report, it noted that lotteries and other games of chance, such as bingo, were extensively carried out by non-profit, community-based organizations in Canada despite their formal prohibition under the existing law (Campbell 1994, 229). The committee observed that the police were often reluctant to enforce laws against well-intentioned community organizations. This reluctance, according to the committee, caused two problems: contempt for the law and ineffective control (Osborne 1989, 50). Accordingly, the joint committee recommended new legislation that would provide workable laws capable of effective enforcement. In line with the reforms introduced, the committee also called for some relaxation of existing prohibitions with respect to the control, sale, and consumption of alcohol. The joint committee, however, concluded that there should be no state lotteries in Canada (Campbell 1994, 234). The recommendations would not be acted on until late 1967 (Osborne and Campbell 1988, 23). Table 5.1 condenses the key amendments and notable developments in the history of gambling in Canada.

Table 5.1

Chronology of amendments and developments regarding the legal status of gambling in Canada

Date	Amendment or development
1892	*Criminal Code* of Canada first enacted, incorporating gambling offences.
1901	Exemption for raffles at any bazaar held for charitable and religious objects.
1906	The phrase "lottery scheme" inserted into the *Criminal Code*.
1909-10	Select Committee of House of Commons convened to inquire into horse race betting.
1910	Betting limited to horse racing tracks.
1917	Order-in-council suspends betting as "incommensurate" with war effort.
1919-20	Royal Commission in [sic] Racing Inquiry convened to examine horse race betting.
1920	Race track betting reinstated using a parimutuel system.
1922	Offence created for betting on dice games, shell games, punchboards, coin tables, or wheels of fortune.
1925	Select games of chance, including wheels of fortune, permitted at agricultural fairs and exhibitions.
1938	Gambling on the premises of bona fide social clubs permitted if operators did not exact a percentage of the stakes.
1954	Game of three-card monte added to the list of prohibited games.
1954	Special joint committee of House of Commons and Senate convened to examine need for law reform in regard to lotteries. Recommends no state lotteries but calls for greater clarity in existing provisions.
1969	Federal and provincial governments allowed to conduct lotteries. Charitable gambling is broadened under provincial licence but remains exempted at fairs and exhibitions.
1973-85	Federal-provincial conflict over authority to conduct lotteries.
1985	Provinces delegated exclusive authority to manage and conduct lotteries and lottery schemes, including games conducted via a computer, video device, or slot machine. Betting on horse races via telephone permitted.
1998	Prohibitions against dice games removed from *Criminal Code*.

The Process of Legalization: The Modern Context
The liberalization of gambling under state regulation began in 1967 when then Minister of Justice Pierre Trudeau introduced an omnibus bill to amend several aspects of the *Criminal Code*. The proposed amendments included

- removal of criminal sanctions for abortion, homosexual practices between consenting adults, and lottery schemes;
- allowing federal and provincial governments the option of conducting state lotteries;
- the broadening of charity gambling;
- the continuation of the existing exemption for agricultural fairs and exhibitions;
- the creation of a new exemption for gambling at public places of amusement under provincial licence. (Osborne 1989, 59)

In 1968, when Parliament was dissolved for a general election, the bill was abandoned. However, when the Liberal Party was re-elected under the leadership of Trudeau, the House of Commons passed an identical bill in 1969. Thus began the transformation of gambling from federal prohibition to provincial regulation.

From the mid-1970s to the mid-1980s, the federal and provincial levels of government were embroiled in an acrimonious legal battle with respect to jurisdiction over lotteries and lottery schemes. The details of this battle are beyond the scope of this discussion.[4] It suffices to say, however, that court actions were halted when the provinces and the federal government reached a contractual agreement to amend the *Criminal Code* to allow the provincial level of government exclusive control over lotteries and lottery schemes. The amendment took effect in 1985 and permitted the provinces, alone or in partnership with other provinces, to operate lotteries and lottery schemes through a computer, video device, or slot machine.

The current provisions of the *Criminal Code* dealing with gambling are set out in "Part VII: Disorderly Houses, Gaming, and Betting." Part VII provides definitions of the following terms: disorderly houses, bawdy houses, betting houses, gaming houses, gaming, betting, and lotteries. This section also presents a number of presumptions with respect to disorderly houses and establishes a series of prohibitions related to betting, gaming, lotteries, and games of chance. Part VII also lists exemptions from these prohibitions that have facilitated the expansion of legal gambling under provincial operation and regulation. The two sections of the *Criminal Code* that are most germane to an understanding of permitted gambling in Canada are (1) section 204, which, in addition to exempting private betting between individuals, has permitted betting on horse racing since 1920 via a parimutuel system operated under the auspices of the federal minister of agriculture and agri-food;[5]

and (2) section 207, subtitled "Permitted Lotteries." It is under section 207 that the transformation and expansion of gambling in Canada over the past thirty-five years has occurred. Section 207 legalizes the creation and operation of lotteries run by any of the bodies specified in section 207(1)(a) to (d). As well, it provides for the regulation of such schemes under provincial laws and under terms and conditions of licences that may be granted pursuant to provincial authority. In other words, section 207(1) permits lotteries to be created and operated by a province or under licence by charitable or religious organizations, by a board of a fair or exhibition, or by any other person to whom a licence has been issued if the ticket cost does not exceed two dollars and the prize does not exceed $500. It is under these *Criminal Code* provisions that provinces have been granted exclusive authority to operate and/or license particular forms of gambling. As a consequence, all Canadian provinces and territories conduct or permit gambling to some extent.

The two formats that now dominate Canadian gambling are (1) EGMs, such as video lottery terminals (VLTs), which are available in all provinces except Ontario and British Columbia in age-restricted premises such as pubs and cocktail lounges; and (2) casino gambling, which in addition to the traditional "green felt" table games now offers a variety of electronic gaming devices such as slot machines. Lotteries – once the primary source of government gambling revenues – have now been eclipsed by revenues derived from electronic gaming machines and casinos.

In the twenty-four years since the 1985 amendment, legal gambling in Canada has become a big business. Today there are approximately 37,782 venues in which to gamble legally in Canada. In 2007-8, there were over 92,000 EGMs in casinos, bars, lounges, and racetracks; 30,800 lottery ticket outlets; 45,000 charitable gambling licences; 66 permanent casinos with 2,000 gambling tables; and 248 race tracks and tele-theatres (Canadian Partnership for Responsible Gambling 2007-8). According to recent data developed by the Canadian Partnership for Responsible Gambling (CPRG), government-run gambling (bingo, EGMs, table games, and lotteries) generated a "gross profit" of $13.7 billion in 2007-8.[6] After paying costs of approximately $6.7 billion associated with generating gambling revenues, government-run gambling produced a "net profit" of just over $7.0 billion with virtually an equal split of the gross profit between provincial governments and gaming service providers (estimated from data provided by the CPRG [*ibid.*]). In addition to government-run gambling, provincially licensed charitable gambling generated revenues of just over $1 billion across Canada. Horse racing gambling revenue produced a total of nearly $400 million. Thus, in 2007-8, a total of approximately $15.1 billion in gross gambling profits was generated in Canada. On the other hand, the per adult loss in

Canada in 2007-8 averaged $547 and ranged from a low of $355 in New Brunswick to a high of $871 in Alberta (*ibid.*).

With the growth of the volume of dollars involved in legal gambling in Canada, employment in the gambling industry has also risen dramatically. In 1992, 11,000 people were employed in the gambling industry. In 2007, 46,000 were employed (Marshall 2008). As a proportion of provincial government revenue, gambling constituted 2.3 percent of all revenue raised by government and ranged from a low of 1.3 percent in Prince Edward Island to a high of 4.7 percent in Alberta (Canadian Partnership for Responsible Gambling 2007-8). While provincial governments are the single largest beneficiary of gambling revenues, it is to be noted that other levels of government also garner a share of gambling revenues, albeit much smaller. More specifically, under the terms of the agreement that resulted in the 1985 amendment to the *Criminal Code,* an amount is paid annually (adjusted according to the consumer price index) to the federal government. Each province contributes a share calculated proportionally to its lottery sales. In 2007-8, the amount contributed by the provinces under this agreement amounted to approximately $64 million and represented about 0.9 percent of net profits (*ibid.*). In several provinces, revenue-sharing agreements have been negotiated with some municipalities. Under these relatively recent agreements, municipal governments received approximately $182 million or approximately 2.6 percent of net profits in 2007-8 (*ibid.*). It is thus apparent that all levels of government in Canada are now reliant to some extent on revenues derived from gambling sources.[7]

Gambling and Canadian Public Opinion

Criminologists are interested in various aspects of public opinion regarding law, crime, and criminal justice primarily because of the possible relationship between such opinion and public policy (Zimmerman, Van Alstyne, and Dunn 1988). Julian Roberts (1992) claims that public officials' beliefs about public opinion influence criminal justice policy. The public's views concerning gambling may be relevant to an understanding of the development of gambling policy and its potential future directions. Although there is little available in the way of national, systematic, or time-series data on the attitudes of Canadians towards gambling, there are nevertheless many existing studies that provide valuable insights into the connection between public opinion and policy formation on the issue of gambling.

Suzanne Morton (2003) characterized the attitudes of Canadians towards gambling as ambivalent for most of the twentieth century. However, beginning with the 1969 *Criminal Code* amendment, gambling was transformed from a stigmatized minor vice to an acceptable activity that was regarded as appropriate and perhaps necessary to fund the Canadian welfare state.

Morton shows how official condemnation co-existed with unofficial toleration during the first half of the twentieth century. She also points to the
steady public lobby, beginning in the 1930s, that looked for reform and
liberalization of the gambling laws. While the rhetoric of anti-gamblers and
legal regulators remained relatively constant from 1919 to 1969, Morton
maintains that there was uneven enforcement of the gambling laws. As well,
there were noticeable shifts in public opinion towards more liberal attitudes
in both the 1920s and 1950s, at least partly as a function of economic conditions. Morton summarizes a series of post-Second World War Gallup polls
that showed a gradual increase in support for legalized lotteries and sweep-
stakes, which reached a 79 percent approval level by 1969. Thus, public
attitudes towards this type of gambling shifted over time from viewing it as
a vice that should be prohibited to an acceptance of its inevitability, one
from which society should benefit.

In March 1984, shortly before the 1985 amendments to the *Criminal Code*,
the Gallup poll asked: "On the whole, are you in favour of, or opposed to
government-run lotteries?" On a national basis, 76 percent of Canadians
were in favour, 16 percent opposed, and 8 percent uncertain. However, in
regard to the 1985 *Criminal Code* amendment, which finalized the transfer
of authority over legal gambling from federal to provincial jurisdiction and
legalized computer, video, and slot machine-style gambling, the government
legislated without public input, creating a source of continuing public controversy (Smith and Wynne 2004). The terms of the amendment were actually negotiated by provincial and federal authorities responsible for culture,
fitness, and amateur sport – authorities that were not typically involved in
criminal law revisions. As Judith Osborne and Colin Campbell (1988) have
commented, Parliament merely "rubber stamped" the amendment in the
interests of ending the acrimonious conflict over lotteries and expediting
funding for the sake of the 1988 Calgary Winter Olympics. As they noted,

> following a conspicuous absence of public hearings or discussions, the lot-
> teries bill was given first reading in the House of Commons on 10 October,
> second and third readings on 6 November, and finally passed after less than
> three hours of debate; in the Senate it was given first reading 7 November,
> second reading on 27 November, and third reading and assent on 20 De-
> cember. It was proclaimed in force on the final day of the year. (Osborne
> and Campbell 1988, 24-25)

Although legal gambling has burgeoned in the years since this amendment, debate continues regarding the appropriate levels and types of gambling that should be allowed in Canadian communities. Recent public
opinion on gambling issues has been the subject of only a few polls and

surveys. While six in ten Canadians reported partaking in gambling in a 1998 poll, 73 percent felt that problems associated with gambling had increased in their province over the past couple of years (Ipsos News Centre 1998). In the same poll, 58 percent indicated that increased revenues do not offset the problems caused by gambling. VLTs and casinos were the formats viewed as being most harmful to the community (42 percent and 41 percent, respectively), while charity lotteries were perceived as the least harmful (10 percent), and 86 percent believed that governments had become addicted to the money generated from gambling (*ibid.*).

In the only random national survey of adult Canadian views on gambling, Jason Azmier (2000) reported that 43 percent felt that their governments should be doing more to restrict gambling in their province, while 47 percent were satisfied with the current levels of restriction. However, there was strong support for increased government accountability regarding gambling policy, with 84 percent agreeing (61 percent strongly) that governments should hold public consultations before introducing new forms of gambling. Sixty percent of the same sample agreed that gambling problems had increased in their province in the past three years; 24 percent perceived the overall impact of gambling to be negative compared to 9 percent who agreed that gambling had had an overall positive impact on their community; and 68 percent disagreed that gambling had improved the quality of life in their province compared to only 14 percent that felt it was beneficial. There was strong disagreement with current policies allowing VLTs in bars and lounges, with 70 percent agreeing (49 percent strongly) to restrict VLTs to casinos and race tracks. However, while 41 percent believed that VLTs should be banned altogether, 43 percent disagreed, although the results favoured a complete ban among those with a strong preference. Respondents did see gambling as a legitimate means for provincial governments to raise revenues, with 67 percent preferring it to raising taxes. However, a strong anti-gambling sentiment is suggested among the 19 percent who preferred to raise revenues through increased taxes.

To the extent that it can be gauged from these limited data, Canadian public opinion on the issue of gambling seems ambivalent. On the one hand, Canadians generally view gambling as an acceptable community activity, due perhaps to its perceived inevitability and its use as a source of revenue for governments and charities (Azmier 2001a). On the other hand, many Canadians feel there should be more restrictions on gambling, with the strength of such feelings varying with the type of gambling (for example, VLTs), the location of venues, and the perceived social costs of gambling. However, as Azmier (2001a, 15) has argued, "gambling policy continues to evolve in Canada with only a minimum of opportunity for public involvement in the decision-making process."

Contentious Issues in Canadian Gambling Policies

This section broaches several contentious issues related to how Canadian provincial governments conduct, manage, and regulate legal gambling. In addition, key issues regarding the control and prevention of gambling-related crime and problem gambling are considered.

Ontario Gaming Legislation Review

In 1996, the law firm of Morris, Rose and Ledgett was retained by the Ontario Lottery Corporation to provide a legal analysis of Ontario's gaming market. A private sector proposal seeking the implementation of VLTs based on the Windsor Casino model triggered the review. The analysis, entitled the *Review of Gaming Legislation in Ontario*, ultimately led the provincial government to abandon an intended introduction of VLTs. However, because the analysis challenged the way that existing gambling formats were conducted and managed, the report was not submitted to an all-party provincial justice committee as originally intended, nor was it released to the public.[8] In reviewing the VLT proposal, the authors of the report found it necessary to analyze the Windsor Casino model on which the VLT proposal was premised, assess charitable gaming, and evaluate the overall legislative framework for gaming in Ontario (Morris, Rose and Ledgett 1996). The legal analysis identified the following matters as possible contraventions of the gambling provisions of the *Criminal Code*.

Broad Interpretation of Criminal Code Gambling Provisions

When Ontario implemented casino gambling in Windsor in the early 1990s, the province adopted a hybrid ownership, management, and operation model. Under this model, casinos are owned, controlled, and regulated by the Ontario government but run by private sector operators. As part of the regulatory structure, two provincial government Crown agencies were initially formed to divide the responsibility for overseeing casino gambling (Alfieri 1994). The Ontario Casino Corporation was made responsible for the business and operating functions of casinos, while the Gaming Control Commission was mandated to undertake registration, enforcement, and audit duties. Interested private sector casino operators were invited to respond to a request for proposals, specifying how they would meet various economic, tourism, security, and civic improvement objectives.

The authors of the *Review of Gaming Legislation in Ontario* argued that this structural arrangement for the management and operation of the Windsor Casino was inconsistent with *Criminal Code* provisions since it was unclear just who was actually *conducting* and *managing* the gambling operation when private sector interests were involved as operators.

As noted earlier, the *Criminal Code* places the onus for conducting and managing "lottery schemes" on provincial governments. The only exemptions are for charitable or religious organizations and fairs or exhibitions licensed by the province. Given that the Ontario casino model is not charity based, and it is arguable whether the Ontario government is in fact conducting and managing the casino games, the Windsor Casino model may be in violation of *Criminal Code* gambling provisions. By the same logic, the authors of the report concluded that the proposed Ontario VLT implementation plan, based on the Windsor Casino operation, was also of questionable legal status. Since the legal principles underpinning the hybrid government ownership/private sector-operated model have never been tested in court, Ontario casinos continue to operate under this arrangement.

Delegation of Authority to Conduct and Manage Gaming Events
As noted earlier, while licensed charities or religious groups can be authorized to conduct and manage lottery schemes to raise monies for worthy causes, a potential problem arises over the involvement of private operators hired to run licensed gambling events. Private operators are allowed to help run gambling operations, but the authorized agent (government/charity/exhibition association) must take "an active and direct participation in ... supervision ... and day-to-day operations" (Donovan and Welsh 1998, A26). The issue then becomes whether licensed organizations can truly claim to be conducting and managing the proceedings as required under section 207(1)(b) of the *Criminal Code* when there is hands-on involvement by private operators in running the gaming events. The *Review of Gaming Legislation in Ontario* makes the case that licensed charities are usually too far removed from the gambling activity, thus giving the private operator *de facto* control over the gaming event. While approved by the Ontario government in its policy manual as well as in the terms and conditions of the licence documents, this practice appears to breach the *Criminal Code*. In other words, the authority to conduct and manage gambling events cannot be delegated to a third party, either by the provincial government or by licensed charitable or religious organizations.

Timothy Patrick (2000) concurs that the *Criminal Code* exemptions granted to provincial governments and charitable and religious organizations to conduct and manage lottery schemes cannot be delegated to another party. In Patrick's view, private sector entrepreneurs who participate in the profits of gambling machines and who provide business plans, management skills, premises, and staff to facilitate machine gambling are indeed conducting and managing an electronic gaming lottery scheme and, in so doing, are violating the *Criminal Code*. However, offering a contrary view, Patrick Monahan and Gerold Goldlist (1999) have argued that, with respect to gaming conducted under section 207(1)(a) of the *Criminal Code*, provinces are able to enter into contractual agreements with private sector interests to assist in the day-to-day operation of a lottery scheme and are furthermore not constrained in how they distribute revenues derived from provincial gaming schemes.

Use of Proceeds from Charitable Gambling

The *Criminal Code* dictates that the proceeds from a licensed gambling event are to be used for charitable or religious purposes. At issue is the involvement of private sector interests that are afforded significant portions of the gambling proceeds. The authors of the *Review of Gaming Legislation in Ontario* claimed that 42.5 percent of the annual gross wager on Ontario charitable bingos in 1995 was diverted to the private sector in the form of expenses rather than distributed for charitable and religious objects or purposes (Morris, Rose, and Ledgett 1996). In 1997, the provincial government in British Columbia sought to introduce EMGs in order to increase its revenues from gambling. New regulations were introduced that would have increased the overall level of gaming revenues for charitable organizations but would have also directed the largest proportion of the revenues to government coffers. Under the province's plan, proceeds from existing licensed charity bingo events were to be pooled with revenues from electronic games. One-third of the revenues were to be directed to charities to a guaranteed minimum of $118 million annually. The province would direct the other two-thirds to its consolidated revenue fund. A number of charitable groups in British Columbia successfully challenged the province by arguing that the plan contravened section 207(1)(b) of the *Criminal Code*, which does not authorize proceeds from charity lottery schemes to be directed to the government. In an interpretation of section 207(1)(b), a 1998 ruling in the Supreme Court of British Columbia held that the provincial government could not appropriate revenues generated by charitable or religious organizations under section 207(1)(b) (*Nanaimo Community Bingo Association v. British Columbia (Attorney General)* 1999).

The trial judge noted that the government's plan for gambling expansion authorized for-profit management companies to receive a proportion of the proceeds of gaming derived from charitable lottery schemes without regard to what constitutes a reasonable charge for their gaming services. The ruling thus determined that the percentage of revenues allocated to private operators granted them an entitlement regardless of the actual value of the services they provide. This action also breached the intent of section 207(1)(b), which specifies revenues be directed to charitable or religious purposes. In short, the Supreme Court of British Columbia's decision in *Nanaimo Community Bingo Association* had significant repercussions for charitable gaming in British Columbia. In response to the ruling, the province, through the British Columbia Lottery Corporation, assumed direct control of casino and bingo operations in order to introduce electronic gaming machines. As well, it was apparent that the private sector companies could no longer assume such a large share of the gambling revenue, which was legally intended for the benefit of community-based charitable or religious organizations.

In other provinces, such as Alberta and Ontario, private sector companies also played a role in providing gaming services to charitable organizations under arrangements that were similar to the ones that had contravened the *Criminal Code* in British Columbia. Questions therefore arose across the country regarding the consistency and legality of the interpretations of the *Criminal Code*. And other questions arose over who had the ability and authority to challenge the varying interpretations that were evident across the provinces.

Regulation of EGMs

Section 207(4)(c) of the *Criminal Code* grants provincial governments exclusive jurisdiction over electronic gaming machines (including computers or video devices used for gaming purposes) and stipulates that the exemptions for religious and charitable organizations as well as fairs and exhibitions that hold for other gambling formats do not apply to electronic gaming. In other words, exempt groups cannot be licensed to conduct and manage EGMs. Nevertheless, in some provinces, EGMs are housed in casinos, race tracks, and liquor-licensed premises, which means that some exempt groups (for example, exhibition associations) are nevertheless profiting from electronic gambling. Similarly, the owners of bars and lounges are benefiting from the machines that are located in their establishments. In Alberta, for example, VLT retailers receive 15 percent of the annual net profits per machine (the remaining 85 percent goes to the government). Since an average VLT produces approximately $20,000 profit, entrepreneurs with multiple EGMs on site can make upward of $400,000 per year with little effort and minimal financial risk (Smith and Wynne 2004). Again, the intent of the provisions of the *Criminal Code* that grant exclusive jurisdiction over gambling to provincial governments may be compromised since sizable portions of gambling revenues are directed towards the private sector interests for allowing EGMs on their properties. In response, Monahan and Goldlist (1999) have posited a dissenting perspective and maintain that provinces are unfettered in their contractual agreements with private operators and are not constrained with respect to the terms of compensation to be paid.

A new twist on the division of EGM proceeds stems from what gaming manufacturers call the "recurring revenue model." In addition to selling EGMs outright to Canadian provinces, some manufacturers lease the machines in return for a proportion of the profits (a percentage of the profits as opposed to a flat daily rate). This joint partnership arrangement raises some fundamental questions (1) is the "conduct and manage" requirement for provincial governments breached if they do not own the machines; and (2) can the public interest in terms of product safety and gaming machine integrity be protected when provincial governments and private sector manufacturers share a vested interest in revenue maximization? Critics have thus questioned whether or not the terms of the *Criminal Code* are strictly applied to gaming machines. As a further illustration, Roger Horbay (2004), a software developer, has doubts about who really conducts and manages electronic gaming. In Horbay's view, conducting and managing EGMs entail complete control over the gaming software. Since gaming machine manufacturers retain proprietary rights to their software, questions arise as to who is the actual "controlling mind."

A further concern over the operation of Canadian electronic gambling machines pertains to the use of unbalanced reel games. An unbalanced reel game is one where there is a shortage of winning symbols on some reels. Players of these machines see combinations of winning symbols above or below the centre line and gain the mistaken impression that they just missed a large payout or that the machine is easier to beat than it really is (Falkiner and Horbay 2006). Unbalanced reel games are widespread in Canada and are seen as problematic for consumers because they are intentionally deceptive and there is no way for players to know how the machines actually work. Falkiner and Horbay maintain that unbalanced reel games are fraudulent not only because they do not meet the standard of a fair game but also because the unbalanced reel design takes advantage of those who are susceptible to becoming problem gamblers.

Other questions pertaining to the operation of EGMs include uncertainties over how odds and pay-out rates are determined and over who regulates the regulators. Since law enforcement agencies generally do not have the technical expertise to investigate complaints regarding the integrity of EGMs, they invariably depend on technical advice from provincial gaming regulators – the very authorities that have sanctioned the machines. This state of affairs raises questions about the adequacy and independence of checks and balances in the overall gambling regulatory process.

In late 2006, frustrated by Ontario provincial government indifference to their concerns, a Canadian group, Gambling Watch Network, supported by the United Church of Canada, formally registered a complaint with the Canadian Competition Bureau, alleging that EGMs were cheating the public. However, in mid-2007, the Competition Bureau rejected the complaint on the grounds of "technical deficiencies," including the failure of the complainants to identify their ages. Subsequently, the bureau advised the group that, even if a resubmitted complaint was determined to be technically compliant with the complaints procedure, the bureau would be unable to pursue it due to competing priorities (Horbay 2009).

Internet Gambling

Section 207(4)(c) of the *Criminal Code* specifies that only provinces can operate computer-based lottery schemes. Thus, the code, as presently crafted, does not allow for charitable organizations or private sector operators to operate online gambling within Canada. Moreover, an Internet-based gambling operation conducted and managed by a provincial government cannot take bets from residents of other provinces without the consent of the other provincial governments. Recently, the governments of Nova Scotia and British Columbia, through their lottery Crown corporations, initiated online lottery schemes restricted to residents of their respective provinces and thus in compliance with existing law.

What critics find troublesome in Internet betting schemes is the relative openness of access. Internet gambling games are offered free of charge to anyone who has a computer and Internet access. To wager for money, however, players must register and establish an account, typically using a deposit drawn on a credit card. Given the private and solitary nature of computer betting on the Internet, in tandem with the universality of access to the Internet, online gambling is extremely difficult for police to monitor. While the *Criminal Code* may prohibit Canadians from participating in gambling on a website located in another country, there is no mechanism to effectively enforce the prohibition within the country (Kelly, Todosichuk, and Azmier 2001). According to a report prepared by the Canada West Foundation on Internet gambling, it is a breach of the *Criminal Code* for a private, commercial, Canadian-based gambling site to accept bets from Canadian citizens. The criminal prosecution of Starnet Communications International in 1999 demonstrated that police and prosecutors are able to proceed against a commercial Internet gambling site that operates in Canada (Hosenball 1999). The fact remains, however, that Canadians have the ability to gamble at offshore Internet sites with relative impunity (for further information, see Lipton 2003).

It is also interesting to note that the Quebec-based Kahnawake Mohawk First Nation has operated extensive online gambling sites since the late 1990s through the Kahnawake Gaming Commission. It licenses and regulates some thirty gambling websites operated through Internet servers physically located on their tribal lands (Lipton 2003; Kelly, Todosichuk, and Azmier 2001). Located on the outskirts of Montreal, the Kahnawake Mohawks assert that they are a sovereign nation and entitled to grant gaming licences for lottery schemes. While the Kahnawake Mohawks are arguably violating the *Criminal Code* and while the Quebec and federal governments, together with the provincial police, have investigated their Internet gambling activities, no action has been taken to halt the operations. Even though Internet gambling is not yet a popular activity for Canadians (less than 2 percent of the adult population report having gambled on Internet sites), Canadian authorities will nevertheless need to deal with these policy and law enforcement dilemmas (Kelly, Todosichuk, and Azmier 2001). Of course, as provincial governments continue to expand their repertoire of gaming products through online media, it is likely that Canadian provinces will assert their legal monopoly in this domain as well.

Internet Horse Race Wagering

Critics of the Woodbine Entertainment Group website, which facilitates online betting on horse races in Ontario, formally sought to have federal and provincial authorities explain how and why the online betting operation received approval, alleging that it violates sections 206 and 207 of the *Criminal Code*. Permission had been granted to the website operators based on the minister of agriculture's interpretation that the 1985 amendment to the *Criminal Code,* which allowed betting on horse racing via telephone, extended to betting via the Internet (another telecommunications device). Queries by a Montreal-based problem gambling counselling firm, Viva Consulting, regarding the legal status of the online betting site to the federal minister of justice and the illegal gambling unit of the Ontario Provincial Police were ignored. According to Viva Consulting, given the concerns surrounding Woodbine's entry into Internet wagering, pertinent *Criminal Code* and regulatory questions included (1) does the minister of agriculture's ruling on Internet betting contravene provisions of the *Criminal Code;* (2) how can non-governmental interests be permitted to conduct online betting schemes; and (3) are regulatory and law enforcement agencies capable of acting impartially and independently on complaints against government-approved gambling operations?[9]

Quebec VLT Class Action Lawsuit

In 2001, Québec City lawyer Jean Brochu brought a class action lawsuit against Loto Québec, claiming that it had failed to warn players about the potential dangers of the 15,000 VLTs housed in over 4,000 bars in the province (*Brochu v. Société des Loteries du Québec,* 2002). The genesis of the legal action stemmed from Brochu's own battle with a gambling addiction. As a result of his out-of-control VLT play, Brochu lost his car and home and was disbarred from practising law because he stole $50,000 to cover his gambling debts.[10] Brochu was suing on behalf of 119,000 Quebecers (a figure derived from a Quebec problem gambling prevalence survey) and asking for $700 million in damages and an admission of liability from Loto Québec and the EGM manufacturers who provided the machines. At present, five defence law firms are involved (the law firm for Loto Québec and four representing machine manufacturers). As of November 2009, the lawsuit is ongoing.[11] Whatever the outcome, this case will be a watershed decision – one that favours the plaintiffs will likely lead to a spate of similar lawsuits. However, a decision in favour of the gaming operators may lead to the government's willingness to increase the number and availability of EGMs.

Bill S-11

A private member's bill sponsored by Senator Jean LaPointe was introduced in 2004 seeking to amend the *Criminal Code*'s provisions that empower provincial and territorial decision making in regard to VLTs. In essence, Senator LaPointe sought to have VLTs removed from convenience locations such as bars, lounges, and restaurants and restricted to designated gambling venues such as casinos and race tracks. The impetus for Bill S-11 was Senator LaPointe's belief that readily accessible VLTs are a major contributor to problem gambling and, hence, create negative social impacts. Debate on Bill S-11 has included expert testimony from Hal Pruden, counsel for the Criminal Law Policy Section at Justice Canada; Jason Azmier, senior policy analyst for the Canada West Foundation; and Jeff Derevensky and Rina Gupta, scholars representing the International Centre for Youth Gambling Problems and High-Risk Behaviors. Discussion on this bill has focused on two main issues (1) how dangerous are VLTs, and (2) what repercussions would there be for the federal government, provincial governments, and private business owners if this bill was enacted?

Compelling evidence was presented to the Senate hearings on these issues suggesting that (1) 70 percent of Canadians agree that VLTs should be restricted to gambling venues only; (2) there is no positive economic outcome associated with VLT play since VLT revenues invariably leave the local communities for provincial coffers, while the community is left to deal with the social damage created by problem gamblers; and (3) VLTs are responsible for almost three-quarters of the negative costs of gambling (Canada 2004). While committee members generally agree that VLTs are hazardous, they have been presented with the following scenarios that would likely occur if this legislation came to pass. First, there would be the prospect of provincial litigation against the federal government on the grounds that the 1985 agreement that gave provinces the exclusive authority to manage and conduct lottery schemes contains a clause stating "this agreement may only be amended or terminated by the unanimous consent of the provinces and the Government of Canada" (*ibid.*). Second, ambiguous terminology in the *Criminal Code* dealing with "slot machines," "video devices," "computers," and "dice games" would need to be clarified. And, third, the provinces may hold back their annual gambling revenue payments to the federal government as part of the previously noted 1985 agreement (which when adjusted to the consumer price index would have amounted to $63.5 million in 2007-8) (Canadian Partnership for Responsible Gambling 2007-8). Bill S-11 presented an interesting dilemma for legislators – namely, were the social problems created by convenience location EGMs worth provoking federal-provincial acrimony? The answers perhaps become apparent when, after passing third reading, Bill S-11 was allowed to die on the order paper when Parliament was dissolved on 29 November 2005.

Cross-National Lessons for Canada

The comparative analysis presented in this section begins with a brief review of the nature and scope of gambling in three countries (Australia, Great Britain, and the United States), followed by a synopsis of each country's national gambling study and the identification of key regulatory issues. The section concludes with suggestions for improvement to Canada's regulatory structures based on policies and practices in the countries we observed. The countries were selected for comparison for particular reasons. All three countries are English-speaking nations and have similar legal systems and traditions. In addition, they are industrialized countries with free-market economies and broadly espouse similar cultural values. They also evidence a variety of legal gambling formats, considerable annual wagering totals, and high per capita gambling expenditures. Notwithstanding these parallels, there are significant differences among the countries in terms of their gambling operations and regulatory frameworks. These differences derive largely from the fact that Australia and the United States, like Canada, have federal systems of government, while Great Britain, on the other hand, has a unitary system. In other words, the division of legislative powers between central and state or provincial governments in Australia, the United States, and Canada has generally resulted in less federal government control over gambling and its regulation. Table 5.2 highlights similarities and differences in the way in which gambling is managed and conducted in Canada and the comparative countries. Each of these three countries' gambling regulatory models has strengths and weaknesses. Gleaning from what strategies were effective and which were ineffective in the countries we examined, the following observations on bolstering Canadian gambling policies and regulatory regimes are tendered.

Canadian Gambling Study

A Canadian national gambling inquiry is long overdue. Indeed, a recommendation for a national review of gambling activity in Canada was made in 2001 by the Canada West Foundation in its report *Gambling in Canada: Final Report and Recommendations* (Azmier 2001b). As is the case with other controversial policy issues, gambling policy is entangled in a myriad of political, moral, social, and economic concerns that polarize positions. Given that legal gambling is now a $15.1 billion a year industry in Canada, it behooves us to know the extent of this enterprise: who gains and who loses from the activity; whether net community benefits are being maximized; how gambling policy is rationalized and implemented; how gambling is

Table 5.2

Cross-national comparisons

Variable	Australia	Great Britain	United States	Canada
Legislative authority	Individual states and territories determine which gambling formats are allowed.	As of 2005, gambling is governed by the *Gambling Act*.	Individual states determine the legal gambling formats offered within their borders; the federal government is involved only if the gambling issue is related to a power granted it by the US Constitution.	Under the federal *Criminal Code*, provinces are delegated authority to manage, conduct, or license permitted gambling formats.
Legal gambling formats[a]	Poker machines (over 200,000); casinos (14); thoroughbred, harness, and dog racing through on-course parimutuel wagering and bookmakers and off-course betting shops; sports betting; lotto and scratch tickets; keno; bingo; and Internet gambling.	National lottery; betting shops (private book-makers who take wagers on sports events, horse races, election results, and so on); casinos (133); horse racing; bingo; slot machines that offer both small and large prizes (no minimum age is required to play the small prize machines).	Lotto and scratch tickets; slot machines and video lottery terminals; horse and dog racing; casinos (914[b]); bingo; sports betting and off-track horse wagering in a few states.	Lottery products such as lotto, scratch tickets, and sports betting; pull-tabs; bingo; raffles; casinos (66); slot machines and VLTs; and thoroughbred and harness racing.

▲

▼ *Table 5.2*

Variable	Australia	Great Britain	United States	Canada
Gambling on First Nation lands	No concessions have been made to allow gambling on Aboriginal lands.	No recognized First Nation groups.	Indian tribes are considered to be sovereign entities with powers that are at least as great and sometimes greater than the states where they reside. Under the terms of the federal statute, the *Indian Gaming Regulatory Act*, commercial gambling already authorized by a state can be offered on tribal lands. At present, over one-third of American tribes provide casino gambling, and two-thirds of them offer bingo.	First Nations require provincial approval to offer commercial gambling on their reserves. Currently, three provinces (Ontario, Saskatchewan, and British Columbia) offer casinos; proposals for the creation of First Nation casinos have been approved in Manitoba and Alberta; and in Nova Scotia, 50 percent of revenues from the Sydney Casino are split among First Nations who have signed gaming agreements with the province.
Problem gambling prevalence rates	In a national study using a variant of the South Oaks Gambling Screen, the Productivity Commission (1999) reported that 2.1 percent of Australian adults had "significant or severe problems" as a result of their gambling behaviour. A further 2.8 percent of the sample were considered to be "at-risk" gamblers.	A British gambling study conducted by GamCare showed between 0.6 percent and 0.8 percent of those aged sixteen and over to be problem gamblers.	A survey conducted for the US National Gambling Impact Study Commission (1999) using the NODS (a DSM-IV-based measure of problem gambling) showed that a combined 4.2 percent of adult Americans scored as "at-risk," "problem," or "probable pathological" gamblers.	A national survey using the Canadian Problem Gambling Index indicated that 5 percent of adult Canadians qualified as "at-risk" or "problem gamblers" (Marshall and Wynne 2004).

	Australia	United Kingdom	United States	Canada
Problem gambling support services funding	The primary responsibility for providing problem gambling treatment services rests with state and territorial governments. The funds to pay for these services come from levies on the gambling industry. The total funding for problem gambling support services for all of Australia in 1999 was $15 million (Productivity Commission 1999).	A Responsibility in Gambling Trust of £3 million per year is contributed by the gambling industry to pay for problem gambling services. GamCare, a national counselling agency, is the primary provider for these services.	Most individual states that have an established gambling industry provide some funds for problem gambling services. These funds come from gambling licence fees, taxes, or operations. Generally, state contributions to problem gambling services have been modest and well below those given to other human service programs. For example, the state most dependent on gambling revenues, Nevada, allocates $0 for problem gambling services.	All provincial governments subsidize problem gambling prevention, treatment, and research programs. However, the funding varies considerably from province to province (for example, Nova Scotia allots $6.41 per person over eighteen years of age compared to New Brunswick's $1.25. In 2007-8, the average across Canada was $3.53 per adult person. (Canadian Partnership for Responsible Gambling 2007-8).
National gambling study	Productivity Commission (1999).	Department for Culture, Media and Sport (2001).	National Gambling Impact Study Commission (1999).	None.

Notes:
a   The legal gambling offerings noted may not be available in all areas of the country.
b   US casinos range widely in terms of size, elegance, and density per state (for example, some states do not allow casinos, while Nevada, with 366 casinos, has 40 percent of the nation's total).

regulated; whether gambling consumers are protected adequately; and whether the social harms resulting from excessive gambling are being properly addressed. Our observation that there is a need for a national gambling inquiry is suggested not only because the other countries examined have followed this path but also because of the perceived deficiencies in current Canadian gambling regulatory policies and practices. The need to assess and to provide guidelines on gambling policy for future generations is paramount. Supporting this view, Margaret Beare (1989, 177) contends that the expansion of legal gambling in Canada has created a sense of ambiguity that has "resulted in inconsistent policy, limited research and evaluation, inadequate funding for gaming regulation and enforcement, and little concern for the potential social consequences of gambling." Although her study is now twenty years old, Beare's comments remain valid today.

Clarifying the Roles and Obligations of Governments

Why are Canadian governments involved in providing gambling opportunities? Given the perceived inevitability of gambling, Canadian legislators have often claimed that it is appropriate for governments to conduct, manage, license, and regulate legal gambling as a way of constraining such negative impacts as organized crime involvement, the corruption of public officials, and unfair gambling practices. However, can it be assumed that the various levels of government oversee gambling mainly to protect the public's welfare, or are they motivated more by revenue generation in spite of the harms that may result? Both positions are relevant given the official rhetoric used in Canada to justify governmental authority to operate and regulate gambling. However, there is an inherent conflict between revenue maximization and social responsibility objectives. Canadian jurisdictions currently perform multiple roles in the provision of gambling goods and services, including licensing, managing, conducting, marketing, promoting, operating, and regulating the activity as well as garnering most of the profits.

Government self-regulation in regard to gambling, however, is questionable public policy for several reasons. For example, an inherent tension arises between the dichotomous roles played by government, namely revenue generation versus the protection of citizen welfare. To wit, certain gambling formats (EGMs) are addictively potent but, at the same time, are highly lucrative revenue sources. The policies and practices of provincial governments over time suggest that they have repeatedly been prepared to accept the gambling addiction of some citizens as a business trade-off for the sake of generating provincial government revenue. As well, self-regulation has tended to blunt transparency and accountability, has led to special treatment for private sector industry partners (such as granting regional monopolies), has created inconsistency between jurisdictions in terms of how gambling is regulated and how *Criminal Code* provisions are interpreted, and has contributed to a systemic unwillingness to address the long-term impact on the public's welfare, such as the consequences of problem gambling.

Recognizing and correcting these policy dilemmas would mean that governments could not conduct, manage, regulate, and profit from gambling at the same time. Except for the provision of lottery products, this conflict of interest is avoided in Australia, Great Britain, and the United States by licensing private corporations and/or Indian tribes to conduct and manage gambling enterprises. Without the imperative to maximize gambling revenues, individual jurisdictions can regulate gambling rigorously and impartially. In this scenario, state gambling revenues are indirect, coming from licensing fees, taxes on corporations that operate gambling, and income taxes paid by gambling industry employees. Overall, less state revenue is generated, but the profit-maximizing and regulatory roles of the state are separated. An alternative solution, though not currently in use in the other countries examined, is to allow states to manage, conduct, and profit from gambling but be regulated by a completely independent body with oversight powers akin to those of auditor generals or ethics commissioners. Of the four countries examined, Great Britain is the only one with a national gambling policy and the only one where gambling is regulated by the national government. In Australia, where gambling regulation is decentralized, scholars have called for a greater federal government presence in gambling policy and regulation on the grounds that the federal government is more likely to be guided by principles of public and national interest and thus be in a better position to mitigate interstate competition. As some commentators have suggested, the federal government would be less likely to make hasty decisions based on short-term economic pressures and be unduly influenced by the gambling industry (Costello and Millar 2000).

Responsible Gambling and Harm Minimization
Lately, the terms "responsible gambling" and "harm minimization" have been used by governments to indicate a concern for mitigating the individual and social damage associated with widespread legal gambling. While responsibility in this regard is a progressive step, it is to be noted that efforts in this area have been tentative and inconsistent (hiring social responsibility directors and incorporating modest responsible gaming features in the design of new gambling machines). Ostensibly, the reason for moving slowly on this issue is that effective responsible gambling policies and practices may result in declining gambling revenues. Despite overwhelming and incontrovertible evidence that EGMs are the game of choice for problem gamblers, provincial regulators have done little to mitigate the harms associated with machine gambling.

Lottery products are the most popular gambling format, with about 60 percent of adult Canadians participating at least once a year. Despite being the most lucrative gambling format for provincial governments, EGMs are played by only 15-20 percent of adults annually, but revenues are high because those who do use the machines do so frequently and intensely (Williams and Wood 2004). It is estimated that about one in fifteen adult Canadians (6.3 percent) are at risk of developing gambling problems, and demographic factors that increase this risk include gender, since men are somewhat more likely to become problem gamblers than are women; education, since those with less than a post-secondary education are at greater risk of developing gambling problems; and ethnicity, since those from an Aboriginal background are three times more likely than those in the general population to be at risk for problem gambling. Finally, the gambling format that places players at most risk for problem gambling is the EGM (Odegaard 2004).

It is a truism in the administration of legal gambling in Canada that, when revenue generation priorities and social responsibility clash, economic exigency wins. For example, the Ontario government recently reassessed its gambling policies in light of a study that found that 35 percent of the province's gambling revenues come from the 5 percent of the population that are problem gamblers (Williams and Wood 2004, 6). The New Gaming Strategy to Focus on a Sustainable Responsible Industry is supposed to "put social responsibility front and centre in the delivery of gaming in Ontario" (Horbay 2005, n.p). A critic of the publicized Ontario policy shift maintains that it gives the appearance that social responsibility objectives have been given a higher priority, but, in reality, attention has simply been diverted from the social and economic damages caused by "years of uncontrolled gambling expansion" (*ibid.*).

A key point raised about gambling regulation in the Australian Productivity Commission's (1999, ch. 12: 16) report is that "governments' failure to follow good regulatory process and design principles, compounded by and combined with revenue raising imperatives, may well have led to perverse regulatory outcomes in gambling." Consequently, the Productivity Commission recommended that the overriding goal of all gambling public policy should be to maximize net community benefits. This has resulted in a concerted effort by Australian state governments and territories to implement stringent harm minimization strategies.

Making social responsibility the focal point of gambling policy requires a more forceful and pre-emptive approach than has been the case so far in Canada. A comprehensive responsible gambling policy implies a commitment to probity and to addressing duty-of-care obligations, even if it means reduced gambling revenues. A recent report issued by the Independent

Pricing and Regulatory Tribunal of New South Wales (2004), entitled *Gambling: Promoting a Culture of Responsibility*, provides a state-of-the-art approach to responsible gambling policy. According to the New South Wales report, an exemplary responsible gambling strategy consists of three main elements:

- informed choice – being able to make decisions about a gambling format on the basis of adequate information about the nature and foreseeable consequences of the activity and without controlling influences;
- consumer protection – implementing measures to discourage risky behaviours and to minimize the incidence, prevalence, and negative consequences of problem gambling;
- counselling measures – various programs to assist those who are developing or have developed gambling problems to stop or control their intemperate behaviour and to blunt the negative impacts of these behaviours on the gamblers themselves, their families, friends, employers, and the wider community.

Along with these responsible gambling building blocks, the report calls for government transparency, active monitoring and enforcement of responsible gambling regulations, and the need for evidence-based research to inform decision makers. In general, Canadian provincial governments do a satisfactory job of providing problem gambling counselling and prevention programs, but they are deficient in the areas of informed choice and consumer protection. For example, Canadian gamblers are not well informed about the probabilities of winning or gambling machine pay-out ratios, nor are they given instructions about how EGMs work. Based on the standards provided by a New South Wales study, Canadian jurisdictions have been lax in implementing certain consumer protection measures. For example, casinos in some provinces extend credit and offer cheque-cashing services, but self-exclusion programs generally exist only for casino patrons and are relatively easy to circumvent. Furthermore, research has shown that bill acceptors on gambling machines and gambling location automatic transaction machines exacerbate problem gambling behaviour, yet they remain a standard feature in Canadian gambling venues. As well, while the maximum bet on a New South Wales gambling machine is $10, some Canadian provinces offer machines that take $100 bets.

Canadian provincial governments also tend to lack transparency on gambling issues, are seldom open to public input about their gambling policies, and are often averse to having research evidence guide policy decisions. Presumably, challenging questions and contrary research findings threaten gambling revenues. However, by adopting defensive stances with regard to their gambling policies and operations, governments violate their covenant to promote the public interest. In this section, we have sought to explore gambling policies and regulatory frameworks in three countries for the purpose of informing legal gambling policies and regulations in Canada. In our view, existing Canadian legal gambling regimes fall short of the laudable goal of maximizing net community benefits. Achieving this goal requires that gambling be regulated in an uncompromising and impartial fashion and that social responsibility becomes the paramount objective of all gambling policy.

Final Observations
This chapter has shown that there are contentious legal, behavioural, and public policy issues raised by the legalization and expansion of many forms of gambling. For example, we have seen how questions have been raised concerning the legality of the interpretations by some provinces of certain *Criminal Code* amendments pertaining to gambling. There is, as well, an absence of consistency in the way in which these gambling amendments have been applied by different provincial governments. We have also observed that the *Criminal Code* amendments and their interpretation raise questions regarding the division of powers between the federal and provincial governments. How can a proper balance be maintained between local provision and regulation of gambling formats and national consistency in the interpretation and implementation of the *Criminal Code*?

Despite the legalization of many forms of gambling, a number of unwanted and harmful behaviours associated with gambling have persisted and, in some cases, increased. In particular, criminal behaviour and gambling remain linked in a number of ways, and new social problems such as "excessive" or "problem" gambling have arisen – the latter associated with the availability of EGMs. A range of provincially funded educational and therapeutic programs directed at preventing and ameliorating problems associated with these new forms of deviance has emerged.

Finally, we have highlighted a number of public policy questions raised by the legalization and expansion of gambling. Most generally, how can the benefits and costs of legal gambling be balanced and the unintended but negative consequences of legalization be mitigated? How should public opinion and values enter into the policy process with respect to the regulation of gambling? Yet perhaps the most crucial policy issue concerns the potential conflicts of interest that arise for provincial governments when they both regulate and promote gambling. Provincial governments have become increasingly dependent on the enhanced revenue generated by the expansion of legal gambling. Therefore, they have a vested interest in the promotion and expansion of gambling. At the same time, these governments now have almost exclusive power to regulate and control gambling activity.

The potential for conflicts inherent in this situation is of pressing concern from both the perspective of public welfare and the integrity of governmental institutions.

Social theory can help place these specific issues regarding the legalization and expansion of gambling within a broader context, explicate the underlying social, economic, and political forces contributing to changes in the social control of gambling, and result in a clarification and generalization of the questions involved. Each of the four theoretical perspectives that follow provides insight into the sources and effects of the changes observed in the social control of gambling in Canada.

The Consensus Perspective

One perspective on the criminal law regards it as an expression of a fundamental consensus in society with regard to certain values and norms. This view of law and punishment emphasizes the expressive and symbolic functions of the criminal law and its enforcement (Durkheim 1960, 1984). From this perspective, then, change in consensus regarding fundamental values should result in legal change, with behaviours once regarded as crimes being decriminalized or legalized. Applied to the topic of gambling, this perspective would argue that the legalization of many forms of gambling in Canada reflects a declining consensus around gambling as a moral evil or vice. While it seems clear that public opinion did not play a major role in producing the 1969 and 1985 *Criminal Code* amendments, it is also evident that public attitudes towards gambling did shift over time towards greater toleration and an acceptance of legalized gambling. Thus, there appears to be evidence of some consensus for aspects of legalized gambling. However, it remains unclear to what extent such consensus has facilitated the *Criminal Code* amendments or, rather, has been the result of these legislative changes. Furthermore, Canadian public opinion remains generally ambivalent towards gambling, particularly with respect to certain types and locations as well as the appropriate balance to be struck between benefits and costs. Thus, public policy concerning some aspects of gambling lacks a strong consensus and could result in a backlash against some government regulations. Consensus or functional theory suggests, then, that there are limits on the extent to which legislation and regulation can diverge from the widely held views of the public.

The Interest Group/Conflict Perspective

A second theoretical perspective recognizes a major limitation of Durkheim's functional approach, namely a failure to consider the role of power and interest group activity in legal change. Rather than a consensus on fundamental values, this perspective conceptualizes society as being constituted by a variety of interest groups in competition and conflict over scarce resources (Quinney 1970; Akers 1994; Akers and Hawkins 1975). Interest groups with greater power are better situated to influence the legislative process to protect their interests and/or values. While there are a variety of interest group/conflict theories, they all emphasize that law, including criminal law, represents, expresses, and protects the specific interests and/ or values of particular groups or segments within society. Applied to gambling legislation, this perspective looks for indications of the influence of business groups such as the leisure industry, including private sector gaming corporations, trade associations, charitable groups, and entrepreneurial individuals in lobbying for the decriminalization of gambling.

Morton's (2003) discussion of the appearance in the early twentieth century of both legislative reform groups and an anti-gambling lobby may represent an example of the interest group/conflict perspective. However, there is a lack of evidence of any significant public or interest group involvement in the 1969 and 1985 amendments. Yet as a result of these amendments and the subsequent expansion of legalized gambling, a number of "special interest" groups have arisen – primarily consisting of non-profit, community-based charitable organizations such as social, cultural, and amateur sporting groups – interested in exerting influence on public policy regarding the social control of gambling. This perspective also focuses attention on provincial governments as the major "interested actors" in the evolution of the social control of gambling in Canada. This is certainly evident in the federal-provincial struggle over gambling in the 1970s and 1980s and the 1985 *Criminal Code* amendments. However, it is perhaps even more apparent since provincial governments have taken on the dual role of major promoter and financial beneficiary of legalized gambling. This perspective suggests, then, that it is unlikely that provincial governments will cede any significant regulatory power over gambling back to the federal government or, indeed, to any other agency.

The Managing Consent Perspective

Another, less comprehensive, perspective has been developed to draw on the historical and cultural realities of Canada's political economy to interpret strategies used by the federal government for governing in a neo-conservative environment (Hatt, Caputo, and Perry 1990, 1992). Termed managing consent, "this strategy emphasizes the generation of public support while avoiding direct, open, and hostile confrontation ... An effort is made to institutionalize conflict and turn political problems into technical and administrative ones" (*ibid.*, 246). These authors suggest that a number of external and domestic factors act to constrain federal public policy development. Most important for our purposes are federal versus provincial powers. The practice of devolving federal responsibilities to lower levels of government has allowed the federal government "to insulate itself from criticism by shifting frustrations and concerns from its own terrain onto that of the provinces" (*ibid.*, 247).

The *Criminal Code* amendments of 1969 and 1985 seem to exemplify the strategy of "managing consent" on the part of the federal government. Maintaining the criminal prohibitions on certain forms of gambling (for example, keeping a common gaming house, "unlicensed" gambling formats), while decriminalizing a variety of widely acceptable gambling activities by placing them under provincial authority, is one way of managing the competing federal and provincial powers. However, this may also have represented a way in which the federal government could "insulate itself from criticism" from segments of the population opposed to gambling expansion and from concerns regarding the possible increased social costs of such action (*ibid.*, 247). While ceding social control to the provinces, as well as much of the revenue-generating potential of legalized gambling, the federal government also effectively withdrew itself from the responsibility of dealing with the various problems associated with gambling expansion. In this way, the federal government can be seen as simultaneously decriminalizing a variety of now widely acceptable activities while upholding the public condemnation of some remaining public vices.

The Neo-Liberal State Perspective
A recent theme in the literature of social control is the mutation of welfare capitalism with the primacy of the social activist state into neo-liberalism with its emphasis on individualism and minimal state structure and a preoccupation with the containment of risk (Garland 1996, 2001; Hudson 2003; O'Malley 1999). Neo-liberalism allows the state only a minimum of functions, including the punishment and control of the dangerous and predatory in relation to crime (Hudson 2003). Among the cultural characteristics of late modernity noted by David Garland (2000) are hyper-individualism, distrust of the state, and the dominance of economic rather than social reasoning. Garland (1996, 2001) argues that the problem of crime control in late modernity demonstrates the limits of sovereign states. They can no longer govern by means of sovereign commands to obedient subjects and therefore "see the need to withdraw or at least qualify their claim to be the primary and effective provider of security and crime control" (Garland 1996, 449).

Garland (*ibid.*) discusses several strategies devised by the administrative machine of the state to adapt to its crime control limitations. One of these is to "define deviance down" either by filtering it out of the system altogether or by lowering the degree to which certain behaviours are criminalized and penalized (see also Moynihan 1992). Thus, behaviours that were once routinely prosecuted may be decriminalized, or the police may decide that they will no longer use scarce investigative resources on certain offences that have a low likelihood of detection and/or a low priority for the public.

Several aspects of the neo-liberal/minimal state perspective apply to key features of the changes observed in the social control of gambling. For example, "economic reasoning" has become an important feature of the discussion regarding the regulation of gambling, particularly in view of the huge profits that are generated. However, even at the outset of the federal-provincial negotiations surrounding amendments to the *Criminal Code,* economic considerations were much more influential than social considerations. We have also observed, beginning with the amendments to the *Criminal Code,* several instances of the "minimal state defining deviance down." The federal government has shifted much of the regulatory control to the provinces, which in turn, have used various means for downloading the control of licensed gambling to Crown corporations and private sector gambling interests. As a result of the low priority assigned to such crime by the public police, these agencies have acquired much of the responsibility for the prevention of gambling-related crime on their premises as well as some of the law enforcement responsibilities (Smith and Wynne 2004; 1999). This fits Garland's (1996, 452) "responsibilization strategy" – whereby central government seeks to act on crime indirectly by seeking to activate action on the part of non-state agencies and organizations rather than directly through state agencies. Perhaps paradoxically, this may result in an extension of social control as these gambling enterprises employ a variety of surveillance techniques over all customers in efforts at situational crime control. With this privatization of the social control of licensed gambling, along with the increased tolerance of gambling by the public, there is some evidence that the criminal justice system is assigning enforcement a lower priority. Concomitant with the emergence of neo-liberal states, an emphasis on consumer-driven, service-based, free-market economies, and a general downsizing and outsourcing of the functions of the welfare state, politicians began to recognize that legal gambling could undercut criminal elements, bolster state budgets, and generate funds for charitable and non-profit organizations – all while curbing increases in taxation. In short, a neo-liberal worldview took root based on the premise that, if gambling could not be suppressed, then at least some public good should come from it. In turn, greater public acceptance of legal gambling allowed criminal justice authorities to relax their formal surveillance of illegal gambling, believing that resources could be better spent monitoring more serious crime (Smith and Wynne 1999).

In a similar vein, Sytze Kingma (2004) has argued that the liberalization and expansion of gambling were part of an international phenomenon that saw state gambling public policy shift from an "alibi model" to "risk model" principles. Although discussing gambling in the Netherlands, Kingma's analysis applies to the gambling policies of other industrialized nations, including Canada. According to Kingma (*ibid.,* 49), an "alibi model" was in vogue prior to gambling's expansion and was typified by tightly regulated gambling under the following conditions: (1) legalization that was intended to avoid illegal markets; (2) the discouragement of private profiteering; and (3) gambling proceeds that were directed towards social programs such as welfare, sports, and other "worthy causes." A "risk model" subsequently emerged along with, and as a result of, global gambling expansion in the 1980s and was exemplified by: (1) gambling being viewed as a legitimate form of commercial entertainment; (2) a belief that gambling revenues should augment government coffers and spur the economy; and (3) a belief that gambling "markets" require state control to minimize the risks of addiction and crime (*ibid.;* see also Smith and Campbell 2007).

Using Jurgen Habermas' (1975) "legitimation crisis" as an explanatory tool, Kingma (2004) postulated that the paradigm shift occurred during the 1970s and 1980s, when legislation lagged behind aggressive gambling practices, ultimately creating a situation where "politics gave in to market demands without convincing and conclusive (legal) justification (*ibid.,* 55). The upshot of this policy inversion was gambling proceeds being largely redirected from decentralized welfare initiatives towards government coffers and the introduction of new gambling formats designed not as intrinsically pleasing, recreational amusements but, rather, as systems for profit maximization (Smith and Campbell 2007).

James Cosgrave (2006, 5) has characterized this redirection as a shift from local to global markets and a "colonization" of gambling by both the gambling industry and the state, working collaboratively in what Gerda Reith (2007, 36) regards as a "symbiotic relationship." No longer a threat to the rationality essential to the work/production ethic of modernist capitalism, gambling has been thus commodified as a legitimate leisure activity and constituted as a fundamental aspect of the consumption ethic prevalent currently in late modernity (Reith 2007; Cosgrave 2006).

The "containment of risk" is another theme from this perspective that seems applicable to the social control of gambling. When the social costs involved in gambling expansion are considered, the relatively small percentage of "problem gamblers" often dominates discussion in lieu of a broader debate focused on public welfare. In conjunction with this attention to risk assessment and harm minimization for "problem gamblers," the degree of social control over gambling may actually be extended, at least for segments of the population, through monitoring and/or restricting their gambling behaviour and instituting various treatment regimes. As Reith (2007, 50) has pointed out, the emergence of problem gambling as an unintended consequence of liberalized, commercialized gambling illuminates "some of the contradictions of modern consumer societies, namely, the increasing emphasis on individual self-control through freely willed practices of consumption that accompanies the reduction in external forms of regulation in economic and social life." The emphasis on individual self-control is evident in the development of responsible gambling strategies, wherein state and commercial interests actively promote the notion that individuals are responsible for holding their "inappropriate" gambling consumption to acceptable levels and by providing an array of "experts" in the form of psychologists, counsellors, and other treatment specialists who actively work both to constitute and cure the problem gambler. In this sense, the self-imposition of norms and values conducive to appropriate gambling consumption is achieved, and therapy itself becomes a form of regulation (*ibid.,* 45 and 50).

Ultimately, the delegation of authority over gambling from the federal government to the provinces, at the very least, is a tacit admission that gambling no longer stands as a matter warranting criminal prohibition. Indeed, as much of the preceding discussion confirms, Canadian criminal law has been used principally to consolidate provincial authority over gambling as a revenue-raising instrument and to expand its availability rather than restrict it in any meaningful sense. Jean-Paul Brodeur and Genevieve Ouellet (2004, 27) have considered the use of the criminal law for the purpose of creating a "limiting monopoly," wherein government control of particular activities is justified on the basis of protecting the public. Such an example resides in the *Controlled Drugs and Substances Act,* wherein the intent is to restrict both the availability and use of substances deemed to be potentially harmful if used improperly.[12] Instead, Canadian criminal law in regard to gambling has been used principally to consolidate and legitimize a provincial government "expansionist monopoly" (*ibid.*). The use of the criminal law as an instrument of provincial fiscal policy rather than as a means for preventing or mitigating social harm thus raises fundamental questions about the purpose and role of law in a modern democratic society. At a minimum, the use of the criminal law to consolidate a provincial monopoly over gambling in Canada strikingly reveals the extent to which the demarcation between "criminal behaviour" and "acceptable behaviour" is largely the outcome of political processes.

Acknowledgments

The authors would like to acknowledge the research assistance of three undergraduate students: Lora Lee, Ayren Messmer, and Jessica Sherman. Gary McCaskill provided much appreciated word-formatting support. We also acknowledge the contribution provided by our interview subjects in the United States, Great Britain, Australia, and Canada. We are grateful for the support given to this project by Rob Simpson and the Ontario Problem Gambling Research Centre and by Vicki Williams and the Alberta Gaming Research Institute. Harold Wynne provided important and helpful comments on an earlier draft of this chapter. We are also especially thankful for the Law Commission of Canada's support and for the opportunity to participate in its "what is a crime?" project. The Law Commission of Canada's senior research officer, Steve Bittle, oversaw the project. His sage advice contributed in immeasurable and positive ways to the original report. More recently, we benefited from the relevant and challenging issues raised by the anonymous reviewers of this chapter.

Notes

1 The shorter *Oxford English Dictionary* provides the following definition of "gamble": "to play games of chance for money; to stake money on some chance." Interestingly, a search of recent textbooks on gambling did not reveal a succinct definition.
2 *Criminal Code*, R.S.C. 1985, c. C-46.
3 See subsequent discussion of public opinion data.
4 Readers interested in the details of this conflict and the terms of its settlement are referred to Labrosse (1985), Osborne and Campbell (1988), Osborne (1989), Campbell (1994), and Campbell, Hartnagel, and Smith (2005).
5 In a parimutuel system, bettors technically wager among themselves rather than with a bookmaker. Payouts to winners are a function of the total amount bet (or "handle"), divided by the number of winning selections; thus, bettors themselves determine the odds. In practice, operators of the parimutuel pools deduct a percentage (or "takeout") from the handle as a profit for themselves and to pay the owners of the winning horses (Abt, Smith, and Christiansen 1985, 83).
6 "Gross profit" includes the government share of gambling revenues plus the expenses associated with its delivery. "Net profit" represents the amount of gambling revenue that accrues to government after expenses have been deducted (Azmier 2005, 2). Some gambling observers refer to "gross profit" as the "win" or the amount equal to that lost by gamblers.
7 It is noteworthy that in 2007-8 total net gambling revenue accruing to the government was slightly over $7 billion, while that accruing to charitable and community-based non-profit organizations from their licensed gaming activities was approximately $0.5 billion (Canadian Partnership for Responsible Gambling 2007-8). While it would be important and interesting for future research to compare the extent to which the various levels of governments direct additional gambling funds to charitable and non-profit organizations versus what they direct to traditional line budget expenditures, this type of analysis is beyond the purposes of the present chapter.
8 Even though the report was never released officially to the public, a leaked copy became available (Donovan and Welsh 1998) and is available online at Review of Gaming Legislation in Canada, http://www.cbc.ca/news/background/gambling/pdf/gambling_report2.pdf.
9 See Bailey (2004).
10 See Thorne (2002).
11 For further complications in this lawsuit, see CTV.ca, http://montreal.ctv.ca/servlet/an/local/CTVNews/20090520/mtl_vlt_report_altered090520/20090520/?hub=MontrealHome.
12 *Controlled Drugs and Substances Act*, S.C. 1996, c. 19.

References

Abt, V., J.F. Smith, and E.M. Christiansen. 1985. *The Business of Risk: Commercial Gambling in Mainstream America*. Lawrence, KA: University of Kansas Press.

Akers, R. 1994. *Criminological Theories*. Los Angeles: Roxbury.

Akers, R., and R. Hawkins. 1975. *Law and Control in Society*. Englewood Cliffs, NJ: Prentice Hall.

Alfieri, D. 1994. "The Ontario Casino Project: A Case Study." In *Gambling in Canada: The Bottom Line*, ed. C. Campbell, 85-91. Burnaby, BC: Criminology Research Centre, Simon Fraser University.

Azmier, J. 2000. *Canadian Gambling Behaviour and Attitudes: Summary Report*. Calgary, AB: Canada West Foundation.

–. 2001a. *Gambling in Canada: An Overview*. Calgary, AB: Canada West Foundation.

–. 2001b. *Gambling in Canada: Final Report and Recommendations*. Calgary, AB: Canada West Foundation.

–. 2005. *Gambling in Canada 2005: Statistics and Context*. Calgary, AB: Canada West Foundation.

Bailey, S. 2004. "Woodbine Internet Betting Site under Fire as Justice Investigates." *VIVA Consulting,* http://www.vivaconsulting.com/advocacy/woodbine.html.

Beare, M. 1989. "Current Law Enforcement Issues in Canadian Gambling." In *Gambling in Canada: Golden Goose or Trojan Horse,* Proceedings of the First National Symposium on Lotteries and Gambling, ed. C. Campbell and J. Lowman, 177-94. Burnaby, BC: Simon Fraser University.

Bowal, P., and C. Carrasco. 1997. "Taking a Chance on It: The Legal Regulation of Gambling." *Law Now* 22, 2: 28-30.

Brodeur, J., and G. Ouellet. 2004. "What Is a Crime? A Secular Answer." In *What Is a Crime? Defining Criminal Conduct in Contemporary Society,* ed. Law Commission of Canada, 1-33. Vancouver and Toronto: UBC Press.

Campbell, C. 1994. *Canadian Gambling Legislation: The Social Origins of Legalization,* PhD diss., Simon Fraser University, Burnaby, BC [unpublished].

Campbell, C., T. Hartnagel, and G. Smith. 2005. *The Legalization of Gambling in Canada.* Report prepared for the Law Commission of Canada, Ottawa, ON.

Campbell, C., and G. Smith. 1998. "Canadian Gambling: Trends and Public Policy Issues." *Annals of the American Academy of Political and Social Science* 556: 22-35.

–. 2003. "Gambling in Canada: From Vice to Disease to Responsibility: A Negotiated History." *Canadian Bulletin of Medical History* 20, 1: 121-49.

Canada. 1956. *Report of the Joint Committee on the Senate and the House of Commons on Capital Punishment, Corporal Punishment, and Lotteries.* Ottawa: Queen's Printer.

–. 2004. *Proceedings of the Standing Senate Committee on Legal and Constitutional Affairs, Dec. 1 and 2.* Ottawa: Queen's Printer.

Canadian Partnership for Responsible Gambling. 2007-8. *Canadian Gambling Digest,* http://www.cprg.ca/articles/Canadian_Gambling_Digest_2007_2008.pdf.

Cosgrave, J.F., ed. 2006. *The Sociology of Risk and Gambling Reader.* New York: Routledge.

–. 2009. "Introduction: The Shape of Legalized Gambling in Canada." In *Casino State: Legalized Gambling in Canada,* ed. J. Cosgrave and T. Klassen. Toronto: University of Toronto Press.

Cosgrave, J.F., and T. Klassen. 2001. "Gambling against the State: The State and the Legitimation of Gambling." *Current Sociology* 49, 5: 1-15.

Costello, T., and R. Millar. 2000. *Wanna Bet?* St. Leonards, Australia: Allen and Unwin.

Department for Culture, Media and Sport. 2001. *Gambling Review Report.* London: Department for Culture, Media and Sport.

Dixon, D. 1991. *From Prohibition to Regulation: Anti-Gambling and the Law.* Oxford: Clarendon.

Donovan, K., and M. Welsh. 1998. "Ontario's Casinos Illegal, Secret Report Says." *Toronto Star,* 31 October, A26.

Durkheim, E. 1960. *The Division of Labour in Society.* Glencoe, IL: Free Press.

–. 1984. "The Evolution of Punishment." In *Durkheim and the Law,* ed. S. Lukes and A. Scull, 102-32. Oxford: Basil Blackwell.

Falkiner, T., and R. Horbay. 2006. "Unbalanced Reel Gaming Machines." Paper presented at the International Pokies Impact Conference, Melbourne, Australia.

Garland, D. 1996. "The Limits of the Sovereign State." *British Journal of Criminology* 36, 4: 445-70.

–. 2000. "The Culture of High Crime Societies." *British Journal of Criminology* 40, 3: 347-75.

–. 2001. *The Culture of Control.* Oxford: Oxford University Press.

Habermas, J. 1975. *Legitimation Crisis,* trans. T. McCarthy. Boston: Beacon.

Hatt, K. 1992. "Criminal Justice Policy under Mulroney, 1984-1990." *Canadian Public Policy* 18, 3: 245-60.

Hatt, K., T. Caputo, and B. Perry. 1990. "Managing Consent: Canada's Experience with Neo-Conservatism." *Social Justice* 17, 4: 30-48.

Horbay, R. 2004. "EGM Transparency: An Essential Element of Product Safety and Consumer Protection." Paper presented at the International Problem Gambling Conference on Myths, Reality, and Ethical Public Policy, Halifax, NS, 4-6 October.

–. 2005. "Guest Editorial." *Canada's Gambling Watch Network Weekly Newsletter,* 24 January, 15.

–. 2009. Personal communication. 11 November.

Hosenball, M. 1999. "Sex, Bets, and Bikers." *Newsweek,* 18 October, 50-51.

Hudson, B.A. 2003. *Understanding Justice.* Buckingham, UK: Open University Press.

Independent Pricing and Regulatory Tribunal. 2004. *Gambling: Promoting a Culture of Responsibility.* Sydney, Australia: Independent Pricing and Regulatory Tribunal.

Ipsos News Centre. 1998. CTV/Angus Reid Group Poll, Press Release, 10 March.

Kelly, R., P. Todosichuk, and J. Azmier. 2001. *Gambling@Home: Internet Gambling in Canada.* Calgary: Canada West Foundation.

Kingma, S. 2004. "Gambling and the Risk Society: The Liberalization and Legitimation Crisis of Gambling in the Netherlands." *International Gambling Studies* 4, 1: 47-67.

Labrosse, M. 1985. *The Lottery ... From Jacques Cartier's Day to Modern Times.* Montreal: Stanke.

Lipton, M. 2003. "Internet Gaming in Canada." Paper presented at the Global Gaming Exposition, Las Vegas, NV, 17 September.

Marshall, K. 2008. *Perspectives on Labour and Income: Gambling,* Catalogue No. 75-001-x. Ottawa: Statistics Canada.

Marshall, K., and H. Wynne. 2004. "Against the Odds: A Profile of At-Risk and Problem Gamblers." *Canadian Social Trends* 73: 25-29.

Monahan, P., and G. Goldlist. 1999. "Roll Again: New Developments Concerning Gaming." *Criminal Law Quarterly* 42, 2: 182-226.

Morris, Rose, and Ledgett. 1996. *Review of Gaming Legislation in Ontario.* Report prepared for the Ontario government, Toronto, ON, http://www.cbc.ca/news/background/gambling/pdf/gambling_report2.pdf.

Morton, S. 2003. *At Odds: Gambling and Canadians 1919-1969.* Toronto, ON: University of Toronto Press.

Moynihan, D.P. 1992. "Defining Deviance Down." *American Scholar* 62, 1: 17-30.

National Gambling Impact Study Commission. 1999. *Final Report.* Washington, DC: Government Printing Office.

Odegaard, Siri. 2004. "Gambling in Canada." *The Wager* 9, 28: 1, Brief Addiction Science Information Source, http://www.basisonline.org/2004/07/the-wager-vol-1.html.

O'Malley, P. 1999. "Volatile and Contradictory Punishments." *Theoretical Criminology* 1, 3: 175-96.

Osborne, J.A. 1989. *The Legal Status of Lottery Schemes in Canada: Changing the Rules of the Game.* LL.M. diss., Faculty of Law, University of British Columbia, Vancouver [unpublished].

Osborne, J.A., and C.S. Campbell. 1988. "Recent Amendments to Canadian Lottery and Gaming Laws: The Transfer of Power between Federal and Provincial Governments." *Osgoode Hall Law Journal* 26, 1: 19-43.

Patrick, T. 2000. "No Dice: Violations of the Criminal Code's Gaming Exemptions by Provincial Governments." *Criminal Law Quarterly* 44, 1: 108-26.

Productivity Commission. 1999. *Australia's Gambling Industries,* volumes 1-2. Canberra, Australia: Productivity Commission.

Quinney, R. 1970. *The Social Reality of Crime.* Boston, MA: Little, Brown.

Reith, G. 1999. *The Age of Chance: Gambling in Western Culture.* London: Routledge.

–. 2007. "Gambling and the Contradictions of Consumption." *American Behavioral Scientist* 51, 1: 33-55.

Roberts, J.V. 1992. "Public Opinion, Crime, and Criminal Justice." In *Crime and Justice: A Review of Research,* ed. M. Tonry. Chicago, IL: University of Chicago Press.

Smith, G.J., and C.S. Campbell. 2007. "Tensions and Contentions: An Examination of Electronic Gaming Issues in Canada." *American Behavioral Scientist* 51, 1: 86-101.

Smith, G.J., and H. Wynne. 1999. *Gambling and Crime in Western Canada: Exploring Myth and Reality.* Calgary, AB: Canada West Foundation.

–. 2004. *VLT Gambling in Alberta: A Preliminary Analysis.* Edmonton, AB: Alberta Gaming Research Institute.

Thorne, D. 2002. "Quebec Lawsuit a Warning to Alta Researcher." *Newscan* 4, 16: 1, Responsible Gambling Council, http://www.responsiblegambling.org/articles/041902_16.pdf.

Williams, R., and R. Wood. 2004. *The Demographic Sources of Ontario Gaming Revenue*. Report prepared for the Ontario Problem Gambling Research Centre, Guelph, ON.
Zimmerman, S.E., D.J. Van Alstyne, and C.S. Dunn. 1988. "The National Punishment Survey and Public Policy Consequences." *Journal of Research in Crime and Delinquency* 25, 2: 120-49.

List of Cases

Nanaimo Community Bingo Association v. British Columbia (Attorney General), [1999] 2 W.W.R. 428 (B.C.S.C.).
Brochu v. Société des Loteries du Québec, [2002] J.Q. No. 1062 (Q.L.).

Afterword
Marie-Andrée Bertrand

Reflections on Crime in Contemporary Criminology

While these case studies, and other works initiated by the Law Commission of Canada, move us well beyond formalistic, static, and objectified studies of "crime," do they push us hard and far enough? And, more importantly, do they challenge us to engage in questions about the truly harmful social conduct of our times? The preceding studies are a step in the right direction, examining as they do how crime becomes defined in practice and misused by the state, and by the powerful more generally, to protect a conception of social order inspired by neo-liberalism. There is far too little research done on this subject and from this perspective in Canada. Except for two short periods in the mid-1970s and 1980s, Canadian criminology has been seemingly uninterested in critiquing the concept of crime and even less interested in uncovering the miscarriages of justice perpetrated by political and economic powers (Ratner 1984; MacLean 1986; McMullan and Ratner 1982; O'Reilly Fleming 1985).[1]

A review of the article "Criminology Research and Criminal Justice Policy in Canada: Present Trends and Future Prospects," under the editorship of C. Murphy and P. Stenning (1999), shows that the "penal question" – meaning prisons, prison reformation, penal politics and practices, sentencing, and parole – is the subject that has attracted the most attention in the past twenty to thirty years (Woods 1999; Stenning 1999). While this subject lends itself to radical questions regarding crime, the legitimacy of criminalizing certain forms of behaviours, and the proportionality of the sentence with the harm done, the researchers' preoccupations point in a very different direction. Rather, what concerns them is the cessation of government financial support to university research centres in criminology and the closing of the research divisions at the Ministry of Justice and at the offices of the solicitor general, as if research was a good thing in itself, whatever its object and perspective. Second in quantitative importance come the subjects of police (Murphy 1999), youth justice (Doob 1999), the treatment of Aboriginal persons within the criminal justice system (La Prairie 1999), and the drug question (Erickson 1999). Here, too, the critique of the researchers is focused squarely on the lack of funding, but it has been expanded to encompass concerns regarding the limited impact of criminological research on penal policies. While this disconnect between criminological research and penal policies is identified and described, it remains inadequately theorized and, thus, unsatisfactorily explained.[2]

Another review is to be found in the *Canadian Journal of Law and Society* (*CJLS*) under the title "Law as a Means of Exclusion" (Bertrand 1996, 15-18). It deals with issues relating to women and racialized peoples. Here the contributors adopt critical perspectives drawn from feminist theories, or post-colonial and anti-racist perspectives, and target the legal definition of crime as the main source of injustice. In contrast with the theoretical orientations of this thematic issue of the *CJLS*, a great number of criminological studies of the late 1990s and early 2000s offer limited analysis, focusing instead on descriptive accounts of crime victims (Wemmers, Cousineau, and Demers 2004) and "marginal people," such as prostitutes (Paradis and Cousineau 2005), street people and street gangs (Fournier 2003), drug users (Sun et al. 2004), and the typical trajectories of juvenile deviants (Brunelle et al. 2002). The authors of these descriptive accounts pay scant attention to the political and economic issues. For instance, questions such as "are the economic interests of the city and neighbourhood security under threat due to the visible presence of marginalized people?" or "are there possible alliances between the police and shopkeepers to 'clean' the city?" – which hint at the possible complicity between economic and political actors in the processes of criminalization – are not even raised.

Although there are Canadian authors who have been very critical of the limitations posed by the notion of crime itself, and even more embarrassed when it comes to the lack of recognition and sanctions for the most harmful behaviours in our society,[3] the vast majority of Canadian criminologists work as agents of the state attempting to build better "criminal" traps to catch individuals who then feed the criminal justice industry and do little to respond to the real issues that many of these individuals face (see Mosher and Hermer, Chapter 1 in this volume; Brockman, Chapter 2 in this volume).

Beyond Criminology

In sharp contrast to what has been going on in Canadian criminology studies, a cohort of British and Irish criminologists and other social scientists acknowledges that the discipline of criminology has neglected crime studies for forty years and forgotten to engage in critique as it did in the 1970s (Hillyard et al. 2004; Schwendinger and Schwendinger 1970; Taylor, Walton, and Young 1973; Quinney 1973; Mathiesen 1980) and is moving forward to work together at identifying and comprehending the "functors" of crime and renew the discipline through criticism. Their theses could be summed up in the following ways. It is useless and even harmful to study crime as defined by the penal code since the conducts and behaviours defined as crimes do not really involve serious social harm. It is time to recognize that governments and big business, and not individuals or small groups, are the greatest perpetrators of injustice and inequalities. They are the authors of serious wrongdoings that impact on entire populations (Tombs and Hillyard 2004, 30-54). We must recognize the moral indifference of political and big business leaders, which penal legislators are unable or unwilling to see (Pemberton 2004, 67-83). For example, despite the number and seriousness of physical injuries attributable to working conditions, legislators do not turn to criminalization mechanisms to stop these tragedies. Instead, they leave these matters in the hands of standard- and procedure-setting bodies. Indeed, within the present state of criminal law, it is unthinkable and un-feasible to enact effective penalties and financial sanctions for such wrong-doing, because all the "guilty," or even suspect, companies would sooner quit the country, leave the employees jobless, and abscond with their capital (Tombs 2004, 156-77). As for political power and its own illegal activities, it is incapable of acting to identify, let alone correct, its own transgressions. It practises a form of organizational deviance that is impossible to sanction by the penal code or even by civil law. Although this is a significant prob-lem, few have attempted to investigate how and with what means we can regulate legislators who violate their own laws (Ward 2004). Moreover, central governments are not the only ones that contravene their own norms and act with moral indifference. Provincial authorities do the same and are akin to individual criminal offenders. Similarly, municipal and regional authorities, while neglecting to take the appropriate measures to protect the lives and welfare of their citizens, fuel stereotypes, undermine civil society, and contribute to the impoverishment of particular geographic areas. In *Beyond Criminology,* a geographer demonstrates that the two vari-ables most closely associated with homicides are not the characteristics of the perpetrator or those of the victim, nor the *modus operandi,* but, rather, the material environmental factors – neglected premises and poverty (Dor-ling 2004, 178-91).

In sum, according to the two authors of the introduction to *Beyond Criminology,*

> there are good reasons why this is an important moment to rehearse the criticisms and debate the issues around criminology and social harm. To begin with, van Swaaningen, in his recent analysis of critical criminology [references deleted], has argued that the "heyday" of critical criminology has passed away from epistemological and socio-political questions and

returned to its old empiricist orientation as an applied science ... fuelled by the political issues of the day, and geared by the agenda of its financiers. (Hillyard and Tombs 2004, 10)

They are right. Since the end of the 1970s and mid-1980s, in Canada at least, criminology has not often enough examined its proper goals. We must go further. However, should we follow the example of our British and Irish colleagues when they suggest renaming the discipline and refocusing on a serious subject – not *"crime as defined by the law"* but, rather, the really serious social harms that the criminal codes are careful not to define? In *Beyond Criminology*, Hillyard et al. (2004) propose a new discipline: *zemiology*, meaning the study of serious social harms that impact entire populations. This new field would utilize concepts developed in political science and economics. In *Toxic Capitalism*, Frank Pearce and Steve Tombs (1998) revisit Antonio Gramsci's (1971) notion of hegemony, showing how political leaders and the dominant classes have managed to successfully transmit their views to their subordinates and, according to Gramsci himself, to society as a whole.

The concept of hegemony is usefully employed to understand not only the repressive actions of both welfare officers and concerned citizens in scrutinizing the conduct of welfare recipients but also the alliance of professionals with the penal system to filter down physicians' delinquencies and de-escalate punishment. Gramsci's theory also sheds light on the way that Ontario welfare officers have acted as the instruments for the implementation of Conservative government policies (Mosher and Hermer, Chapter 1 in this volume). Gramsci (1971) illustrates how the dominant classes succeed in imbuing their economic projects with a "historical inevitability" that legitimizes corporations, the professional and technical elite, and the public officers assigned to manage the economy, to run the government, and to ensure the "security" of citizens. Although each of these subgroups develops its own rationale, they are all interdependent, sharing strategies and utopias. All conspire to instill a way of thinking that legitimizes the exploitation of human, natural, and industrial resources – a thesis that is very close to that of Jonathon Simon (2007, 233-57) when he analyzes the workplace. Recalling the deaths attributable to working conditions, the International Labour Organization inventoried two million such deaths in 2000 alone (5,000 per day), a number that experts say is only the tip of the iceberg (Tombs 2004). However, even with the best of will, the criminal justice system cannot put a stop to such major harms and wrongdoings, because it is hampered by irremediable conceptual disadvantages. It is limited to considering individual responsibility, the guilty mind, and no more. How can the criminal law work for the common good and rein in the great predators and polluters with such inadequate instruments and philosophies? Notwithstanding these critical limitations, the existing laws do have some practical utility. For instance, Tombs reminds us that the rationality of the apparatus can be turned against those who make the rules. As Tombs says, "in the area of corporate offending, the law retains some deterrent potential, since it is aimed at organizations that claim rationality for themselves and operate on the basis of calculability" (*ibid.*, 176).[4]

Since a fundamental criticism of criminology and penal law is possible in Great Britain, what makes it so difficult here in Canada? In a recent issue of the *Canadian Journal of Criminology and Criminal Justice*, which considered the thematic issue "law, society, and critique in Canada," fifteen authors attempted to answer this question (volume 48, 5, September 2006). This thematic issue points us to an answer residing in the current social and political climate – in the *neo-liberal ethos* that makes it very difficult or even impossible to think critically. In the words of Woolford, Hogeveen, and Martel (2006, 631-32), "critical scholarship is becoming increasingly restrained by an almost all-encompassing neo-liberal ethos." Yet is this answer not simultaneously too simple and too sweeping? Does it not aim to exonerate Canadian criminology from all responsibility, laying blame solely on a neo-liberal environment with a near-totalizing effect? Yet an equally neo-liberal atmosphere reigns in Great Britain! How can we explain that in Tony Blair's time some universities managed to overcome this hegemony, as evidenced not only in *Beyond Criminology* (Hillyard et al. 2004) but also in *Toxic Capitalism* (Pearce and Tombs 1998) and in *Unmasking the Crimes of the Powerful* (Tombs and Whyte 2003)? Could it be because they have been working in a more interdisciplinary manner than Canadians rather than concentrating on criminology alone? Do they enjoy a stronger tradition of criticism? Perhaps the conservatism and relative absence of fundamental debate in Canadian criminology are traceable to a perception of criminology as a profession rather than as a body of knowledge that should constantly revise its hypotheses and suppositions?[5] The discipline, as it is now, is content to produce a yearly crop of hundreds of graduates, destined to be commandeered by the government and instructed in the smooth functioning of institutions and the constraints of penal law rather than the art of critical reflection (Brockman, Chapter 2 in this volume).

When it comes to Canadian criminological research, the editors of the special review note that further obstacles to critical thought sometimes arise from the researchers' proximity to the state apparatus, which requires them – as appendages of this apparatus – to develop and pursue issues of interest to the government (Martel, Hogeveen, and Woolford 2006, 633-46). They note also that the organization of scientific research in the human sciences in Canada and elsewhere provides an ever-decreasing space for free research since it imposes ever-increasing constraints on researchers. It demands proof of relevance and usefulness for projects, partnerships, and other subtle mechanisms that serve the neo-liberal ideology (Chunn and Menzies 2006,

663-80). As for the organization of teaching, it discourages interdisciplinary studies and favours economic rationalism, traditional careers, and the "financial" success of the institution (Ratner 2006, 647-62).

Conclusion

Thanks to the initiative of the Law Commission of Canada, citizens, professional groups, and researchers have been invited since 2001 to reflect on criminology, reconsider the relative harmfulness of behaviours defined as crimes, and interrogate the effect of criminalization. The participants in the debate have awakened from their lethargy in the face of social harm on a grand scale, the impacts of which far exceed those of existing penal infractions. Many of us are wondering, yet again, what really is the harm caused by many of the "offences" included in the *Criminal Code*. Do such behaviours warrant criminalization, and how do we stop the more grievous social wrongdoings that are untouched by the existing criminal law system? The discipline of criminology has never before been able to mobilize sustained, critical investigations of these questions. And if we are persuaded by the editors of the *Canadian Journal of Criminology and Criminal Justice* issue on "Law, Society, and Critique in Canada," there is little room for optimism that things will change in criminology itself. It was the Law Commission of Canada that was in the best position to ask the hard questions, mobilize reflection, and issue collections of studies that shed light on the limits of law and its application in the pursuit of justice.

Sadly, as noted in the Introduction, the commission received its own death sentence in 2006 from the minister of justice, who simply abolished it. This gesture aptly illustrates the prevailing political climate and especially the views of the elected Conservative representatives on the importance of democratic consultation and critical reflection. Speaking of critical reflection, the initiative launched by the commission in 2001 did not go too far. Rather, it did not go far enough. Of course, it was also hampered by a growing lack of funds, an anti-intellectual and conservative context, and the neo-liberal mood. Nevertheless, what it should have done was to go further. Instead of focusing on crime, it should have revealed sooner and more dramatically the lies and misconceptions at the heart of the legal notion of crime, not only by demonstrating the relativity, changing nature, underlying interests, and unfair impacts of the law and its application but also by questioning the very word "crime" and by working against the tide to raise awareness in this regard. Although "crime" should be reserved for the most serious offences, it is not in law. This is clearly illustrated by Janet Mosher and Joe Hermer (Chapter 1 in this volume) and by Lisa Chartrand and Cora Weber-Pillwax (Chapter 3 in this volume). What the law calls "crime" will never get at the most serious miscarriages of justice perpetrated by government, corporate, and economic powers. The authors of the *Criminal Code* will always find good reasons to exclude the serious harms committed by the powerful, or else judges and lawyers will filter down the suspicions, accusations, and prosecutions as we have seen in Joan Brockman's study (Chapter 2 in this volume).[6] The very rules of criminal law (individual responsibility and a guilty mind) impede justice ministries, judges, and the prosecution from pursuing charges against the perpetrators of serious crimes committed by the powerful.

So why not adopt a new name for the discipline, zemiology, which addresses the real perpetrators of serious wrongdoing – that is, the people who murder on a daily basis and major transgressors who perpetuate deadly working conditions, toxic environments, and poverty? Why not, through zemiology, examine the economiċ motivations of legislators, who dictate, as they wish, the prohibition and liberalization of behaviours? Why not recognize in our studies the role of governments who refuse (or are unable) to assume their due responsibilities as guardians of the common good because their ceaseless and ever-increasing appetite for revenues blinds them to all other concerns? Would legislators agree to define as "criminal" an activity that fills the government's coffers, as is the case, in part, with gambling? As it stands now, however, "criminology perpetuates the myth of crime" (Hillyard and Tombs 2004, 11). Why not teach and research zemiology and replace the study of crime with that of economics and politics and then look for the best means to pursue social and penal justice?

Acknowledgment
Translated from French by Margaret McKyes.

Notes
1 However, there were, and still are, notable exceptions to this statement, found, for example, in the works of Snider (2004, 2006) and Boyd, Chunn, and Menzies (2001), among others, which are discussed later in this chapter.
2 It is not that researchers ignore the problems that plague criminological research. The reviewers write: "All police researchers must grapple with the fundamental tension between doing research which may contribute to the protective and freedom enhancing aspects of public policing or its potentially oppressive and coercive quality" and "government goals, such as the provision of public peace and security through surveillance, threat, and legal force, present very real opportunities for abuse, misuse, bias, and possibilities for mistake and waste" (Murphy 1999, 205). The diagnostic comes later – none of the conditions required is there to effectuate the necessary inquiry.
3 See, for example, Boyd, Chunn, and Menzies (2002); Boyd, Chunn, and Menzies (2001); Pearce and Tombs (1998); and Glasbeek (2002).
4 The author deplores the fact that many enterprises, corporations, businesses, professional associations, and even universities have hung onto the misconceived idea that major corporate crime is not really crime.
5 Joan Brockman (2003, 288) suggests that many criminologists work as criminal justice technicians for the state rather than questioning how the criminal law is defined and enforced against one group as opposed to another.
6 *Criminal Code*, R.S.C. 1985, c. C-46.

References
Bertrand, M., ed. 1996. "Introduction: Law as a Means of Exclusion." *Canadian Journal of Law and Society* 11, 2: 15-18.
Boyd, S. 2002. *Toxic Criminology: Environment, Law, and the State in Canada.* Halifax: Fernwood Press.
Boyd, S., D. Chunn, and R. Menzies, eds. 2001. *[Ab]Using Power: The Canadian Experience.* Halifax: Fernwood Press.
Brockman, J. 2003. "The Impact of Institutional Structures and Power on Law and Society: Is It Time for Reawakening?" *Law and Society Review* 37, 2: 283-94.
Brunelle, N., et al. 2002. "Trajectoires types de déviance juvénile: Un regard qualitative." *Canadian Journal of Criminology* 44, 1: 1-32.
Chunn, D., and R. Menzies. 2006. "'So What Does All of This Have to Do with Criminology?' Surviving the Restructuring of the Discipline in the Twenty-First Century." *Canadian Journal of Criminology and Criminal Justice* 48, 5: 663-80.
Doob, A. 1999. "Youth Justice Research in Canada: An Assessment." *Canadian Journal of Criminology* 41, 2: 217-24.
Dorling, D. 2004. "Prime Suspect: Murder in Britain." In *Beyond Criminology: Taking Harm Seriously,* ed. P. Hillyard et al., 178-91. London: Pluto Press.
Erickson, P. 1999. "A Persistent Paradox: Drug Law and Policy in Canada." *Canadian Journal of Criminology* 41, 2: 275-84.
Fournier, M. 2003. *Jeunes filles affiliées aux gangs de rue à Montréal: Cheminements et expériences.* Les cahiers de recherches criminologiques, cahier no. 39. Montréal: Centre international de criminologie comparée.
Glasbeek, H.J. 2002. *Wealth by Stealth: Corporate Crime, Corporate Law, and the Perversion of Democracy.* Toronto: Between the Lines Press.
Gramsci, A. 1971. *Selections from the Prison Notebooks of Antonio Gramsci.* Ed. and trans. Q. Hoare and G.H. Smith. London: Lawrence and Wishart.
Hillyard, P. 2004. "Introduction." In *Beyond Criminology: Taking Harm Seriously,* ed. P. Hillyard et al., 1-9. London: Pluto Press.
Hillyard, P., et al. 2004. *Beyond Criminology: Taking Harm Seriously.* London: Pluto Press.
La Prairie, C. 1999. "The Impact of Aboriginal Justice Research on Policy: A Marginal Past and an Even More Uncertain Future." *Canadian Journal of Criminology* 41, 2: 249-60.
MacLean, B.D. 1986. *The Political Economy of Crime: Readings for a Critical Criminology.* Scarborough, ON: Prentice-Hall.
Martel, J., B. Hogeveen, and A. Woolford. 2006. "The State of Critical Scholarship in Criminology and Socio-Legal Studies in Canada." *Canadian Journal of Criminology and Criminal Justice* 48, 5: 633-46.
Mathiesen, T. 1980. *Law, Society, and Political Action: Towards a Strategy under Late Capitalism.* New York: Academic Press.
McMullan, J.L., and R.S. Ratner. 1982. "Marxism and the Study of Crime: A Critical Review and Appraisal of 'Policing the Crisis.'" *Canadian Journal of Sociology* 7, 2: 231-39.
Murphy, C. 1999. "The Current and Future State of Police Research and Policy in Canada." *Canadian Journal of Criminology* 41, 2: 205-15.
Murphy, C., and P. Stenning, eds. 1999. "Criminology Research and Criminal Justice Policy in Canada: Present Trends and Future Prospects." *Canadian Journal of Criminology* 41, 2: 127-30.
O'Reilly Fleming, T., ed. 1985. *The New Criminologies in Canada: Crime, State, and Control.* Toronto: Oxford University Press.
Paradis, G., and M. Cousineau. 2005. *Prostitution juvénile: Étude sur le profil des proxénètes et leur pratique à partir des perceptions qu'en ont des intervenants-clés.* Les cahiers de recherches criminologiques, cahier no. 42. Montreal: Centre international de criminologie comparée.
Pearce, F., and S. Tombs. 1998. *Toxic Capitalism: Corporate Crime and the Chemical Industry.* Toronto: Canadian Scholars' Press.

Pemberton, S. 2004. "A Theory of Moral Indifference: Understanding the Production of Harm in Capitalist Society." In *Beyond Criminology: Taking Harm Seriously,* ed. P. Hillyard et al., 67-83. London: Pluto Press.

Quinney, R. 1973. *Critique of Legal Order: Crime Control in Capitalist Society.* New York: Little, Brown.

Ratner, R.S. 1984. "Inside the Liberal Boot: The Criminological Enterprise in Canada." *Studies in Political Economy* 13: 145-64.

–. 2006. "Pioneering Critical Criminology in Canada." *Canadian Journal of Criminology and Criminal Justice* 48, 5: 647-62.

Schwendinger, H., and J. Schwendinger. 1970. "Defenders of Order or Guardians of Human Rights?" *Issues in Criminology* 5, 2: 123-57.

Simon, J. 2007. *Governing through Crime: How the War on Crime Transformed American Democracy and Created a Culture of Fear.* New York: Oxford University Press.

Snider, L. 2004. "Poisoned Water, Environmental Regulation, and Crime: Constituting the Non Culpable Subject in Walkerton, Ontario." In *What Is a Crime? Defining Criminal Conduct in Contemporary Society,* ed. Law Commission of Canada, 155-84. Vancouver and Toronto: UBC Press.

–. 2006. "Making Change in Neo-Liberal Times." In *Criminalizing Women: Gender and (In) Justice in Neo-Liberal Times,* ed. G. Balfour and E. Comack, 323-42. Halifax: Fernwood.

Stenning, P. 1999. "Criminal Justice Research and Policy in Canada: Implication of Public Service Reform." *Canadian Journal of Criminology* 41, 2: 179-90.

Sun, F., et al. 2004. "Consommation de substances psychoactives et degré de gravité du crime." *Canadian Journal of Criminology* 46, 1: 1-26.

Taylor, I., P. Walton, and J. Young. 1973. *The New Criminology: For a Social Theory of Deviance.* London: Routledge and Kegan Paul.

Tombs, S. 2004. "Work Place Injury and Death: Social Harm and the Illusion of Law." In *Beyond Criminology: Taking Harm Seriously,* ed. P. Hillyard et al., 156-77. London: Pluto Press.

Tombs, S., and P. Hillyard. 2004. "Towards a Political Economy of Harm: States, Corporations, and the Production of Inequality." In *Beyond Criminology: Taking Harm Seriously,* ed. P. Hillyard et al., 30-54. London: Pluto Press.

Tombs, S., and D. Whyte, eds. 2003. *Unmasking the Crimes of the Powerful: Scrutinizing States and Corporations.* New York: Peter Lang.

Ward, T. 2004. "State Harms." In *Beyond Criminology: Taking Harm Seriously,* ed. P. Hillyard et al., 84-100. London: Pluto Press.

Wemmers, J., M. Cousineau, and J. Demers. 2004. *Les besoins des victimes de violence conjugale en matière de justice: Résultats d'une étude exploratoire qualitative auprès de victimes et d'intervenantes en maison d'hébergement.* Collection Études et Analyses no. 28. Montreal: Centre de recherche interdisciplinaire sur la violence familiale et la violence faite aux femmes.

Woods, G. 1999. "Then and Now: Federal Support for Justice Research." *Canadian Journal of Criminology* 41, 2: 171-78.

Woolford, A., B. Hogeveen, and J. Martel. 2006. "An Opening." *Canadian Journal of Criminology and Criminal Justice* 48, 5: 631-32.

Contributors

Marie-Andrée Bertrand (D. Crim., University of California, Berkeley, 1967) has taught and researched in criminology, sociology of law, feminist and critical theory at the University of Montreal School of Criminology and International Centre for Comparative Criminology since 1968. From 1969 to 1973, she was a member of the (Canadian) Commission of Inquiry into Non-Medical Drugs (LeDain Commission). In her minority reports, she recommended the legalization of all illegal substances and state controls over their production and sales. Her main research areas are drug policies and the "question of women" in penal law. She has been invited to teach and do research at the Onati International Institute for the Sociology of Law (Spain), the Hamburg Institute of Criminology (Germany), the Berkeley School of Criminology (United States), the Faculty of Law at the University of Alberta, the Department of Sociology at the Centre d'études sociologiques sur le droit et les institutions pénales (France), and the McGill Centre for Research on Women. She now teaches epistemology in the PhD Program on Human Sciences at Montreal University and is an affiliated researcher with the International Center for Comparative Criminology at the same institution. Her latest books are *Les femmes et la criminalité* (2003) and *Prisons pour femmes* (1999). Her most recent articles are on the gender and colour of the law, feminist theory as a theory of knowledge, the dual legal status of cannabis, reasonable accommodations, and the question of women.

Joan Brockman is a professor in the School of Criminology at Simon Fraser University and a member of the Law Societies of British Columbia and Alberta. She teaches courses on crimes and misconduct in the professions, corporate crimes and misconduct, gender in the courts and the legal profession, criminal procedure and evidence, and wrongful convictions. Her publications include *Gender in the Legal Profession: Fitting or Breaking the Mould* (2001) and (with V. Gordon Rose) *An Introduction to Canadian Criminal Procedure and Evidence* (2010, 4th edition). She recently received a Social Sciences and Humanities Research Council of Canada grant to begin research towards her next project, *The Construction of Deviant Professionals: Sex, Lies, and Bill(k)ing the State.*

Colin S. Campbell has studied and written about Canadian gambling policy developments for over twenty-five years. In addition to having worked extensively in western Canadian charitable casino operations, Campbell has provided research and consultation services to private and public sector organizations. Prior to teaching in the Department of Criminology at Douglas College, he provided research services and policy advice to the Commission of Inquiry into the Nanaimo Commonwealth Holding Society. Campbell's academic research has focused on government regulatory policies with respect to gambling in Canada. He is a frequent speaker at national and international conferences on gambling, has edited two books on gambling in Canada, and is a past member of the Board of Directors of the Responsible Gambling Council.

Lisa Chartrand is a lawyer and member of the Law Societies of Alberta, British Columbia, and Manitoba. She has a Bachelor of Laws degree from the University of Alberta and Master of Laws degree from the University of Manitoba. Chartrand's LL.M. thesis focused on Métis Aboriginal rights in western Canada and the impact of contemporary negotiated agreements on those rights. She has numerous years of experience working with Aboriginal collectives, communities, and governments. She is currently the registrar of the Métis Settlements Land Registry with the province of Alberta. In addition to this position, Chartrand has also been delegated the ministerial responsibility to maintain the Métis Settlements Membership List, which is governed according to provincial legislation. As co-principal researcher and writer for this project, Chartrand draws not only on her experience as a lawyer working with Aboriginal collectives on rights-based matters but also from her experience as a Métis person and community member.

Timothy F. Hartnagel is professor emeritus in the Department of Sociology at the University of Alberta, specializing in criminology, and has served as the director of the department's BA program in criminology. In addition to teaching the course on introductory criminology, he has taught crime and public policy and social structure and crime, and he has supervised a number of MA and PhD students. He is the co-author of *Fractured Transitions from School to Work* (1996) and editor of the text *Canadian Crime Control Policy* (1998). He has published widely in professional journals, including *Criminology, Journal of Research in Crime and Delinquency, Canadian Review of Sociology and Anthropology, Canadian Journal of Criminology,* and *Criminal Justice*. His current research includes an investigation of punitive attitudes towards offenders and on gambling and crime. He has received funding from various agencies, including the Social Sciences and Humanities Research Council of Canada and the Alberta Gaming Research Institute. He has previously been appointed as a visiting fellow at the Institute of Criminology at Cambridge University and a visiting scholar at the Center for the Study of Law and Society at the University of California Berkeley.

Joe Hermer is an associate professor of sociology and criminology at the University of Toronto. His work examines contemporary strategies of regulation and order, with a particular interest in poverty and marginalized populations. Hermer is the author of *Regulating Eden: The Nature of Order in North American Parks* (2002) and *Policing Compassion: Begging, Law, and Power in Public Spaces* (forthcoming 2010). He is co-editor (with Janet Mosher) of *Disorderly People: Law and the Politics of Exclusion in Ontario* (2002).

Frédéric Lemieux is an associate professor at The George Washington University. He is also the Director of the Police Science and the Security and Safety Leadership programs at GWU. He has conducted studies on informal control mechanisms, on deviant behaviours, and on the functioning of criminal intelligence as a formal social control tool. Lemieux has also published various journal articles that examine social control and crime in the context of a major disaster situation. He is also the author of books on criminal intelligence and homeland security issues in general, and his most recent book is *International Police Cooperation* (2010).

Janet Mosher is an associate professor at Osgoode Hall Law School. Her teaching and research interests centre on woman abuse, poverty, welfare reform, and access to justice. She was the principal investigator of an academic and community-based collaborative research project examining abused women's experiences in Ontario's welfare system, *Walking on Eggshells: Abused Women's Experiences of Ontario's Welfare System* (2004), and is a co-editor with Joe Hermer of *Disorderly People: Law and the Politics of Exclusion in Ontario* (2002).

Nadège Sauvêtre earned a Master's degree in criminology (University of Montreal) and in psychology (University of Nantes). She was a research assistant at the International Center for Comparative Criminology, and she was appointed as project manager regarding the research project on incivilities. Sauvêtre presently works as a strategic analyst for a municipal police department in the province of Quebec.

Garry J. Smith is a gambling research specialist with the Alberta Gaming Research Institute. Smith has been investigating gambling issues for over twenty-five years, during which time he has produced numerous scholarly articles for academic journals, contributed scientific reports for governments and private sector corporations, and presented before national and international audiences. He is frequently called on by North American media outlets to comment on gambling issues and teaches a university course on the subject. Smith's current research interests include the social and economic impacts of gambling, public policy issues related to gambling, crime and gambling, and sports gambling.

Cora Weber-Pillwax is an associate professor in the Indigenous Peoples Education graduate specialization in the Department of Educational Policy Studies at the University of Alberta. She has over forty years of experience in education, post-secondary as well as public schooling, and has lived and worked primarily in northern Cree and Métis communities. She has served Aboriginal communities and peoples as a teacher, educational administrator, researcher, and community processes facilitator. Her research focus is on Indigenous knowledge systems and how these impact on, or are evident within, Aboriginal health and education and the lived contexts of contemporary Aboriginal communities, peoples, and persons.

Index

Ontario College of Physicians and
Surgeons, 61-65, 70-71
Ontario Disability Support Program Act
(ODSPA), 21, 29
Ontario Health Insurance Plan Fraud
Squad, 62
Ontario Medical Association (OMA), 57, 75
Ontario Municipal Social Services
Association: on fraud task force, 23
Ontario Provincial Policy Fraud Investiga-
tion Unit, 61-62
Ontario Works Act (OWA): on contractual
obligations, 9, 23, 28-29, 32, 40-41; on
eligibility for social assistance, 9, 20-24,
26, 29-30, 40-41, 43; on entitlement, 9,
27-29, 34; and incidence of fraud, 20-21;
and receipt of income, 32-36; reforms to
social assistance regime, 9, 18, 21, 29

physicians. *See* health care professionals
Pimatsowin Weyasowewina, 93, 123
poverty, conceptualization of, 27, 29,
135-36
problem definers, 77
problem gamblers, populations at risk of,
7, 166, 172(t), 176, 183; support services
for, 173(t)
professional misconduct. *See* health care
fraud
professional problem, 76
prosecution: crimes of the powerful,
75-76, 195; of health care fraud, 53, 61,
65, 69-71, 73; of welfare fraud, 9, 18, 20,
22, 24-25, 34, 40, 47, 74(t)

Quasi-criminal: and health care fraud,
54, 61, 63, 65, 70-71; and traditional
Aboriginal practices, 6, 14

R. v. MacDiarmid, 72
R. v. Maldonado, 30, 32-34
R. v. Olan, 31, 34
R. v. Powley, 113-14, 116
R. v. Scott, 68, 71-72
R. v. Sparrow, 118
R. v. Théroux, 32-33
R. v. Van der Peet, 117-18
R. v. Zlatic, 32
regulation: of intimate relationships, 31,
37-38, 40; legal forms of, 5-6, 17, 23, 31,
34-35, 43, 47, 101, 104, 107-11, 154,
160; of oneself, 11; of professionals, 10,
54, 59; social forms of, 5-6, 17, 19, 46-47,
118; through crime, 5-6, 13, 48, 116,
122, 131-32, 135, 148; through
discourses of criminality, 6, 8-9, 12-13,

18, 29, 44-45, 48; through surveillance,
6, 8-9, 14-15, 18, 27, 37, 41, 182
relocation programs, 109-10
responsibilization: and gambling, 7, 182;
and welfare receipt, 48
responsible gambling, 175-77, 184
Review of Gaming Legislation in Ontario,
162-64
risk, carriers of, 9, 11-12; containment of,
11-12, 181, 183; creation of, 9; discourse
of, 12; and gambling, 169, 172(t),
176-77, 181-83; and welfare, 11, 25,
43-44

self-determination, 119
self-regulating organization (SRO), 54,
59-63, 65-66, 69-71
self-regulation: government and gambling,
174, 183-84; of professions, 11, 54, 59-60,
75; and self-responsibilization, 7, 11-12,
28
self-responsibilization. *See* self-regulation:
self-responsibilization
social assistance. *See* welfare
Social Assistance Reform Act (SARA): and
welfare fraud as a problem, 19, 21, 28, 38
social capital, 173
social cohesion: and response to incivilities, 130-31, 137, 145; variation in
levels of, 5, 147-48
social control: absence linked to levels of
criminality, 130-31, 148; of gambling,
153-54, 179-83; in housing communities, 131, 135-37; informal methods of,
5, 76, 92, 135, 137, 148-49
social disorder, perception of, 139, 142;
physical signs of, 130, 132-33, 140;
preventative strategies to, 133-35; in
relation to community ties, 130-31, 134,
136-37, 148-49
social harm: and gambling, 7-8, 154, 161,
174-76, 178; non-criminal solutions to,
53, 76, 183-84
social housing: housing cooperatives, 5,
131-32, 137-42, 144(t)-49; low-income
housing, 4-5, 8, 131-32, 137-38, 142;
management modes, 4-5, 131-32, 138,
140-44(t), 147-49
social marginality, 13-14, 38, 139, 190
social norms, 1, 12, 122, 179, 184, 191
socio-demographic characteristics, 131,
136-37, 145-46
spouse: constitutional challenge to definition, 38; defined for welfare purposes,
30, 37-38; *Family Law Act*, 37, 39; and
intimate relationships, 31, 37-39, 41-42,

LAW AND
SOCIETY

Patrick James
*Constitutional Politics in Canada after the Charter: Liberalism,
Communitarianism, and Systemism* (2010)

Louis A. Knafla and Haijo Westra (eds.)
*Aboriginal Title and Indigenous Peoples: Canada, Australia,
and New Zealand* (2010)

Stephen Clarkson and Stepan Wood
*A Perilous Imbalance: The Globalization of Canadian Law and
Governance* (2009)

Amanda Glasbeek
Feminized Justice: The Toronto Women's Court, 1913-34 (2009)

Kimberley Brooks (ed.)
Justice Bertha Wilson: One Woman's Difference (2009)

Wayne V. McIntosh and Cynthia L. Cates
Multi-Party Litigation: The Strategic Context (2009)

Renisa Mawani
*Colonial Proximities: Crossracial Encounters and Juridical Truths
in British Columbia, 1871-1921* (2009)

James B. Kelly and Christopher P. Manfredi (eds.)
*Contested Constitutionalism: Reflections on the Canadian Charter of Rights
and Freedoms* (2009)

Catherine E. Bell and Robert K. Paterson (eds.)
Protection of First Nations Cultural Heritage: Laws, Policy, and Reform (2008)

Hamar Foster, Benjamin L. Berger, and A.R. Buck (eds.)
The Grand Experiment: Law and Legal Culture in British Settler Societies (2008)

Richard J. Moon (ed.)
Law and Religious Pluralism in Canada (2008)

Catherine E. Bell and Val Napoleon (eds.)
First Nations Cultural Heritage and Law: Case Studies, Voices, and Perspectives (2008)

Douglas C. Harris
Landing Native Fisheries: Indian Reserves and Fishing Rights in British Columbia, 1849-1925 (2008)

Peggy J. Blair
Lament for a First Nation: The Williams Treaties in Southern Ontario (2008)

Lori G. Beaman
Defining Harm: Religious Freedom and the Limits of the Law (2007)

Stephen Tierney (ed.)
Multiculturalism and the Canadian Constitution (2007)

Julie Macfarlane
The New Lawyer: How Settlement Is Transforming the Practice of Law (2007)

Kimberley White
Negotiating Responsibility: Law, Murder, and States of Mind (2007)

Dawn Moore
Criminal Artefacts: Governing Drugs and Users (2007)

Hamar Foster, Heather Raven, and Jeremy Webber (eds.)
Let Right Be Done: Aboriginal Title, the Calder Case, and the Future of Indigenous Rights (2007)

Dorothy E. Chunn, Susan B. Boyd, and Hester Lessard (eds.)
Reaction and Resistance: Feminism, Law, and Social Change (2007)

Margot Young, Susan B. Boyd, Gwen Brodsky, and Shelagh Day (eds.)
Poverty: Rights, Social Citizenship, and Legal Activism (2007)

Rosanna L. Langer
*Defining Rights and Wrongs: Bureaucracy, Human Rights, and
Public Accountability* (2007)

C.L. Ostberg and Matthew E. Wetstein
Attitudinal Decision Making in the Supreme Court of Canada (2007)

Chris Clarkson
*Domestic Reforms: Political Visions and Family Regulation in
British Columbia, 1862-1940* (2007)

Jean McKenzie Leiper
Bar Codes: Women in the Legal Profession (2006)

Gerald Baier
*Courts and Federalism: Judicial Doctrine in the United States, Australia,
and Canada* (2006)

Avigail Eisenberg (ed.)
Diversity and Equality: The Changing Framework of Freedom in Canada (2006)

Randy K. Lippert
*Sanctuary, Sovereignty, Sacrifice: Canadian Sanctuary Incidents,
Power, and Law* (2005)

James B. Kelly
*Governing with the Charter: Legislative and Judicial Activism and
Framers' Intent* (2005)

Dianne Pothier and Richard Devlin (eds.)
*Critical Disability Theory: Essays in Philosophy, Politics, Policy,
and Law* (2005)

Susan G. Drummond
Mapping Marriage Law in Spanish Gitano Communities (2005)

Louis A. Knafla and Jonathan Swainger (eds.)
Laws and Societies in the Canadian Prairie West, 1670-1940 (2005)

Ikechi Mgbeoji
Global Biopiracy: Patents, Plants, and Indigenous Knowledge (2005)

Florian Sauvageau, David Schneiderman, and David Taras, with Ruth Klinkhammer and Pierre Trudel
The Last Word: Media Coverage of the Supreme Court of Canada (2005)

Gerald Kernerman
Multicultural Nationalism: Civilizing Difference, Constituting Community (2005)

Pamela A. Jordan
Defending Rights in Russia: Lawyers, the State, and Legal Reform in the Post-Soviet Era (2005)

Anna Pratt
Securing Borders: Detention and Deportation in Canada (2005)

Kirsten Johnson Kramar
Unwilling Mothers, Unwanted Babies: Infanticide in Canada (2005)

W.A. Bogart
Good Government? Good Citizens? Courts, Politics, and Markets in a Changing Canada (2005)

Catherine Dauvergne
Humanitarianism, Identity, and Nation: Migration Laws in Canada and Australia (2005)

Michael Lee Ross
First Nations Sacred Sites in Canada's Courts (2005)

Andrew Woolford
Between Justice and Certainty: Treaty Making in British Columbia (2005)

John McLaren, Andrew Buck, and Nancy Wright (eds.)
Despotic Dominion: Property Rights in British Settler Societies (2004)

Georges Campeau
From UI to EI: Waging War on the Welfare State (2004)

Alvin J. Esau
The Courts and the Colonies: The Litigation of Hutterite Church Disputes (2004)

Christopher N. Kendall
Gay Male Pornography: An Issue of Sex Discrimination (2004)

Roy B. Flemming
Tournament of Appeals: Granting Judicial Review in Canada (2004)

Constance Backhouse and Nancy L. Backhouse
The Heiress vs the Establishment: Mrs. Campbell's Campaign for Legal Justice (2004)

Christopher P. Manfredi
Feminist Activism in the Supreme Court: Legal Mobilization and the Women's Legal Education and Action Fund (2004)

Annalise Acorn
Compulsory Compassion: A Critique of Restorative Justice (2004)

Jonathan Swainger and Constance Backhouse (eds.)
People and Place: Historical Influences on Legal Culture (2003)

Jim Phillips and Rosemary Gartner
Murdering Holiness: The Trials of Franz Creffield and George Mitchell (2003)

David R. Boyd
Unnatural Law: Rethinking Canadian Environmental Law and Policy (2003)

Ikechi Mgbeoji
Collective Insecurity: The Liberian Crisis, Unilateralism, and Global Order (2003)

Rebecca Johnson
Taxing Choices: The Intersection of Class, Gender, Parenthood, and the Law (2002)

John McLaren, Robert Menzies, and Dorothy E. Chunn (eds.)
Regulating Lives: Historical Essays on the State, Society, the Individual, and the Law (2002)

Joan Brockman
Gender in the Legal Profession: Fitting or Breaking the Mould (2001)

Printed and bound in Canada by Friesens
Set in Stone by Artegraphica Design Co. Ltd.
Copy editor: Stacy Belden
Proofreader: Dallas Harrison